HEINEMANN
SCHOOL
MANAGEMENT

Understanding and Managing Bullying

DELWYN TATTUM
ET AL

HEINEMANN
SCHOOL
MANAGEMENT
Understanding and Managing Bullying
Delwyn Tattum *et al*
Heinemann Educational
A division of Heinemann Educational Books Ltd.,
Halley Court, Jordan Hill, Oxford OX2 8EJ

OXFORD   LONDON   EDINBURGH
MADRID   ATHENS   BOLOGNA   PARIS
MELBOURNE   SYDNEY   AUCKLAND   SINGAPORE   TOKYO
IBADAN   NAIROBI   HARARE   GABORONE
PORTSMOUTH NH (USA)

ISBN 0 435 800434

Typeset by Taurus Graphics, Kidlington, Oxon.
Printed in Great Britain by Clays Ltd, St. Ives plc.

Contents

SECTION III: HELPING VULNERABLE CHILDREN

Contributors

Delwyn P. Tattum (Editor)

Peter Blatchford, Senior Lecturer, Department of Educational Psychology and Educational Needs, Institute of Education, University of London.

Alice Charach, Psychiatrist, C.M. Hincks Research Institute, Toronto, Canada.

Wendy Craig, Doctoral Candidate, Department of Psychology, York University, Toronto, Canada.

Danielle Drouet, Coordinator for Special Educational Needs, Waverley School, London.

David Gillborn, Lecturer in Sociology of Education, Institute of Education, University of London.

Graham Herbert, Curriculum Coordinator, Salendine Nook High School, Huddersfield.

Ton Mooji, Senior Researcher, Institute of Applied Social Research, Catholic University of Nijmengen, The Netherlands.

Dabie Nabuzoka, Research Fellow, Community Health Research Unit, University of Zambia.

Debra Pepler, Associate Professor of Psychology, Department of Psychology, York University, Toronto, Canada.

John Pitts, Reader in Applied Social Science, West London Institute, Brunel University.

Ken Rigby, Associate Professor, Institute of Social Research, University of South Australia, Adelaide.

Erling Roland, Associate Professor, Centre for Behavioural Research, Stavanger College of Education, Norway.

Sonia Sharp, Research Associate, Department of Psychology, University of Sheffield.

Phillip Slee, Lecturer in Human Development, School of Education, Flinders University, Adelaide, South Australia.

Peter Smith, Professor of Psychology, Department of Psychology, University of Sheffield.

Delwyn Tattum, Reader in Education, Cardiff Institute of Higher Education, Cardiff.

David Thompson, Director of M.Sc. Educational Psychology Course, Department of Psychology, University of Sheffield.

Irene Whitney, Research Associate, Department of Psychology, University of Sheffield.

Suzanne Ziegler, Chief Research Officer, The Board of Education for the City of Toronto, Canada.

Understanding the Complex Nature of Bullying

1 What is bullying?

Delwyn Tattum

Bullying is the most malicious and malevolent form of anti-social behaviour practised in our schools. As pupils, teachers or parents we have experienced or witnessed it and, in fact, research evidence indicates that it is more prevalent and damaging to children than most adults are prepared to accept. The perpetrators are found in nursery classes, infant, junior and secondary schools: their conduct includes name-calling and teasing; jostling and punching; intimidation and exclusion; and even spreading of malicious rumours, maiming and murder. The victims for their part suffer the physical and psychological abuse of their persons, isolation and loneliness, insecurity and anxiety arising from the threatening atmosphere which surrounds them. At its most insidious bullying focuses on vulnerable children who are regarded as being different.

Sadly, there is a misplaced belief amongst some adults that if bullies are ignored they will stop bullying. Others hold to the view that it is an inevitable part of growing up which will pass without their intervention. There are even those who subscribe to the view that bullying is 'good' for children, as it teaches them to 'look after themselves'.

These views are completely inconsistent with the concept of a 'caring' school or teachers who are in 'loco parentis'. Children look to adults to protect them from the excesses of more aggressive peers. Adult intervention may at times be inept or even insensitive, but it can be effective if the response is early and firm. It may involve little effort for the adult but bring considerable relief for the child. To do nothing is at best to give the impression that bullying is not regarded as serious and at worst to condone the abuse of a member of the school community by others. There is no doubt that bullying challenges teachers and other adults to look very closely at their own attitudes to the behaviour and the children involved.

For if we do not resolve marked ambiguity in our own attitudes we are unable to give the support, guidance and protection to which children are entitled.

▮▮▮ Towards understanding the problem

As a prelude to examining the nature of bullying, it is important that we discuss three fundamental issues which are central to our understanding and management of the problem.

1 **There is bullying in all schools, regardless of age-range, type, locality or composition of intake.**

It is the characteristics of schools which makes such a categorical statement possible. They bring together large numbers of children and young people from a variety of home backgrounds and amongst them will be some who, as a result of their upbringing, will be more aggressive and violent than others. They will have learned that in order to get your own way you must be prepared to be more physically intimidating and verbally abusive than your peers. It is also the case that the design and structure of schools provide ample hidden places where bullying can take place away from the eyes of adults.

The other factor that makes the above contention possible is the scale of the problem. A national survey in Norway showed that some 15 per cent of pupils are engaged in bullying – 6 per cent bullies and 9 per cent bullied. (The Norwegian campaign is dealt with in greater detail by Erling Roland, Chapter 2.) The United Kingdom has approximately 9 million pupils in full-time education in the maintained and non-maintained sectors. Fifteen per cent of that figure would be in excess of 1.3 million children in 'special need' of care and support. Given this figure it is difficult to envisage any school exempt from having bullying pupils.

It is important that we further develop this central point because unless headteachers and teachers accept this statement they will not take steps to manage and reduce the problem. They will argue that it is a nonsense to address a non-existent problem. Unfortunately, there are headteachers who maintain that bullying does not take place in their schools. Their self-deception would not be so serious if its consequences were not so harmful to children and their families. For the claim discourages pupils from admitting to being bullied and makes them feel different and inadequate as the *only* pupil who does not conform to the school's image of its pupils. Parents too will be reluctant to tell the staff that their child is being victimised, as they anticipate that they will not be believed.

Therefore, it is important that every school communicates to pupils and parents their awareness that bullying takes place and that it is behaviour which will not be tolerated.

2 Bullying relates to other forms of anti-social behaviour.

Pupils who are aggressive towards their peers are also most likely to direct that aggression towards teachers, other adults and property, that is, they will disrupt lessons, abuse ancillary staff, vandalise property and engage in acts of petty theft. The victims of bullies for their part can display an understandable unwillingness to attend school and many become reluctant attenders. Reid (1988) calculated that 15 per cent of persistent absentees gave bullying as their original reason for truanting. Moreover, Knox (1988) holds that many children who become school phobics give bullying as the reason for their fear. Thus, if a school engages in an anti-bullying programme it will also tackle and reduce other forms of unacceptable behaviour. This optimistic message is supported by the work of Olweus (1989) in Bergen where, following the Norwegian national campaign, he conducted a follow-up study of some 40 schools. His encouraging findings are:

- A 50 per cent decrease in bully/victim problems during the two years following the campaign, with the figures applying to both boys and girls.

- There was no transfer of problems from school to the journey to and from school.

- There was also a reduction in general anti-social behaviour, such as disruption, vandalism and petty theft.

- Truancy figures also dropped and pupils expressed increased satisfaction with their school life, especially reflected in an enjoyment of playtimes.

Erling Roland offers a cautionary word (page 25). In his follow-up study to the Norwegian campaign in Stavanger he found that the most successful outcome occurred in schools which showed the greatest commitment to introducing the campaign, whilst in those schools which did little more than introduce the campaign the extent of reported bullying actually increased. These findings are supported by the work done by schools in the United Kingdom and reported in *Countering Bullying: Initiatives in Schools and Local Authorities* (Tattum and Herbert, 1993). Of the 16 schools which report on their anti-bullying programmes several found that there was a marked increase in the number of pupils who reported that they were being bullied. The increase was regarded by the schools as a measure of the success of their campaign, that is, that having raised the issue and invited pupils to 'tell' they had created a more open climate of trust. They also found that, as they sustained their programme, the reported figures began to decline. Thus, schools which set about managing and preventing bullying as described in this book should resolve to sustain their commitment throughout the year and into subsequent years.

3 Teachers need to examine their own attitudes towards bullying and in so doing examine their personal views on aggressive behaviour in general.

Associated with this issue is the fact that teachers invariably underestimate the extent and severity of bullying in their own schools. This is supported by my own work with many schools where teachers have been surprised and dismayed by the amount of bullying reported by pupils in the school's survey into the problem. This underestimation may in part explain why bullying has not been recognised until recently to be a widespread and persistent problem in our schools.

There are various possible explanations for teachers' (and other adults') underestimation of the incidence of bullying:

■ Bullying is predominantly a secretive activity, carried out in hidden places and away from the eyes of teachers and other adult workers in schools. And whilst this is the case, there is evidence to challenge the notion of teacher ignorance on this matter. For example the Elton Committee commissioned Sheffield University's Education Research Centre to conduct a survey into teacher perceptions of indiscipline; their findings are reported in the Elton Report on *Discipline in Schools* (DES, 1989). As part of the survey a stratified sample of teachers in primary and secondary schools were asked to identify from a prepared list the different types of pupil behaviour they had to deal with the previous week. Table 1 combines data extracted from the report (Tables 1, 2, 9 and 10) which deal specifically with bullying. From the table it is evident that teachers are aware of its nature and incidence, thus challenging the view that bullying is a highly secretive activity and that is why teachers have underestimated its extent. Particularly revealing are the figures relating to teachers' awareness of bullying in their own classrooms – both physical and verbal.

These figures confirm the findings of Stephenson and Smith (1988), who conducted a survey of teachers and final year primary school children in 26 schools in Cleveland. As part of their study they also asked the teachers and 143 children in the top two year groups in one primary school to nominate which pupils in their class were bullies and which were victims. They received a high level of agreement between the nom-

Table 1 The Elton Report: Sheffield University Survey (October, 1989)

Bullying behaviour observed at least once during the survey week by:		
PRIMARY TEACHERS (n = 1200)		
	In class	About school
Physical assaults:		
pushing, punching, striking	74%	86%
Verbal abuse		
offensive/insulting remarks	55%	71%
SECONDARY TEACHERS (n = 3200)		
Physical assaults	42%	66%
Verbal abuse	62%	76%

inations made by teachers and children – .80 correlation. Olweus in his *Aggression in the Schools* (1978) also reported high levels of agreement between the nominations made by pupils of this age and their teachers. Maybe it is because teachers are so aware of bullying that they tend to regard it as an inevitable part of school life. But such an attitude is unacceptable. In an article on bullying I wrote 'it gives the impression, however misplaced, that schools condone aggression and the domination of one pupil by another. Children have a right to an education in a safe, secure learning environment and adults have a responsibility to provide it' (Tattum and Tattum, 1992b).

Other possible explanations, and these will be discussed in less detail, are that:

■ Adults in general frequently dismiss bullying as low-key behaviour or mere horse-play.

■ As observed earlier in this introduction, children are frequently unwilling to tell their teachers or their parents that they are being bullied. In addition to their sense of shame they are unconvinced that the matter will be dealt with discreetly or sensitively.

■ Teachers have contributed to children's unwillingness to tell by frequently dismissing their 'tittle-tattle' or 'tale-telling'. Strongly running through Australian culture is the belief that you 'don't dob on yer mates', that is, one does not tell, grass, split or snitch. It is regarded as most un-Australian to be a 'cobber-dobber' – a theme which is developed by Rigby and Slee in their work on children's attitudes towards bullying (Chapter 9). As teachers we have to teach children the difference between idle tale-telling and reporting acts of intimidation and abuse.

■ It is also the case that bullying challenges teachers and other adults to look very closely at their own attitudes to aggressive behaviour and the children involved. Do we have a sneaking regard for the bully as someone with 'leadership' qualities or a person 'who is able to look after her/himself'? And do we regard victims as wimps, weak, over-protected or mother's pet?

■ Finally, from the many staff training days on bullying I have delivered, it is evident that many teachers do not understand the complex nature of bullying and are unsure about how to tackle the problem at both the individual and school level. The aim of the other contributors is to respond to this need and provide ways to manage, reduce and prevent bullying.

What is bullying?

One of the most comprehensive definitions of bullying is provided by Erling Roland (page 16) but for this section I offer a short definition because it enables us to examine particular factors in bully-victim interaction.

> 'Bullying is the wilful, conscious desire to hurt another and put her/him under stress' (Tattum, 1988).

Firstly, the definition draws attention to the fact that bullies know what they are doing, that is, in the majority of cases it is a planned act. Bullies know that by any civilised standards of behaviour to intimidate or oppress another is wrong and yet they do it. They continue to do it because they get personal satisfaction from dominating another less aggressive and vulnerable person; and they gain social status in the eyes of their peers who follow them or are frightened to oppose them. From the victim's viewpoint, stress is created not only by what actually happens but by the threat and fear of what might happen. The bully does not have to be physically present for the child to be anxious and distressed – he or she may not sleep or want to go to school, suffer from an upset stomach or headaches, avoid threatening places like toilets where the bully or bullies may frequent. Stress is a debilitating condition which can adversely affect a person's ability to concentrate, work or give of their best. In the classroom a child can be pre-occupied with worries about what might happen during break or lunchtime – it can fill his or her mind throughout the day so that he or she is not thinking about work but how to escape from the bully.

In Tattum (1988) and Tattum and Herbert (1990) we discuss six elements of bullying behaviour: nature, intensity, duration, intentionality, numbers involved and motivation. In the following pages each will be dealt with if not in a direct manner. As a way of examining the complex nature of bullying Tattum, Tattum and Herbert (1993) lists five forms of bullying:

- Physical bullying
- Verbal bullying
- Gesture bullying
- Extortion bullying
- Exclusion bullying

Physical bullying can range in severity from a punch to an assault with a deadly weapon, as in the case of Ahmed Ullah, a 13-year-old Asian boy, who was murdered in the playground of Burnage High School in 1986. (A report on the Inquiry by Ian MacDonald Q.C. can be found in MacDonald *et al.*, 1989.)

For most people it is the physical form that comes to mind when they think of bullying, mainly because it is visible. But *verbal bullying* can be equally hurtful and emotionally bruising. It can range from teasing and taunting to abusive comments about a person's appearance, ability, clothes and so on. Particularly disturbing forms of verbal bullying are sexual and racial abuse. The former demeans girls and women, and the latter is an attack on an individual's family, culture and ethnicity. Another vulnerable group are children with special needs and each of these groups are dealt with in detail by the contributors to Section III. The spreading of malicious rumours is another form of verbal bullying.

In the classroom the worst excesses of physical and verbal bullying are discouraged by the teacher's presence, although a teacher's presence does not eliminate them as we noted from Table 1. But *gesture bullying* can be frightening because of the implied threat of more physical violence to follow. Gestures can also carry embarrassing sexual or racist connotations.

Opportunities for *extortion bullying* are greater in schools than they have ever been. Pupils come with sweets, chocolates or crisps for break-time snacks, they have money for bus fares and lunches. They are required to have special equipment for most lessons and they possess expensive, designer-labelled bags and clothing. All of which provide an opportunity for the bully to use physical violence and intimidation to demand payment from the victim. And as with adult extortion the bully will not be satisfied with an isolated act of intimidation.

Exclusion bullying is a subtle and covert form of bullying which is particularly common among adolescent girls – although boys can also isolate a targeted member of the group. The most painful feature of exclusion is that it is carried out by so-called 'friends'. It can destroy a young person's school life, isolating him or her from their important peer group. School is a social meeting place and to be excluded from the intimate camaraderie of teenage culture can undermine a young person's self-esteem and cause untold distress.

How much bullying is there?

The methods used to gather data about the extent and frequency of bullying have been mainly self-report questionnaires, teacher nominations and peer nominations – the first method being most commonly used. The most comprehensive survey into the incidence of bullying was the national survey carried out in Norway in 1983, where self-report questionnaires were used. The results of this survey, as indicated earlier, were that approximately 15 per cent of pupils were involved – 6 per cent as bullies and 9 per cent as bullied. In Chapter 2 (page 20) Erling Roland explains the background to the Norwegian campaign and the results of the survey.

In the UK, the growing body of research is mainly small scale and local, but the evidence is that a higher proportion of pupils are involved. Of interest to primary schools is the work of Stephenson and Smith on bullying in the junior school (1988). In their 1982 survey in 26 schools in Cleveland they collected data from 49 teachers on 1078 year 6 children. They indicated that 23 per cent of their children were involved in bullying: 7 per cent victims, 10 per cent bullies and 6 per cent in the dual role of bully and victim. These disturbing figures would suggest that one in five primary school children are involved in bullying behaviour, and are supported by Ahmad and Smith (1990) who administered a self-report questionnaire similar to the Norwegian instrument to about 2000 pupils in seven middle schools and four secondary schools in the South Yorkshire region. In response to questions on frequency of being bullied, 17 per cent said that they had been moderately bullied (sometimes/now and then) and severely bullied (once a week). Using a similar categorisation of frequency, 6 per cent admitted they had bullied other children. These high figures are also supported in a Sheffield study of two secondary schools (234 pupils) by Yates and Smith (1989), in which the figures, using the same categories given above, were 20 per cent victims and 6 per cent bullies. (For further information about the Sheffield

Project, see Chapter 4.) More conservative figures are provided by Mellor (1990) in his survey of 942 pupils in 10 secondary schools in Scotland. He found incidences of 6 per cent who were bullied 'sometimes or more often' and 4 per cent who had bullied 'sometimes or more often'.

What about young children?

Very young children are also involved in bullying but, as indicated by a number of contributors (Roland, page 25; Pepler *et al.*, page 80), children under the age of 6 have difficulty understanding the concept of bullying. In these studies information has been obtained from parents or teachers. Chazan (1988) reported on the total infant school intake (435) on the Isle of Wight at the beginning of the autumn term. Both teachers and parents completed the Rutter Child Behaviour Scale (Infants) during the children's first term, in which one item is 'bullies other children'. Combining the frequency statements 'certainly applies' and 'applies somewhat', the parents reported that 7.8 per cent of boys and 4.9 per cent of girls bullied other children. The percentages reported by the teachers were 9.5 per cent boys and 7.6 per cent girls. In a national survey by Osborn *et al.* (1984), who administered a modification of the Rutter Scale (retaining the item on bullying) to the mothers of a large national sample of 5-year-olds at home (*n* = 13, 135) and using the same frequency ratings as above, a figure of 13.9 per cent cases of infant bullies was found.

When we consider research involving parents of young children the figures are even higher. From their longitudinal study of child-rearing patterns, *Parents' Perspectives on Children's Behaviour in School*, (1984), Newson and Newson reported that out of a sample of 700 eleven year-olds, the mothers of 26 per cent were aware that their children were being bullied at school, 4 per cent seriously, and another 22 per cent were being bullied in the street.

Bullying worldwide

Increased concern about bullying is evident from many other countries and in addition to information from Norway this book contains contributions from Holland, Canada and Australia. A study in Toronto, Canada, of 211 students from 14 classes (grades 4 to 8) found that 20 per cent were bullied 'now and then' and 'weekly or more often' (Ziegler and Rosenstein-Manner, 1991). Here too the researchers asked the children's parents and teachers about whether they were aware of how often children in the school were bullied, and there was an underestimation in both cases. Fourteen per cent of parents were aware that their child had been bullied 'now and then' or 'weekly or more often'; and when their teachers were asked, 'How many students in your class have been bullied at least once a week in school this term?', as many as 14 per cent replied zero (compared with 6 per cent students) and 7 per cent just 'Didn't know.'

Also using a self-report questionnaire Rigby and Slee (1990) surveyed 676 pupils in three primary schools and one high school in Adelaide, Australia. They found that when they pooled the responses to the question asking, 'How often have you been bullied?', for the categories 'pretty often' and 'very often', the figures were 17 per cent for boys and 11 per cent for girls. In this book Ton Mooij (Chapter 3) reports on his research in The Netherlands. From a sample of 1065 primary aged pupils 8 per cent replied that they had been bullied and 6 per cent had bullied others 'once a week or more'. In his sample of 1055 secondary school pupils the figures were less from the same frequency, namely, 2 per cent bullied and 5 per cent bullying.

Using the same rate of frequency, that is, 'once a week or more often', O'Moore and Hillery (1989) examined the incidence of bullying in four Dublin, Eire, primary schools. The study comprised 783 children of 7–13 years of age and 10.5 per cent were involved in serious bullying (as defined by the above frequency rating) and 8 per cent were seriously bullied.

Finally, in this section on incidence it is important to note that a number of studies report a decline in frequency as children get older. Olweus (1990) demonstrated that the number of victims declined steadily with age for both males and females and that the number of female bullies also declined steadily, but the number of male bullies remained fairly constant between ages 8 and 16. We may in part explain the decline by recognising that young children are more prepared to talk about their problems and turn to adults (not peers) for help. No doubt it is also the case that they are more often bullied in the playground than older pupils simply because as a pupil moves up the school there are fewer older and bigger children to do the bullying. Moreover, adolescents have learned to master the more subtle forms of bullying and also the skills of negotiation which can deflect the bully's attention.

■ Who are the bullies – and who the victims?

From his research into bullying covering well over a decade Olweus provides a *profile of the 'typical bully'*.

'A distinctive characteristic of the typical bully is their aggression towards peers; ... They are, however, often also aggressive toward teachers, parents and siblings. Generally, they have a more positive attitude to violence and use of violent means than students in general. They are often characterised by impulsivity and strong needs to dominate others. They seem to have little empathy with victims of bullying' (Olweus, 1989).

These results have generally been replicated by other studies, including Stephenson and Smith (1988) in the UK. They found that bullies tended to be physically strong, active and assertive; and one could add that they are easily provoked, see insult when none is intended and actually enjoyed aggression. Concerning bullies' school work O'Moore and Hillery (1991) found that they were below average in attainment, had poor concentration, low self-esteem regarding their work and hated school and teachers.

Aware of the dangers of over-simplification Stephenson and Smith distinguished between the typical bully and 'anxious bullies' (18 per cent of their survey population). The latter were defined as having low popularity and low confidence, and also reported as having few likeable qualities and more frequently to have problems at home.

In his *profile of a 'typical' victim* Olweus' findings have also been replicated by other researchers.

'Victims of bullying are more anxious and insecure than students in general. They are often cautious, sensitive and quiet. When attacked by other students, they commonly react with crying (at least in the lower grades) and withdrawal. They have a negative view of themselves and their situation. They often look upon themselves as failures and feel stupid, ashamed and unattractive.

Further, the victims are lonely and abandoned at school. ... If they are boys, they are likely to be physically weaker than boys in general' (Olweus, 1989).

Regarding their work at school Stephenson and Smith reported that, like bullies, victims tended to have poor concentration, poor school attainment and low self-confidence. Besag (1991) highlighted the probable clumsiness of victimised children, and Frost (1991) concluded that they tended to be misfits, because of appearance, lack of friends, or being irritating or unusually compliant. When considering appearance Olweus in his 1978 study found that the over-simplified explanation of being in some way different from the norm made certain children potential targets of bullying. He concluded that children were not singled out for bullying because they are physically different (for example, wear glasses, have speech or language differences, are obese, or have unusual facial expression, posture or dress), but that bullies probably used some oddity in the potential victim as a pretext for bullying. (I shall return to this important point a little later.)

As in their work with bullies, Stephenson and Smith also distinguish between the typical victim and 'provocative victims' (17 per cent of their survey population), who are attention-seekers within the peer group. Findings indicate that they more often complain to their teachers that they are being bullied, though it appears that they actively provoke the bullying. Provocative victims invariably create considerable management and counselling difficulties for teachers.

Disregarding provocative victims, it is difficult to explain bullying as a consequence of the behaviour of the victims themselves. For to do so is tantamount to 'blaming the victim' for the bully's aggressive and abusive behaviour. As one bullied teenager said, 'I don't have a problem – he's got the problem!' and whilst it is the case that the behaviour and demeanour of some victims signal that they are insecure and timid persons who will not retaliate if insulted or attacked, that is only part of the problem. Some children are picked out because they have 'positive' attributes, such as, being clever, or good at games or another subject, or even being physically attractive. As teachers we must not focus on the victim to explain the bully's behaviour and accept that there are children who actually take pleasure from causing pain and distress in others.

Looking ahead

In the next three chapters the overlap between this section on understanding and Section II on the management of bullying will be abundantly evident. For these chapters present the advanced thinking on the problem from research in the United Kingdom, Holland and Norway. Each in turn raises our perception of bullying and progresses to provide a broad sweep of how it can be successfully tackled. Subsequent chapters describe specific areas of school management which need to be organised and administered if a successful whole-school, anti-bullying programme is to be effected.

2 Bullying: a developing tradition of research and management

Erling Roland

Today, we know that bullying is a serious problem among children and adolescents at least in the industrialised parts of the world. In fact, it can be estimated that 5–10 per cent of young people suffer from bullying, and that about the same percentage of the youngsters bully. Until about 1970, bullying was a non-existent phenonomen within social research, but a real problem for children and parents. Sadly, the problem was a private one.

Surprisingly, it was in Scandinavia, probably one of the most peaceful corners of the world, that bullying was first addressed as a concept for research. The pioneer was a Swedish doctor of medicine, Peter Paul Heinemann. His first article (1969) and book (1972) were succeeded by several empirical investigations and programmes of management in Scandinavia and Finland, as both professional and public concern were developing.

In late 1982 this concern was greatly increased when two young people in Norway took their own lives and the local social services reported that these suicides were caused by longstanding bullying of the two youngsters. These incidents were in the news all over Norway, and soon afterwards the Minister of Education announced that the ministry would take action against bullying in Norwegian state schools.

A working group, of which I was a member, was set up to plan a nationwide campaign against bullying. As an integrated part of the campaign, a broad investigation was conducted before the campaign started. Another member of the working party, Professor Dan Olweus, was mainly responsible for this investigation which began in late 1983. The main results from this investigation were published by Olweus in 1985. There were also follow-up investigations to see if the campaign had been effective.

The design of the campaign and some preliminary results were presented at the first international conference about bullying, at Stavanger, Norway, in 1987 (arranged by the Norwegian Ministry of Education and the European Council). At this conference 13 European countries were represented. A main conclusion of this conference was that research and public concern about bullying was very meagre outside Scandinavia. This has now changed, not least because of the work by some of our guests at the Stavanger conference. Several delegates from different European countries contributed to the book *'Bullying: An International Perspective'* (Roland and Munthe, 1989). Today, it is encouraging to notice increasing international concern about the serious problem of bullying, both professional and public.

This chapter is concerned with the main background and developing tradition of research and management in Scandinavia, and especially of my own work in Norway.

▰ Pioneering research

In 1969, Peter Paul Heinemann published the first article about bullying, or 'mobbing', as he called it. This article, which attracted great public interest, was succeeded by a book in 1972, translated into Norwegian in 1973. Heinemann's work was pioneering and the origin of research on bullying. The core of his understanding is that mobbing is a kind of uncontrolled activity conducted by a rather large group of individuals. The main reason for this mass attack is that the group has been disturbed in its ordinary activity by an individual and it is this person who becomes the target of the group violence. When the attack is over, the members of the group again take on their roles as ordinary pupils.

I think it is fair to say that Heinemann's 'accidental mass attack' hypothesis is not the common opinion today. Instead bullying is understood as a quite stable phenonomenon conducted by some children and directed against some particular others. A widely accepted definition today is:

> 'Bullying is longstanding violence, physical or psychological, conducted by an individual or a group and directed against an individual who is not able to defend himself in the actual situation' (Roland 1989a).

This definition includes some important aspects: the activity is violent, it is longstanding and it is conducted by a power agent against a somehow helpless individual.

▪▪ What are the dynamics of bullying?

Most of the research in Scandinavia and Finland concerning the dynamics of bullying has concentrated on the personalities of bullies and victims. Drawing on results from his Stockholm area investigation in the early seventies, Dan Olweus, a leading researcher in the field, has contributed much to this aspect of the problem. One of his main conclusions is that boy bullies are characterised by an 'aggressive trait' and also have weak inhibitions against aggression, and that this is a major explanation for persistent bullying behaviour. The boy bullies are also above normal in physical strength (1978).   *need to still rel.*

Some other aspects of the personality of the bullies have also been investigated, among which are self-esteem and academic ability (Olweus, 1978; Mykletun, 1979; Roland, 1980; Bjørkvist *et al.* 1982). The main results are that the bullies are not very different on general self-esteem and that boy bullies, but not girl bullies, probably are a little below normal on academic ability.

As for the boy victims, Olweus (1978) concluded that they are insecure, low on general self-esteem and below normal academic ability. These results for victims have, in the main, been confirmed by other investigations in Scandinavia (Mykletun, 1979; Roland, 1980) and the results are probably valid for both boys and girls. However boy victims are not especially deviant in outlook although they are below normal on physical strength, according to Olweus.

Besides personality, home conditions have been focused on by Olweus (1980). As part of his Stockholm area investigation among adolescent boys he investigated the connection between some family variables and interpersonal aggression on the part of the boys. His main finding was that both negativism from mother to boy, mother's permissiveness towards aggressive behaviour on the part of the boy, and mother's and father's use of power-assertive discipline methods were correlated with interpersonal aggression on the part of the boy, and that the joint effect of the family variables was substantial, explaining some 25% of the variation on aggression. This result should prove very important for a common understanding of the dynamics of bullying. It could in principle be illustrated as follows: *home*

Family → Personality → Bullying

The main understanding then, is that some unfortunate home conditions generate an aggressive personality on the part of the boy, which is then a main explanation for a persistent tendency to bully others. The victims of this behaviour are in general physically weak and insecure.

A few words should be said about this persistently claimed explanation. It was the connection between home conditions and interpersonal aggression of bullies that was investigated by Olweus (1980). The dependent variable was not bullying, as is clearly demonstrated by the definition of interpersonal aggression used by him. The connection between home conditions and bullying is not shown in this investigation. Some evidence exists, however, for such a direct connection between unfortunate home conditions and bullying: namely a moderate relationship between estimates of positive attitudes towards aggression and bullying (Olweus, 1978). However since this connection is far from complete, one should be very careful not to conclude that the investigated family variables explain the same amount of variation in bullying as they probably do on interpersonal aggression in general. The strength of the connection between family variables and bullying remains to be investigated directly. Note also that the samples studied by Olweus were composed of boys only. Finally, even if the connection between some family variables and bullying should show up to be of about the same strength as that between such variables and interpersonal aggression, the major part of the variation on bullying remains to be explained.

The group or individuals?

In his pioneering work, Heinemann (1972) claimed very strongly that the bullies were ordinary children, without any particular deviant traits. It was when the balance of the group was disturbed by a child demonstrating deviant and interrupting behaviour that the individuals in this groups turned against the deviant in an all-against-one attack. Heinemann drew heavily on group dynamics to explain bullying. In many ways, it is the classic contradiction between understanding a situation or person as cause that is represented by Heinemann and Olweus.

However this is not to say that Olweus has not been concerned about group structures and processes as explanations of bullying (1978; 1981), but in principle he seems to regard group dynamics as secondary to personality. It is the particular personalities of the bullies and the victims that mainly create group structures and escalate the interaction of bullying between the two parties. Unfortunately, such structures and processes have not been documented by Olweus with empirical evidence where bullying is concerned. The only exception may be that boy bullies seem normally to be popular, while victims are below their peers on popularity. But the descriptions of supposed structures and processes go much further than this.

The importance of group dynamics has also been discussed by several other researchers from Scandinavia and Finland (Hauge, 1973; Ekman, 1977; Hohr, 1983), including myself (Roland, 1980). The theoretical approaches and explanations have been different and also contradictory. But a common problem has been lack of empirical evidence for the different conclusions, just as it has been for Heinemann and Olweus. A further step to illustrate Nordic research on bullying then should be to include group dynamics but to give this aspect a secondary status:

$$
\begin{array}{c}
\text{Family} \rightarrow \text{Personality} \rightarrow \text{Bullying} \\
\updownarrow \\
\text{Group dynamics}
\end{array}
$$

The aspect of group structures and processes may have been over-estimated by Heinemann as causes for bullying. At the beginning of the eighties, enough evidence existed to conclude that some pupils were involved in bullying more than others, and that personality counts. But personality variables did not explain the majority of the variance on bullying. The 'situation' then, should be addressed in a more systematic way, both theoretically and empirically.

The way to stop bullying

Each of several different investigations about bullying was conducted in one or a few schools and these investigations came up with quite different figures about the extent of the problem. The figures for victims varied from 2–3% up to 20%, and the percentages for bullies were also quite different from one study to another. The investigations were conducted at both small and big schools, schools in rural and urban areas and so on. Also the methods of investigation varied. Despite this variation both professionals and the public saw bullying as a serious problem in schools in Scandinavia and Finland at the beginning of the eighties, and programmes of management were started.

In the Nordic countries and especially in Sweden and Norway, a programme of management worked out by Anatol Pikas (1976) was widely accepted. Pikas, like Heinemann, was mainly concerned about group processes of bullying. In fact, Pikas has always claimed that 'mobbing' should also be the correct term in English, to emphasise the group and not the individual aspect of bullying (1989). In fact, it was his understanding of group processes that was the core of the programme, called in my translation, 'The way to stop bullying'.

The two principles of the programme were:

- To split and then reunite the group of bullies.
- To co-operate with the bullies.

Pikas was able to see that the bullies would stick together if they were in the first place addressed together. Consequently, he recommended that the teacher or the school psychologist should meet first with the bullies one by one. In this way, the individual bullies would be much easier to handle compared with a first meeting with the whole group. These individual meetings should be conducted sequentially so that the bullies should not get the opportunity to talk with each other. Then the teacher should meet with all of them to reunite the group and make further plans.

The co-operative aspect was taken care of by the teacher by appealing to the individual bullies and the whole group about the victim's difficult situation. By this approach the bullies were not only expected to stop their own bullying but also to be brave and assist the victim if bullied by others. Pikas reported that this programme had worked well in several cases and it was adopted by many school psychological services and schools.

The minister takes action

In the beginning of 1983, shortly after the alarming reports of two suicides caused by bullying, the Norwegian Ministry of Education arranged a hearing for some 15 school politicians and professionals about the problem of bullying. I can well remember the key question asked by the minister, Tore Austad, at the beginning of the hearing: 'Do we have enough knowledge about bullying to take action at a national level?'. The answer was 'Yes', and the minister announced to the Norwegian mass media that the ministry would initiate a national campaign against bullying to start in autumn 1983 after a planning period.

The ministry set up a working party, headed by the Deputy Education minister, to prepare the campaign and during the spring and summer of 1983 the programme was worked out. It was composed of two main parts:

- A campaign to prevent and to stop bullying.
- An investigation to estimate the amount of bullying in Norway.

A 'package' of written material and a video were produced. The main elements were an article and some short papers for the headteachers and teachers, and a brochure for parents. As for the profile of the campaign, the article by Olweus and Roland, (1983) was a most important part. It had two sections, 'Background' and 'Management'. Under background, we outlined a definition of bullying and key empirical findings, mostly home conditions and personalities of bullies and victims, besides estimates of the amount of the problem. The approach, then, was the now familiar: **home** → **personality** → **bullying** structure, supplemented with some comments on group processes. Part II, about management, was mainly composed of the key elements of the two already published programmes of management (Pikas, 1976; Roland, 1983). The article was not an original contribution to the knowledge of bullying but mainly a review of research and an integration of already known principles and methods of management.

All the other material – the brochure for parents, some short papers for headteachers and teachers and the video – were based on the main ideas of the article. The film was composed of some cameos of bullying in primary school and in secondary school, plus some ideas for prevention and intervention. This film could be shown to teachers, pupils and parents. The schools had to buy or rent the film, at a subsidised cost. All other material in the 'package' was free and it was distributed to all schools by the ministry.

Besides the programme of management it was decided to conduct a nationwide survey to estimate the level of bullying before the campaign was started. A questionnaire for pupils and instructions for administration of the investigation were worked out and distributed to all state primary and secondary schools in Norway to be used in a specific week in autumn 1983. A few days later, all the schools received the package of written materials from the Ministry of Education.

In this way concern about bullying had reached a climax in Norway and we were ready for probably the largest social experiment in the school system of our country. But a period of at least ten years had been necessary to build the platform for the Norwegian campaign. This period can be illustrated in this way (Roland, 1989):

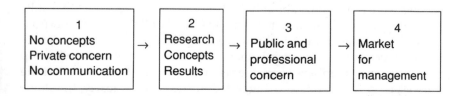

Both the announcement by the minister of the campaign and the introduction of it were widely referred to in the mass media and the campaign therefore was well known among pupils, parents and teachers.

The nationwide baseline investigation

The nationwide investigation was conducted at the beginning of October
1983. All the 3500 primary and secondary schools in Norway were
invited to participate and about 90% did so.

An anonymous questionnaire to the pupils, grades 2–9, was used to
establish a baseline before the campaign. About 10% of the schools
(about 83 000 pupils) were chosen by the National Bureau of Statistics as
a representative sample. Dan Olweus analysed the answers from these
schools.

Nearly 10% of the pupils, grades 2–9, reported that they were bullied,
slightly more boys than girls. The percentage of victims decreased with
increasing age at primary level but not at secondary level. As a mean,
about 7% of the pupils reported that they had bullied peers at school
now and then or more often. For girls, the percentage of bullies slightly
decreases with increasing age but this is not the case with boys. The percentage of bullies is about twice as high for boys than for girls at grade 2
and the difference increases with increasing age. Olweus used the criterion 'now and then or more often' to identify the victims and the bullies.
In this case, 'more often' means one or more times a week. If the often
used criterion of 'once a week or more often' had been used, the figures
would most probably have been less than those he reported. Two follow-
up investigations among the schools in the sample were conducted, one
in Bergen and one in Rogaland, each sub-sample containing about 40
schools.

Short-term effects in Bergen

Olweus (1991) has reported remarkable short-term effects in Bergen.
About one year after the campaign the number of victims in the Bergen
schools were reduced by about 50%. This was estimated from the results
of a follow-up study in which exactly the same definition and questionnaire was used as in the baseline investigation. One year later this new
low level persisted. However, it should be noted that between follow-up
investigations, members from the research team in Bergen visited the
schools, reported results and suggested further work. Clearly, the short-

term effect of the campaign was remarkable and very promising but what of the longer-term effect of such a large-scale campaign?

■■■■ Longer-term effects in Rogaland (1983–1986)

In Rogaland, 37 of the 40 schools in the sample took part in the follow-up study in October 1986, three years after the baseline investigation and the campaign. As in Bergen, exactly the same definition of bullying and the same questionnaire were used. There is no indication that the campaign was adopted or used in different ways in Bergen and Rogaland. One major difference is that the research team in Rogaland did not intervene in any way in the schools in the period between the baseline and follow-up investigations to make the situation in Rogaland as similar as possible to the rest of the country.

The overall changes from 1983 to 1986 have been reported by Roland (1988). The main trend is that the level of bullying in Rogaland has increased slightly during these three years, most especially among the youngest pupils. The increase for girls was very slight, but for boys (grades 4–9, 11–16 years) rose from 3.6% being bullied in 1983 to 5.2% in 1986, and those admitting to bullying rose from 4.1% to 5.1%.

The trend was regarded as a disappointment, but it can be concluded with greater certainly that this not very promising trend is not a consequence of the campaign but a tendency that appeared inspite of it. This can be seen by taking a closer look at the results at schools that were a little, moderately or seriously engaged in the campaign in 1983.

■■■■ The follow-up research

Information about the level of bullying was collected by questionnaires given to the pupils in October 1983 and in October 1986, grades 2–9. All questions referred to 'this term' (about 20 August to October). Key questions were about 'bullying' and 'exclusion'.

Bullying was defined to the pupils as both verbal and physical attacks conducted by one pupil or a group of pupils towards a pupil who is not able to defend him or herself. I will call this 'open bullying'. The pupils were also asked if they were excluded and were alone during the breaks. Pupils who are excluded in this way will also be reported as victims of bullying. The pupils were asked 'how often' the exclusion and open bullying took place, ranging from 'seldom' to 'several times a day'. Only those who reported incidents once a week or more often will be counted as victims or bullies. Only results from grades 4–9 are reported because some younger pupils had problems filling in the questionnaires.

The degree of involvement in the campaign in autumn 1983 was estimated on the basis of information from the headteacher and teachers at each school. One or two teachers were interviewed at small and middle range schools, three teachers at big schools. Both the headteachers and the teachers were independently asked detailed questions about what was done at their school, that is, materials used, meetings, in-service days etc. Four values were used (graded 1–4) to estimate the degree of engagement by the school, and these were carefully assessed and recorded.

Value 1:   The school did nothing more than conduct the investigation.

Value 2:   The school conducted the investigation and the results were presented to the staff and discussed.

Value 3:   The school conducted the investigation, the results were presented and discussed, and the teachers used the material in the package in class and/or at a parents' meeting to some degree.

Value 4:   The school conducted the investigation, presented and discussed the results, and demonstrated a serious and planned use of the package towards pupils and parents.

Results of the follow-up

The results between engagement and changes in bullying behaviour which were found for excluded and openly bullied pupils and for the bullies, showed clear, though not major differences.

Openly bullied pupils

In 1986, a total of 3.75% of the pupils reported that they were openly bullied, 4.52% of the boys and 3.12 of the girls. The percentage for primary schools is more than double that for secondary schools. The long-term effects of the campaign in primary and secondary schools showed an almost straight connection between engagement and positive changes in primary schools. This general tendency was demonstrated for both boys and girls. The tendency in secondary schools was similar but weaker.

Bullies

In primary schools, approximately the same tendency as for excluded and openly bullied pupils was demonstrated. There was a substantial connection between engagement in the campaign and positive change. The tendencies are mainly the same for boys and girls. The long-term effect for bullies in secondary schools was not as clear as in primary schools. The most negative change is in schools that were moderately involved in the campaign, while there is a minor positive change at schools that were actively involved both for boys and girls. At the secondary level, one should notice that more schools were moderately or actively involved in the campaign compared with the number of schools which were engaged to only a small degree. The figures then are most reliable at schools that were moderately or actively involved in the campaign.

What was found?

From 1983 to 1986 the percentage of excluded and also openly bullied pupils was quite stable in Rogaland but the percentage of bullies increased (Roland, 1988). Inspite of this a substantial and positive long-term effect of the Norwegian campaign against bullying was demonstrated in Rogaland. A clear and nearly straight connection between degree of engagement in the campaign and positive change was mainly found for both excluded and openly bullied pupils and for bullies. This tendency was most clearly demonstrated at primary level. The only exception to this tendency was found for bullies at secondary level but even for these pupils the best results were achieved at schools that were actively involved in the campaign.

The results were reported only for grades 4–9 (11–16 years) because some of the younger pupils had difficulties answering the questionnaire in a reliable way. The results for this age group were analysed however, and showed that the level of bullying increased in an alarming way from 1983 to 1986. The results are, as I say, uncertain ones. But an interesting point to note is that in 1986 level 2 and 3 pupils had not started school in 1983 when the campaign was conducted which indicates, in the same way as the substantial connection between involvement and positive change, that the long-term effect of the campaign was positive. But at the same time, it is alarming that the level of bullying increased in Rogaland and probably also in Norway in this three-year period inspite of the good effect of the campaign.

Finally, when one compares the short-term effects in Bergen with the longer-term effects in Rogaland, a few conclusions are very clear:

- The structure of the changes is approximately the same but the short-term effect is much stronger than the long-term effect.

- Only 2–3 schools in Rogaland continued their systematic work against bullying after the autumn of 1983, according to the interviews with the headteachers and the teachers. This is probably a major explanation for the difference between the short- and long-term effect.

It is clear from the two follow-up investigations that the Norwegian campaign against bullying had a positive effect. However, it showed the importance of schools establishing stable routines for actions against bullying. The accidental 'now and then' approach could possibly make the situation worse and not better.

A new programme

Some main conclusions from the follow-up research of the Norwegian campaign have been used to design a new project.

- The main principles of management used in the Norwegian Campaign (Olweus and Roland, 1983) are effective according to the short- and long-term effect studies.
- The short-term effect is much stronger than the long-term one and the explanation seems to be that only 2–3 schools out of 37 in Rogaland established routines to continue the good work that was initiated by the campaign.
- The long-term effect is better at primary schools than at secondary schools.

These conclusions have been important for the design of a new programme called 'A System Approach'.

'A System Approach'

The new programme is different from the Norwegian campaign programme. An important focus is the 'the good start' principle and also the 'system' principle (Roland, 1989) is more central. Finally, bullying is taken as an integrated part of a general programme for classroom management and not an isolated element. The reason for this is to achieve a permanent and general concern by the teachers about understanding and managing bullying. This system approach is illustrated on page 27.

The left part of the model illustrates families (F) of the pupils and lines are drawn between the families to demonstrate the possible relationships. The box in the middle is the class, composed of the individual

The system approach model

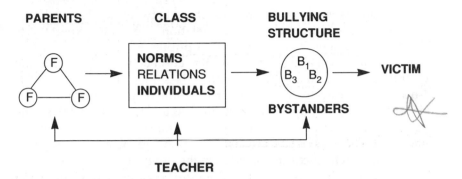

pupils but also of relations between them and group norms. The behaviour in question, in this case bullying, is located at the right of the model.

Thus, bullying is not conceptualised simply as the number of bullies and victims that result from particular home-class conditions but as a pattern of interaction between the bullies and between bullies and the victim. Bystanders of bullying are also included. Lines are drawn between the families, the class and the pattern of bullying to illustrate causal links. Such lines are also plotted from teacher to families, to class and to the bullying pattern. The system model is a conception to analyse central causes of different kinds of behavioural problems, including bullying. The model also is used to highlight principles of prevention and intervention. In this way, the model is flexible, and also where management is concerned. The teacher may focus on a particular kind of behavioural problem or at behaviour in general.

The parents

As an important part of the new programme the teachers were recommended to work closely with parents. This was to establish good relationships with each family but also to be concerned about the network between the different families as illustrated in the model. Good relations between teacher and the different families and also *between* families are regarded as preventative measures. Also, if behavioural problems, including bullying, show up, such networks, already established, can be useful. The parents of the different families then could probably communicate well and also co-operate with the teacher. These principles and procedures for co-operation with the parents are introduced to the teachers as an important part of the system approach.

The class

Great emphasis is put on the relationships between teacher and each pupil in the class. If the quality of these relations is good we expect this to improve the influence from teacher to pupils. High quality teacher-pupils relations will also improve the attraction between the pupils and so contribute to social integration within class. Pupil-pupil relations are also addressed directly in the new programme by principles and methods for profiling the pupils' positions in class and also for formal organisation between pupils. Finally, the importance of prosocial norms, common goals and symbols are focused upon and methods to establish such common references are included in the programme.

Intervention

The programme includes principles and methods for handling behavioural problems in general and bullying in particular when such behaviours occur. As for collective behavioural problems, including bullying, the main steps are:

- To make the individual pupil responsible when the anti-social behaviour takes place.
- To follow up the individual pupils by separate meetings to make clear that the behaviour in question is not acceptable and also to invite the pupil to co-operate.
- To bring the pupils together again to demonstrate that the individual pupils were responsible and co-operative, and build on this to create prosocial norms and patterns of co-operative behaviour.

The bystanders, or even 'neutral' pupils, may be included in this three-step method to stabilise the group of disruptive pupils or bullies.

The theory behind the practice

The programme builds on the following principles:

- The social structure of a class is theoretically separated from the process of behaviour – the social pattern in the model.
- The social structure of a class will contribute to the quality of different kinds of behaviour – the processes.
- The behaviour and social consequences of it may change the structure.

- By contributing to a good social structure of a class the teacher could prevent different kinds of anti-social behavioural problems, not only bullying. And by handling a particular kind of behavioural problem in a constructive way the structure could change to prevent not only this problem but other kinds of problems as well.
- This broad approach is also expected to make the work of the teacher persistent and longstanding because of the economy of the work.
- The social structure of a class, including parents and teacher, will be established quickly and then be difficult to change.

The best effect of the programme then will be in first grade. But also the start of secondary school or even the beginning of a new school year will be a critical period and a potential for a new start.

The project goes into practice

The new project was started in spring 1991 in 9 of the primary schools in Sandnes, a town in the south western part of Norway. A main element of the project is to implement the System Approach of management, for teachers working at grade 1. The best time for the teacher to contribute to a good social system in class is probably in the first year, class one. The whole year but, in particular, the first days and weeks are likely to be of great importance.

The design of the project was:

Spring 1991.	A baseline investigation to estimate the level of bullying and other social aspects at first level in 9 schools and about 20 classes.
Spring 1991– spring 1992.	Implementation of the System Approach for management in class.
	About 20 teachers working at first level in the school year 1991–92. Four seminars and consultations between the seminar days with staff from the research team.
Spring 1992.	A second investigation identical to the first one to estimate the effect on bullying and other social aspects of the System Approach of management.
Spring 1992– Spring 1993.	Seminars and consultations with the new group of first level teachers. Implementing the System Approach, and *adding* the aspect of *bullying*, theory and management, in an *explicit* way.

Spring 1993.   A third investigation identical to the first two to estimate the effect on bullying and other social matters of the *bullying focused* System Approach.

The two versions of the programme (1991–92 and 1992–93) are designed to investigate how focused bullying should be in such an integrated programme. By comparing the results from investigations 1 and 2, we have reason to be optimistic about the effect of the general System Approach. The more bullying focused programme will be finished in spring 1993 and investigation number 3 conducted. The effect on bullying and other aspects of behaviour of the two slightly different programmes will be estimated by comparing results from the three identical investigations. In this way it should be possible to evaluate the extent of the effects of the changed behaviour of year 1 pupils on the rest of the school as they progress into subsequent years. Will the longitudinal 'good start' programme gradually influence the ethos of the school in a positive way?

3 Working towards understanding and prevention in The Netherlands

Ton Mooij

Before 1985 bullying was given hardly any attention in The Netherlands. Since then, however, interest in being bullied and bullying has become more and more widespread. A breakthrough was recognised by the book, *The Scape-Goat in the Classroom* by Bob van der Meer, the Dutch pioneer on this issue (1988). His case studies of children being bullied and suggestions on how to manage the problem alerted teachers and parents, school management, school counsellors and educational policy alike. Since the appearance of the book bullying is a 'hot topic' in the media.

Within five years of van der Meer's book being published four main trends can be distinguished in The Netherlands:

- Within a lot of schools teachers, parents and school management have become aware of bullying as a kind of signal or symptom indicating the quality of the social processes within school and in the school playground. For example, many schools request information or talks about bullying, teachers discuss bullying with each other or with pupils and parents, and teachers and parents work to try to prevent it.

- Social welfare institutions discovered a 'new' subject to work on with schools. The common problem is how to work with bullies and victims and how to reduce bullying behaviour. There are many ways in which this co-operation is carried out: creating conversation groups with bullies and victims; developing lessons on bullying; giving information to bullies, victims, classmates, teachers and parents; creating theatre or role plays on bullying behaviour; making videos with examples of bullying behaviour and how it could be stopped; developing social training programmes for bully and victim, classmates and teachers; institutionalising a bullying policy in school; or appointing one person as a 'trust person' in school. In 1992 a comprehensive overview was published by the National Health Institute.

■ Educational, welfare and justice policy became more and more interested in bullying behaviour because, despite the vivid interest in the topic, so little is 'really' known about bullying in The Netherlands – as in most other countries. Moreover, indications exist that bullying is related to disruptive behaviour of pupils during lessons, to final school drop-out, and to developing a criminal career (Bayh, 1975; Beirn, Kiney and McGinn, 1972; Mooij, 1980, 1992a, 1992b; Olweus, 1984, 1987, 1991; Reich and Young, 1975).

■ Research projects were designed in order to provide more information on bullying in The Netherlands. A first longitudinal project concentrated on social and affective adjustment and development of bullying (about 2500 pupils in elementary education: see Haselager and van Lieshout, 1992a, and b). This project is ongoing. Secondly, I carried out a survey with schools, teachers and about 2000 pupils in elementary and secondary education (Mooij, 1992a). This will be dealt with later. Thirdly, a survey elaborating more violent aspects of bullying with about 5000 pupils in about 100 secondary schools started in 1992 (Mooij, 1992c).

Thus it is evident that interest in understanding bullying and its different aspects, and attempts to reduce or even prevent bullying, have grown rapidly in The Netherlands. In order to give some initial information I will provide the most important results from a research project supported by the Dutch Foundation for Educational Research (Instituut voor Onderzoek van het Onderwijs, SVO), carried out in 1990–92. The research questions were formulated by SVO and intended to clarify the kind, duration, location, and intensity of being bullied and bullying in primary and secondary education in The Netherlands.

The scope of the SVO-Project 0110

In the literature on bullying at least five potential causes for bullying are distinguished. This multi-causal structure has been partly verified by research but not all of the required research has yet been carried out. The following kinds of potential causes seem realistic:

■ **Personal characteristics**: e.g. being a boy or having a high degree of aggressiveness (Olweus, 1978).

- **Early home socialisation characteristics**: e.g. degree of punishment experienced during early youth: a higher degree of punishment and a greater permissiveness of the mother towards her child's acting out of aggressive behaviour stimulate bullying behaviour later on at school (Olweus, 1980). Also, differences between the cultural values and norms at home and at school may disadvantage pupils coming from lower socio-economic backgrounds, which may promote bullying and disruptive behaviour (Willis, 1977).

- **Social processes**: e.g. affective, co-operative, disruptive and power processes between persons or groups have their own rules and characteristics (Lewis, Lippitt and White, 1939; Marsh, Rosser and Herre´, 1978; Mulder, 1977). As bullying processes occur between one or more bullies and one or more victims, these processes are social processes by definition. Affective, co-operative, disruptive and power characteristics may therefore also become relevant in bullying processes.

- **School characteristics**: e.g. within-classroom instructional processes characterised by very little pupil responsibility or by a competitive atmosphere in struggling for scarce good school marks in the yearly grading system, may promote bullying processes between pupils. This occurs because class and school characteristics promote a yearly pupil competition with success for some pupils and lack of success, demotivation and compensating disruptive and bullying behaviour for others (Arbeitsgruppe Schulforschung, 1980; Bowles and Gintis, 1976; Brusten and Hurrelmann, 1973; Mooij, 1979, 1987, 1992b; Willis, 1977). Also, school characteristics like school climate, number of pupils, degree of anonymity of a pupil within the school or the school's environment may be relevant.

- **Societal characteristics**: e.g. the degree of achievement or status orientation within society may promote or even 'legalise' the dominance and power orientation displayed by bullies (Bayh, 1975; Bowles and Gintis, 1976; Karabel and Halsey, 1977).

The scope of the SVO-project was limited by budget and time. The project concentrated on the clarification of bullying concepts, the quality of their measurement, their interrelationships and the relationships with personal, home, class and school characteristics. It was for example hypothesised that:

- Boys are relatively more involved in bullying than girls;
- Parents' or carers'' education and profession ('family background') relates to a child's bullying behaviour;

■ The didactical organisation within the class, and surveillance during free lessons and in the playground during breaktimes, are
related to bullying.

Many other variables were included for explorative reasons.

The method that had to be used was a survey in randomly selected
schools. First, headteachers in elementary education and school-leaders
in secondary education were asked to complete a short questionnaire.
Second, teachers of the participating schools were contacted. They were
teachers of the sixth and eighth classes in primary education (children of
about 9–10 and 11–12 years old, respectively) and teachers of the second
and fourth classes in secondary education (children of about 13–14 and
15–16 years old, respectively). The teachers were asked to complete a
short questionnaire on didactical-organisational aspects of their lessons.
They were also asked to let their pupils complete some questionnaires
and tests. Most important was Olweus' self-report questionnaire on
being bullied and bullying, a sociometric questionnaire asking pupils to
report about the behaviour of their classmates (Haselager and van
Lieshout, 1992a), and a test meant to measure non-verbal intelligence
(Raven's Standard Progressive Matrices).

Thirty primary schools with 45 classes and 1065 pupils and 36 secondary
schools with 43 classes and 1055 pupils co-operated. This gives quite a representative view on being bullied and bullying in elementary and secondary education in The Netherlands. I give selected results here;
complete results and detailed statistical aspects can be found in Mooij
(1992a).

Being bullied and bullying

In agreement with the international literature the percentages on the
self-reported frequencies of being bullied or bullying in Olweus' questionnaire were used to indicate the incidence of being bullied and bullying. The results of the SVO-project show that the incidence of *being
bullied* in The Netherlands during the school-year 1990–91. In general,
these results are in line with results from other European countries
(Roland and Munthe, 1989; Olweus, 1987, 1991; Tattum and Lane, 1989).

being bullied:	primary education:	secondary education:
several times a week	4%	2%
once a week or more	8%	2%
now and then or more	23%	6%

In the same vein, the incidence of *bullying* in The Netherlands during the school-year 1990–1991 ranges between 3% ('several times a week') and 20% ('now and then or more') in elementary education, and between 3% and 16% respectively in secondary education.

being bullied:	primary education:	secondary education:
several times a week	3%	3%
once a week or more	6%	5%
now and then or more	20%	16%

Compared with the results on being bullied in secondary education the percentages on bullying seem somewhat puzzling because bullying occurs more often than being bullied. One possible explanation is that bullies prefer to select victims who are younger (Olweus, 1987).

■■■ Bullying concepts

In order to provide more information on being bullied, bullying and the relationships of these phenomena with other characteristics, at first the relationships between items potentially representing bullying concepts were analysed. The analyses were carried out on the self-reported data of all pupils in the research. The results show that six concepts can be distinguished reliably:

1 **Being bullied directly**: this means being bullied physically and continuously (last school-year, this school-year, during the last five days), everywhere (at school, on the way to and from school), and in different ways (being kicked, being told mean things or called names);

2 **Being bullied indirectly**: being socially isolated: disliking breaktimes, hardly having any good friends in the class, more often feeling lonely at school and during breaktimes, and more often thinking you are less liked than the other pupils within class;

3 **Bullying**: bullying continuously (last school-year, this school-year, during the last five days) and everywhere (at school, on the way to and from school), and saying that he or she likes bullying;

4 **Negative attitude towards bullying**: not liking other children to be bullied, helping a bullied child of their own age, and not liking children who bully other children;

5 **Bullying the teacher**: having watched children who try to bully the teacher, more often co-operating with other pupils in bullying the

teacher, and having done this already more often during the last school-year;

6 **Stopping bullying**: observing that the teacher, other children or other people on the way to and from school are trying to put an end to bullying.

The questionnaire items with respect to each concept were combined in a scale and each pupil's scores on the six scales were computed. As hypothesised, some of these scale-scores are highly interrelated. For example, being bullied directly and being bullied indirectly show a high interrelationship: a bullied child is usually bullied both directly and indirectly (physically and socially, respectively). Furthermore, being bullied is associated with expressing a more negative attitude towards bullying and observing that other people try to stop bullying. On the other hand, bullying is positively related to bullying the teacher (which is, among other things, done by behaving in disruptive ways during the lesson) and related to expressing a positive attitude to bullying. These relationships strengthen the internal validity of the self-reported conceptual framework on bullying behaviour.

What do peers think of a bully?

Because self-reporting on socially undesirable behaviour (like bullying and disruption) may be distorted by ego-centric or ego-defensive mechanisms, it was deemed important to check the self-report information on being bullied and bullying with information from other persons, such as each pupil's classmates.

To accomplish this twelve behavioural characteristics were selected, and each pupil was asked to write down the names of the three pupils who most showed each behaviour in the classroom. These data were factor analysed in order to reveal the underlying relationships between the behavioural characteristics. In factor analysis, characteristics with relatively high interrelationships are grouped together and, if this makes sense, are given a fitting conceptual name. In this 'sociometric' case three groups of characteristics represent three factors conceptualising other pupils' behaviour. The sociometric factors are called: (the other pupil) is a bully; is sympathetic; is a scape goat. The factors were rotated in order to minimise the overlap between them, so the three factorial concepts are relatively independent of each other. Here are the sociometric factors with their most characteristic items:

1 **(the other pupil) is a bully:**
  regularly bullies other children;
  often quarrels with other pupils;
  usually disrupts lessons;
  is not liked at all by me;
  is (the opposite of) very shy;

2 **(the other pupil) is sympathetic:**
  is liked very much by me;
  is my friend;
  is always ready to help somebody;
  co-operates well with other pupils;

3 **(the other pupil) is a scapegoat:**
  is bullied often;
  is not liked at all by mc;
  wants somebody to help him or her.

Factor 1 shows that bullying and quarrelling with other pupils and disrupting lessons are highly correlated and seem characteristic for bullies. This result also confirms the relationship between the self-reported information on bullying and bullying the teacher. Factor 2 integrates liking, friendship and co-operativeness with respect to other pupils. Factor 3 illustrates that being bullied often, not being liked and behaving in a dependent or non-assertive way represent the scape goat or victim. It is important to notice that both bully and victim are not liked or not considered as sympathetic. Without extra instigation a pupil will usually not assist or not help a pupil perceived as a victim or scape goat (because co-operation only occurs with 'sympathetic' pupils: see factor 2). Finally, the factor analysis shows that having particular physical characteristics had no (important) relationships with these three factors.

The classmates' sociometric information can be used to check each pupil's self-report on being bullied and bullying. If a close correspondence exists between the two kinds of concepts, the external validity of a pupil's self-report on being bullied and bullying is supported. In our study the results on peer perception confirmed the external validity of the conceptual framework on bullying.

▓▓ Who is the bully?

Being bullied and bullying relate to other pupil characteristics: a boy bullies other pupils or his teacher more often than a girl does (Olweus, 1984, 1991), and being bullied and bullying decreases with age.

The analysis results revealed the expected relationships: boys bully more than girls; older pupils bully less than younger pupils. Moreover, pupils from lower socio-economic backgrounds (lower occupation and lower education of parents) bullied more and bullied more than pupils from more favoured socio-economic backgrounds. Also, pupils scoring higher on non-verbal intelligence reported being bullied less than pupils scoring lower on this aspect of intelligence.

▰▰▰ The effects of the class and the school

However, such results may be confounded by characteristics from classes or schools. This point needs looking at further. A pupil is part of a class. Pupils within the same class are therefore influenced by the same class processes, such as the teacher's social management or instructional processes. Variation on the pupil level within classes therefore has to be separated from variation between classes. In the same way school variables may influence both pupils and classes within a school in the same way. For example, school disciplinary processes may differ between schools, but within each school the disciplinary rules and expected pupil behaviours are about the same.

It may be possible to disentangle variation on the pupil level and class level by using each pupil's score as a relative score, that is a score relative to the mean score of the pupils in the pupil's class. Once we clarified these 'relative' relationships the results made clear that the relationships between the relative and absolute bullying scores, and the relationships of these scores with a pupil's sex, were comparable with each other. But, *contrary* to the 'absolute' results given before:

- Being relatively older or younger than classmates has *no* significant relationship with bullying relatively more or less. Within a class the relatively older or younger pupils are not the pupils who usually bully.

- Coming from a relatively less or more favourable socio-economic background than classmates has no relationship with bullying relatively more or less.

- Scoring relatively higher or lower on a non-verbal intelligence test than classmates has *no* significant relationship with bullying relatively more or less.

The disappearance of some pupil-level relationships while controlling for class mean scores suggests that significant between-class differences must be present. I looked at these relationships between relative pupil scores focusing on self-reported variables, sociometric variables and non-verbal intelligence variables. The results show groupings of pupil characteristics on being bullied relatively more frequently (factor 1) and on bullying relatively more frequently (factor 2). Moreover, factor 3 groups items on seeing relatively more pupils being bullied and bullying in the class, and bullying and being bullied relatively more. This factor thus represents bullying as a collective social process in the class. Relative degree of non-verbal intelligence appears in factor 4: it has no relationship to being bullied or bullying relatively more, either as an individual or as a social (class) phenomenon. The detailed results are (self-reported data = self; sociometric data = peer):

1 **being bullied relatively more:**
   (self) being bullied directly relatively more;
   (self) being bullied relatively more;
   (self) being bullied indirectly relatively more;
   (peer) being relatively more a scapegoat;
   (peer) being relatively less sympathetic;

2 **bullying relatively more:**
   (self) bullying relatively more;
   (peer) being relatively more a bully;
   (self) being a boy;
   (self) being relatively less negative towards bullying;
   (self) bullying the teacher relatively more;

3 **bullying as a class phenomenon:**
   (self) seeing a larger number of children being bullied within class;
   (self) seeing a larger number of children bullying within class;
   (self) bullying relatively more;
   (self) being bullied directly relatively more;

4 **relative non-verbal intelligence:**
   having a relatively higher degree of cognitive flexibility;
   having a relatively higher degree of structural capacity.

These results confirm that pupil level or within-class bullying (see factors 1 and 2) are separated from between-class bullying (see factor 3). Relative degree of non-verbal intelligence (factor 4) is not related to relative degree of being bullied or bullying. These results again support the external validity of the self-report data: both factor 1 and factor 2 represent conceptually fitting self-reported and sociometric variables.

■ Bullying and teacher, class and school characteristics

On the class level, a factor analysis was done on variables characterising teachers' didactical, organisational and social management behaviour, while mean scores of the pupils in the class on bullying and other pupil variables were also included. The findings covered a range of factors, and the implications are discussed later.

In the matter of school characteristics, a first and rather unexpected result was that, in elementary education, school size has no clear relationship with the pupils' mean scores on being bullied and bullying. In secondary education, however, the larger the number of pupils in school, the less:

- Pupils say they are bullied directly.
- Pupils bully.
- Pupils differ with respect to bullying in school.
- Teachers are bullied by the pupils (by pupils disrupting lessons).
- Pupils see other pupils being bullied or bullying.

■ The prevention of bullying and disruptive behaviour

Now that we have come to understand bullying a little bit more, the question arises whether we could reduce or even prevent bullying and disruptive behaviour of pupils.

Research on the causal determinants of bullying, the bullying process itself, or the reduction or prevention of bullying, is still very scarce. However, it is clear that it is relevant to distinguish different 'levels' to make the bullying problem more understandable and manageable. It seems wise to make use of – at least – the person or pupil level with pupil characteristics, the class level with class and teacher characteristics, and the school level with school characteristics.

In order to construct optimal effects the within-school prevention or early management of bullying and disruptive behaviour should be emphasised from the pupil's first school-day onwards (Mooij, 1982). Only in this way can an efficient and effective attack on bullying and disruptive behaviour be expected. This also implies that the main task to be done rests with teachers and school management and not school counsellors or social welfare professionals from outside school. They usually come to deal with a problem pupil if the integration of the pupil into school is clearly endangered or failed already. This means they become involved at a (too) late point in time.

Prevention of bullying should focus on variables that can be manipulated or influenced by educators at various levels.

At the pupil level

At the pupil level schools should offer each pupil, from his or her *first* school-day:

1 An accepting, child-oriented, positive and warm **atmosphere** combined with short, clear behavioural rules defining for pupils and teachers alike how to create and maintain this atmosphere.

2 Short, clear positive formulations about **rewards** that can be earned by following the behavioural rules.

3 Short, clear formulations describing **punishments** associated with (repeated) trespassings against the behavioural rules.

Furthermore, for each pupil schools should have available:

4 A reliable and valid **accounting system** of educationally relevant characteristics of each pupil's functioning in school throughout the pupil's school career. Such characteristics are, for example: general and specific intellectual characteristics and school achievements, social characteristics and achievements, emotional characteristics, creative characteristics and achievements, athletic characteristics, and motivational characteristics concerning school (Mooij, 1992b).

5 Individual or subgroup based remedial or, on the other hand, enriched didactical **stimulation material**. Providing such material should (also) be based on the pupil's progress in the accounting system (see 4) and be related to the curricula in use.

6 The development of the pupil on the characteristics (see 4) and on the specific didactical stimulation (see 5) should be **evaluated** regularly with teachers and parents or carers.

At the class level

7 The **play and social or learning curricula** must be differentiated into individual, subgroup, and whole-group processes. If necessary because of a pupil's 'weak' or 'strong' characteristics, the pupil must be able to proceed in a subgroup of relatively comparable pupils from the first school-day onwards.

8 The teacher should concentrate on both **management and social aspects** of the play and social or learning processes of each pupil. The necessary behavioural rules (see points 1–3) can be partly adapted to the wishes or characteristics of the pupils and the teacher. The curriculum should be organised in such ways that pupils are as self-responsible and self-regulatory as possible from the first school-day onwards (Alschuler, 1980; US Department of Health, Education and Welfare, 1973).

9 Evaluation of learning achievement of pupils should **not be based on comparison** between pupils (in a class, or in school) but on the individual effort or motivation of the pupil in order to realise the school-work as far as possible according to his or her potentialities.

10 The **curriculum** of the school subjects meant to select pupils should be **individually or subgroup directed**, which implies that being held back or skipping classes does not need to happen. Schooling should become more self-regulated by the pupil and the pupil's real capacities, be more continuous and more directed towards the positive development of each pupil instead of either emphasising a pupil's deficiencies or forcing the pupil to work below his or her capacities or potentialities.

11 In the self-regulatory curriculum the teacher can **concentrate** on the social aspects of individual work or the within-subgroup co-operation of pupils, on the reinforcement of positive learning and social processes, and on ways to (re)integrate pupils who bully and disrupt or who are socially isolated and function in a socially marginal way.

At the school level

12 **Co-ordination** of behavioural rules, the curricula, curriculum flexibility, both remedial and enriched programmes, registration within the accounting system, and the regular evaluation of the development and achievement of pupils.

13 **Support** of and – if necessary – **assistance** in teachers' innovation of rules, curricula, curriculum flexibility, remedial and enriched programmes, registration, the accounting system and evaluation of pupils.

14 If necessary, **school development** in order to provide the educational support of 'weak' or 'strong' aspects of a pupil's functioning in school.

15 If necessary, organising **external advice or in-service training** on the formulation or maintenance of behavioural rules, curriculum procedures, registration or evaluation procedures.

■ A summary of the findings

The main conclusions from the research in the SVO-project are:

- Being bullied and bullying can be measured in reliable and valid ways.
- Bullying behaviour towards other pupils and towards the teacher is related; both kinds of bullying behaviour are related to disruptive behaviour during lessons.
- With respect to bullying behaviour it is necessary to distinguish pupil level characteristics (including the relative position of a pupil in the class), class and teacher characteristics, and school characteristics.
- The causal or longitudinal structure of bullying behaviour and its relationships with pupil characteristics, class and teacher characteristics, and school characteristics, deserves further attention and research.

■ The way ahead

Realising such developmental conditions may be a long road for one school but only a short track for another school. Each school can – depending on its own situation – decide for itself where to start and where to end, and at which point assistance from outside school is needed. It may be wise to start at the pupil level and class level simultaneously, tackling different aspects of the same problem at about the same time. When this is more or less finished the consequent changes on the school level could be worked out and integrated within the school, that is, on all three levels for all pupils, all classes and on the school level. Then a subsequent part of the necessary change could be chosen and attacked in the same way and so on.

Schools can thus gradually come to prevent bullying and disruptive behaviour of pupils by working successively on specific parts of the change programme. The work should occur on three levels: the pupil level, the class level and the school level. This within-school prevention approach also implies that the bulk of the counselling or welfare facilities, funds and activities should be given to and used within schools. For, in so far as bullying and disruptive behaviour occurs within school, school is also the place where this behaviour should be tackled. This demands a reallocation of facilities and professionals. Moreover, intervention research should be adequately designed in order to check, evaluate and support ongoing changes in school practice.

4 Tackling bullying: The Sheffield Project

Sonia Sharp and *Peter K Smith*

'It's just so hard to know what to do … I mean it [bullying] seems so hard to pin down and other times I just know that there is bullying going on but I don't know how to approach it … it's different from other kinds of discipline matters – I feel much less confident somehow … .'

As bullying has gradually become more of a public issue, placed firmly on the educational agenda, so the problems faced by the uncertain teacher quoted above have begun to be addressed. Over the last few years there have emerged a range of materials and approaches which aim to tackle the problem of bullying in schools.

The Department for Education (DFE) Sheffield Bullying Project tried to identify, through evaluation, what kind of methods and approaches are successful in reducing bullying in schools. The project was broadly based on the work of Olweus and Roland in Norway (see Chapter 2).

The Sheffield Survey

Our own work started with a large-scale survey, funded by the Calouste Gulbenkian Foundation. This was carried out in 24 schools in the Sheffield LEA (17 primary, 7 secondary) in November 1990. Its aim was to identify the nature and extent of bullying in a large sample of pupils. Every pupil over seven years of age completed an anonymous questionnaire, providing details of how often they were bullied, how they were bullied, where and who by, as well as whether they had told anyone about it, how they felt about it and whether they had been involved in bullying others themselves. The design of this questionnaire was based on that of Olweus (1991), and its piloting and modification was described in Ahmad, Whitney and Smith (1991).

The detailed findings of this survey, which covers over 6700 pupils and is the largest so far in the UK, were described by Whitney and Smith (1993). They were not dissimilar to findings in Norway and The Netherlands (see Chapters 2 and 3). In brief, the survey established that there was generally more bullying in primary schools than secondary schools. On average, a quarter of pupils in the primary schools had been bullied at least 'sometimes' during the term leading up to the survey, and 10% reported being bullied once a week or more. In the secondary schools, 12% of pupils overall had experienced bullying during that term and 4% at least once a week. There was a steady decline with age in frequency of being bullied but only by sixth form had it reached small enough proportions that the problem could justifiably be disregarded.

Almost every school had classes where the level of bullying was higher than others, alongside classes where bullying was scarcely a problem – suggesting that as every school has its own 'ethos' so may each class within that school. Much of the bullying seemed to be based within the same class or year groups, though children were also often bullied by older children. In primary schools, three quarters of this bullying took place in the playground, either at playtime or lunchbreak. In secondary schools, the problem was more dispersed but the playground was still the most likely site for bullying.

Name-calling was the most frequent form of bullying reported; a proportion of this (though less than a quarter) was racist name-calling, and some amounted to sexual harassment. This was common in both boys and girls. Other bullying behaviours included: physical violence, damage to possessions, extortion, having nasty rumours spread about a pupil or their family, being threatened and exclusion from groups or play. Girls seemed to be more involved in the indirect types of bullying – spreading nasty rumours and excluding from play, while boys tended towards more physical forms of bullying and bullying involving threats.

The majority of pupils did not have sympathetic attitudes to bullies (though a 'hard core' of about 20% did). Rather worryingly, but in line with other findings, many pupils who reported being bullied, even quite frequently, had not told a teacher or anyone at home about this. This was especially so in secondary schools where, although bullying was less frequent, the social pressures against 'telling' seemed to be greater.

Each school received a portfolio of its own results – in effect a 'bullying profile' which clearly identified the general level of bullying, where it happened, whether teachers had been told, and the 'hot spots' for bullying in terms of which classes were most involved. In general, schools found this portfolio very useful and were concerned to act on the information obtained in a positive way.

The Sheffield DFE Bullying Project

This project built on the Sheffield Survey. During the first few months of 1991, each of the 24 schools had received its own survey results. Soon after this, as funding became available from the DFE, these schools were invited to become involved in an intervention project[1]. The intention was that the impetus in each school to respond to their survey findings would be supported by relevant resources and in-service training provided by the research team. The work of each school would be monitored and evaluated with a second survey two years later (November 1992). In this way, the success of intervention and the differential success of different types of intervention could be assessed. Also, definite recommendations could be made on a national basis by summer 1993.

One primary school did not wish to continue after the survey. The remaining 16 primary schools and 7 secondary schools were all involved in the project. Each school had a project coordinator (often the head or deputy head). These schools were asked, as a minimum, to develop a whole-school policy to tackle bullying. This would form the 'core' intervention of the project, since it was felt that it was essential both to the success of more localised interventions and to the continued effectiveness of school action after the project support ceased. Additionally, schools could each choose to select from a range of 'optional interventions': different approaches or materials which had at the time (early 1991) been promoted as ways of reducing or confronting bullying. These interventions fell broadly into three categories:

- Curriculum-based strategies which might involve all pupils and individual staff.
- Strategies which focused on the pupils directly involved in a bullying incident.
- Strategies which involved manipulation of the playground environment either by changing the playground area or improving supervisory systems.

Developing a whole-school policy on bullying

Throughout the project there were organised meetings where project coordinators met together to discuss key issues in policy development. At an early stage in the project, during one of these meetings, a list of six minimum criteria for policy development were agreed.

1 The process by which the policy was developed.

If the problem of bullying was to be effectively tackled – often so embedded in pupil culture, sometimes so deliberately hidden from teacher view – then the involvement of non-teaching staff, parents and pupils themselves was probably crucial. Thus the schools agreed that for this policy, as wide consultation as possible was advisable. There was some initial concern about involving parents, especially with Local Management of Schools and wider parental choice looming large. Would parents think that the school had a greater problem with bullying than other schools in the neighbourhood who were not involved in the bullying project? Fortunately, one or two schools took steps to involve parents in the consultation stage early on in the project. They received a positive response from parents, for whom bullying was a common concern, demonstrating to other more tentative schools that including parents in this important part of the process had many benefits in enhancing not only home-school relationships but also the reputation of the school within the community.

2 Defining what kinds of behaviours constitute bullying.

Pupils, parents and staff should have no doubt about whether or not the pupils had been bullying or been bullied. Arriving at a mutual definition can be an enlightening experience for staff, parents and pupils! We have not worked with any group of people yet who have been in agreement about what is or is not bullying from the start. A clear definition of bullying helps to discourage common rationalisations for bullying behaviour such as 'We were only playing' or 'It's only a bit of fun.'

3 Clear guidelines for action.

It was felt that the policy should clearly define the roles and responsibilities for people who know that bullying is going on – not only the pupils directly involved, but the bystanders, the staff who may suspect that there is a problem and the parents who may be the first adults to know that a problem exists. Preventative strategies also need to be described – how can schools promote cooperative behaviour and reduce the likelihood of bullying occurring at all?

4 Providing ways of telling.

The silence and secrecy that often surround bullying can be the bullying pupil's greatest ally. The perhaps unuttered threat that hangs over the pupil who longs to 'tell' can deter pupils from letting teachers know what is going on. Consequently, bullying problems can remain hidden for a long time. Creating a climate where pupils feel safe to talk about bullying was therefore seen as a key feature of whole-school policy development. Interestingly, the initial survey showed great variation between schools as to whether pupils would talk to a teacher about bullying or not. It seems likely that this is an area where schools can really take action.

Teachers who put bullying on the classroom agenda – therefore giving pupils 'permission' to talk about the things which have been happening to them in and around school – can open a floodgate of reporting. Schools must decide how they are going to handle this in a way which will not discourage pupils from continuing to let staff know if they are being bullied, but will also allow staff time to respond satisfactorily. In an attempt to broaden opportunities for pupils to tell about bullying, three schools in the project have enlisted the help of pupils in setting up a listening service for pupils who are being bullied. This began with training for interested pupils in active listening and basic counselling skills. The pupils who offer the service also accompany pupils who are reluctant to inform staff about their problems to key teachers or act as 'advocates' on their behalf. They do not, however, intervene in a bullying situation on behalf of the bullied pupils or tackle the bullies themselves.

5 Successful communication of a policy.

A policy must not lie on a shelf gathering dust. Schools agreed that thorough communication was an essential ingredient to putting the policy into practice. The policy is normally approved by school staff and by the governing body, but the final version must also be available and perhaps distributed to parents, lunchtime supervisors, pupils, and possibly other persons involved with the school (community police officer, school nurse, etc). This needs to be done regularly and each audience could be targeted in more than one way. How a policy is communicated also has implications for the maintenance of the policy over time.

6 Keeping a policy alive.

Careful consideration needs to be given to how the policy can be kept alive and how new staff, parents and pupils can be introduced to it. Monitoring its success is important and subsequent review ensures that a policy is workable and remains effective over time. Even if a school policy is suitable when first designed and used, the school population is fluid and changes with each new intake. Any anti-bullying policy cannot be carved in stone; it will need to be flexible to meet the variations in circumstances and in bullying behaviour which may occur over time.

Through policy development, bullying behaviour should become an important issue throughout the school community. The message that bullying behaviour is unacceptable should be made very clear and staff, parents and pupils should all know what action they can take if confronted with a bullying situation. Some schools completed this process more quickly, or more thoroughly, than others. The project carefully documented the stages which the schools went through in arriving at a final whole-school policy to tackle bullying. One outcome of the project is the detailed information for other schools who wish to develop their own policies on bullying behaviour.

▇ Tackling bullying through the curriculum

The curriculum provides a natural vehicle for addressing the issue of bullying. Firstly, it can provide an opportunity for awareness-raising about bullying for pupils. In this way, pupils are provided with information about bullying so they understand what it is and how it affects other people. It can enable pupils to reflect on their own behaviour towards others as well as provide a useful basis for informed consultation when schools wish to involve pupils in the devising of the school's policy. At this level, teaching staff can gain insight into the kind of bullying experiences that pupils may be involved in.

Secondly, and at a more challenging level, the curriculum can be used to try to change pupils' behaviour – to reduce the level of bullying amongst pupils, either by tackling the pupils who are bullies or who are being bullied or by motivating the bystanders to take action.

The materials which have been used by the project schools include two videos, one book and one groupwork method.

▇ Drama and video

The videos chosen where *Only Playing, Miss*, produced by the Neti Neti Theatre Company, and *Sticks and Stones*, produced by Central Television. *Only Playing, Miss* is an extended drama about the experiences of a pupil whose father has died. His tormentor taunts him about his father's death and the bullying gradually affects not only the victim but other members of their peer group too. The play goes on to explore how the combined efforts of all the pupils helps to stop the bullying from continuing. Within the project, the video has been used with pupils ranging from Year 4 to Year 11. Although initially concerned that their pupils 'would not take to the video' because of its lack of scenery and its use of signing and Bengali, it has proved a success with even the youngest pupils.

Sticks and Stones contains a series of short narratives and dramatisations aimed at a secondary school audience. The video is presented solely by young people and explores the viewpoints of victim, bully and bystander. This video can be shown in its entirety or can be divided into sections, each part being used to investigate the issue from a different perspective.

With each of the videos, the project team supplied a package of suggestions for activities which would help teachers to stimulate discussion, role play and creative work around the issue of bullying. Francis Gobey from the Neti Neti Theatre Company ran a workshop for teachers who were interested in using drama and role play to explore the issue of bullying with pupils.

Books

The Heartstone Odyssey by Arvan Kumar deals, in the course of an adventure suitable for older junior school pupils, with issues of racial harassment and violence. The story describes the ordeals of a young Indian dancer who is faced by blatant and direct intimidation from members of an extreme right wing group with racist aims. The story combines fantasy and adventure with stark reality as her cause is taken up by a network of very active mice who are already involved in the fight against racial injustice. The book is told to pupils rather than read by individuals.

The story telling method which best conveys the message of the book was introduced to teachers in the project by Sitakumari, who runs the Heartstone Organisation. This organisation is committed to challenging racial bullying and harassment and links pupils in schools throughout the country via *The Stonekeeper* magazine, to which pupils can contribute their own stories, poems and ideas, and local events. The schools who were interested in trying out *The Heartstone Odyssey* were provided with a copy of the book and a subscription to the magazine.

The Quality Circle

This groupwork approach aims to encourage pupils to develop their own solutions to bullying. It also offers all pupils, including those who may not be involved directly in bullying themselves, an opportunity to take an active stance against bullying.

Bullying can be viewed as a social problem which is 'embedded' in pupil culture. Solutions proposed by adults may therefore be less effective in tackling the problem than those developed by pupils. Talking with pupils about the bullying that occurs in their class or school, it is evident that most of them know exactly where the 'hot spots' for bullying are and who is involved. This can sometimes be quite contrary to the perceptions of teachers or other adults in the school community, even those who are in close contact with their pupils.

The Quality Circle process invites pupils to work together to identify the features of the problem as encountered by them. They are introduced to structured activities which enable them to research the extent of the problem, to identify causes and to develop practical solutions. The process itself originates from industry and in Britain it has been applied to education for use with adults (Fox, Pratt and Roberts, 1991). The approach was adapted for use with pupils in the project schools. The process enables the pupils to take a more active role in preventing and responding to bullying. Additionally, the pupils develop skills of problem identification, solution development, planning, communication and presenting their ideas which can be applied to other areas of their educational experience.

The process itself inhibits unpractical or over-idealistic ideas. The kinds of solutions the pupils arrive at tend to be simple, achievable ones such as to overcome boredom at lunchtime by holding a games tournament (which they organise themselves), or running a merit system which allows non-bullying pupils to be rewarded.

Working with pupils involved in bullying

The project looked at two approaches here: the method of common concern, and assertiveness training for victims of bullying.

The method of Common Concern

The method of Common Concern was developed by the Swedish psychologist, Anatol Pikas (1989). It aims to change the behaviour of the pupils involved in the bullying incident and to improve the situation for the person being bullied. It is usually employed when there is a group or gang of children bullying another pupil. The method is carefully scripted and is based on a non-punitive, non-aggressive approach. The teacher leads each pupil, including the victim, through a series of individual 'chats'. On a one-to-one basis, each pupil is encouraged to suggest ways in which they personally can help 'improve the situation' for the person being bullied. Once an improvement has been achieved (which usually means that the bullies simply leave the victim alone), the process finishes with a group meeting which establishes an agreement between the bullies and victim about how they can 'live peacefully together in the same school.' It is not assumed that the bullies and victim will ever become firm friends, rather the final stage emphasises the importance of tolerance.

Although on paper this method might seem rather time consuming, in reality the initial discussions with each pupil usually last no longer than 10 minutes per child. Two 'chats' are usually enough to bring about change (the second round of chats are much shorter) and the final meeting generally takes about half an hour. Thus the total time spent on a bullying situation involving five pupils will amount to approximately 1 hour 45 minutes, spread over a three-week period – as long as the teacher sticks to the script.

Pikas himself had only used the method with gangs of boys. However, teachers in the project schools have been using it with groups of girls as well as individual pupils of both genders. The experience of this method indicates that it is a relatively successful way of stopping the bullying (Cowie, Sharp and Smith, 1991). It also has the advantage that the teacher does not have to respond immediately to the bullying situation – the bullying may have been going on for some time anyway and the teacher can employ the method at the nearest convenient opportunity. However, in the long term, it is unlikely to be a substitute for an effective whole-school policy.

Assertiveness training for groups of victims

These small, safe support groups provide an opportunity for pupils who are experiencing persistent bullying to learn and practise skills and techniques which can help them avoid and escape from bullying situations. With help from members of the project team, teachers in the project schools established and maintained a programme of assertiveness training for groups of pupils in both primary and secondary phases. The group size can vary, and indeed some teachers have used the techniques with individual pupils as well as whole classes and year groups. The skills and techniques introduced to the pupils include saying 'No' and 'No, I don't want to'; handling name-calling and criticism; resisting unwanted pressure; enlisting support from other pupils or bystanders; and various strategies for resolving and avoiding conflict.

The schools differed in how and when the groups were organised – some in lunchtime, some during lesson time. The groups seemed to run successfully with pupils from all ages and both genders. The sessions last between 30 minutes and one hour and usually continue through a half term. The groups provide a forum for pupils to talk about the kinds of bullying they are experiencing as well as how they feel about it. As all the members of the groups share the experience of being bullied, the group provides an empathic support network which in some cases continues beyond the weekly meetings. Pupils discuss strategies they have tried out and how well they felt they worked in practice. The sessions also provide a time when pupils can rehearse different solutions to their own real problems without the fear of 'making a mistake'.

▇ Using the school environment

▇ Playground supervision

As we have seen, up to 75% of bullying in schools occurs in the playground. Certainly, many of the schools, especially in the primary sector, felt concerned about the playground and wished to bring about some kind of change to the way in which this was organised.

Team members developed an overview of strategies available for schools which offered ways of enhancing the quality of pupil play, promoting cooperative behaviour amongst pupils, and implementing effective management systems for playtime and lunchbreak. Schools selected different strategies which they felt suited them and put them into practice.

The role and status of lunchtime supervisors provided a central theme for intervention in this area as they are effectively the managers of the lunchtime period, yet more often than not untrained and poorly paid, at worst, taunted by pupil and patronised by teaching staff. Training sessions for supervisors of the schools provided information about bullying, and described methods of identifying and responding to bullying situations which would help to de-escalate the situation and would serve to reinforce the idea of supervisors as a valued part of the school management system. Efforts to raise the status of supervisors in the eyes of staff, parents and pupils were also emphasised. Enhancing communication between teachers and supervisors via regular meetings helped to enable supervisors to air concerns and put forward good ideas about streamlining the lunchtime systems. These meetings also allow teaching staff to tell supervisors about pupils who may be causing concern, either as bullies or as victims, thus encouraging the supervisors to be more vigilant about those pupils whilst they are on duty.

In many schools, one of the biggest steps towards raising the status of supervisors has been through their inclusion in the process of policy development. They have proved valuable members of working parties and training events and their presence, often voluntary, emphasises their role within the school community.

Changing the playground environment

As in many areas throughout the country, Sheffield is not without its fair share of bleak and barren playgrounds – a stark contrast to the rich learning environment within many classrooms. In conjunction with the Department of Landscape Architecture and with some funds from the Calouste Gulbenkian Foundation, pupils, parents and staff embarked on an extensive improvement programme for the playground in four of the project schools. Pupils in the schools identified problem areas, and produced 'ideal' plans for playground development. From these plans and in consultation with staff, a professional design brief was formulated for each school which provided a detailed plan for immediate, short and long-term change. The design brief combined cheap, easy to achieve ideas with more ambitious and adventurous development plans.

The monitoring process

To identify whether or not the levels of bullying have changed during the process of the project, the original questionnaire was given to pupils in each school after two years. This allowed a fairly straightforward 'before and after' comparison to take place. Schools also carried out a termly monitoring process whereby certain groups of pupils within the school recorded whether or not they have been bullied each day for a week. This process not only helped to identify general levels of bullying but also highlighted those pupils who were being persistently bullied. Lunchtime supervisors and teaching staff on duty also kept their own record of bullying incidents.

The way in which each school approaches whole-school policy development and other interventions was also recorded. Amount of time spent, numbers of pupils involved, details of lesson formats and materials used were collected throughout the project. A picture of action within each school during the two-year period emerged through regular interviews with project coordinators and other staff.

Questionnaires for parents and governors attempted to ascertain their views on how the project proceeded. Parents and governors were interviewed when willing and available. The schools themselves were asked to grade the amount of effort they put into different aspects of the project on a termly basis. Using previously agreed criteria, members of the project team also provided a grade for each school in relation to policy development and intervention implementation. This is added to interview data on views of pupils and staff on how they perceived the project in practice.

Each intervention had a specific monitoring process. The curriculum based interventions were evaluated via pupil questionnaire and comment, alongside teacher interview. Detailed short and long-term follow-up of the pupils involved in bullying incidents where the Pikas method of Common Concern was used, enabled the project team to determine the success of the approach. Self-esteem and use of assertive strategies were measured before and after pupils attended a series of support groups for victims of bullying. The effects of playground change were recorded through interim half-termly monitoring of bullying levels, and pupil and staff interviews.

At the time of writing, the project team planned to use all this information to offer clear guidelines to schools throughout the country about how bullying can be tackled via whole-school approaches and more specific interventions. They believed it would be possible to identify which processes and procedures work well and under what circumstances.

One planned outcome of the project is a package of advice for schools, governors and parents, which is likely to be circulated to schools, by the Department for Education. In addition, it is hoped to publish an edited volume of the research findings, together with an extended practical handbook. These are likely to be available late in 1993. Together with the other initiatives now taking place in the UK, and with the active involvement of concerned schools, it is to be hoped that the problem of school bullying can be reduced considerably over the next few years.

---

[1] The grant holders on the project were P.K. Smith, Y. Ahmad, M. Boulton, H. Cowie, D.A. Thompson; LEA liaison officers were M. Gazzard and D. Pennock; research associate, S. Sharp.

The Management of Bullying

5 Short, medium and long-term management strategies

Delwyn Tattum

If we are to begin to tackle the problem of bullying effectively, we first need to acknowledge its prevalence in our schools and more fully understand its origins and motivation. In Section I we examined the complex nature of the behaviour and indicated the need to raise public, professional and political awareness as to the extent, nature and severity of the problem. As a major proportion of bullying is secretive, we need to devise management strategies which progress beyond the reactive, crisis-management response to be found in many schools, to a more preventative approach, the aim of which is to change attitudes towards bullying and, at the same time, create a school ethos which will not tolerate the oppression of one member by another.

How to manage change

Schools need to work towards a whole-school approach which is consistent with the daily experiences of pupils, teachers and parents. A policy statement must be drawn up and communicated to all. The governing body should be involved in its preparation and promotion, as the 1986 and 1988 Education Acts charge them with legal responsibility for the good conduct and discipline in the school. The Advisory Centre for Education has produced an invaluable information bulletin on *Governors and Bullying* (ACE, 1990). But having a school policy statement is not an end in itself, it needs to be put into practice using the full panoply of management, which progresses from crisis-management to intervention approaches and prevention strategies.

In developing its programme a school needs to initiate methods of supporting individuals who are bullied and also ways of changing the attitudes and behaviour of known bullies. For such intervention to be effective in helping individual pupils, they must operate within a community ethos which openly names and condemns bullying behaviour as totally unacceptable. Thus, before discussing in detail how a school may develop an anti-bullying management programme, it is necessary to examine some of the recommended strategies for dealing with individual bullies and victims.

Some approaches

Recommended approaches which focus on bullies include use of sanctions, with exclusion regarded as the final action in demonstrating to pupils and parents that a school will not tolerate bullying. Other approaches include reasoning with bullies and trying to get them to appreciate how the victim feels. Some writers advocate the use of group pressure as a way of sanctioning bullies but also to encourage other pupils to take responsibility for their more vulnerable school mates. (Rigby and Slee, Chapter 9, write perceptively on this approach.) Lowenstein (1991) proposed that teachers should reward desirable behaviour by the bully, for example, the award of tokens to purchase privileges. Several people (Besag, 1989; Walker, 1989) recommend non-violent conflict resolution as a way of bringing about reconciliation between two parties.

> 'A conflict is a clash between two or more individuals or groups and can be carried out with violent means but does not have to be. Non-violent antagonists in a conflict search for solutions which will enable both sides to at least partially meet their own needs. On an interpersonal level, non-violent conflict resolution does not attempt to avoid conflicts – non-violence cannot be equated with passivity – but rather to deal with them consciously, constructively and imaginatively. . . . Of course, it is not always possible to arrive at mutually beneficial solutions, especially when the power in the relationship is unequally distributed or when one side refuses to even recognise the fact that a problem exists' (Walker, 1989).

Another approach which aims to individualise responsibility is advocated by Pikas (1989) and called the Common Concern method, although it is intended for use in 'mobbing' by adolescent bullying gangs. The approach requires the teacher to talk each member of the gang and the victim through the incident in a non-threatening or non-accusative manner. This process is repeated again during the week in an effort to generate an empathic response from the bullies – arrival at a successful feeling of common concern is achieved when the bullies agree to help the victim. The success of the process is heavily dependent on the teacher's conciliatory skills in bringing the disputants to a resolution of the problem. Whether teachers have these professional skills is questionable; moreover the approach is very time consuming. (See Sharp and Smith, Chapter 4, for a more detailed description of the methods involved.)

Bully courts are another way to influence a bully's behaviour through group pressure and other sanctions. They were pioneered by Laslett (1980, 1982) in a small, day school for maladjusted children. The 'justices' of the court were children who heard complaints about bullying and set punishments, from apologising to or doing something nice for the victims, to such tasks as extra sums, washing the stairs or losing free time privileges. In his 10 years as headteacher Laslett believed that they helped to reduce bullying, helped children to understand bullies and victims, and helped children to learn about making reparation and restitution.

More recently, Brier and Ahmed (1991) and Elliot (1991) have described how bully courts may be used in mainstream schools. Brier and Ahmad's 'bench' consisted of two teachers and five elected children in a primary school. Initially, the children wanted severe punishments for bullying but became more moderate. They claim that the courts helped the children understand the need for codes, laws and sanctions.

In their resource pack 'Action Against Bullying' (1991) Johnson and her colleagues give an assessment of the inherent problems in an approach which grants children judgmental and punitive measures over their peers.

- If the children judge and the teacher observes, the limits of 'punishment' available have to be predefined very strictly The pupils may advocate vengeful measures if given their heads.

- What sort of 'punishment' can be meted out anyway? A punitive response can make the problem worse. How sophisticated a response can the pupils make? What factors can they take into account?

- How will the victim feel? Is the bully court a further humiliation, a proof of weakness? You cannot offer bully courts for some victims and not for others – or can you?

- If the bullies are a gang, will the bully court make them worse? Bully gangs are difficult to handle.
- What will you tell parents? Parents will have to know and agree in advance, otherwise problems will arise. Problems may still arise if a bully pupil goes home in tears after a court 'hearing'. How will the parents react?
- What if the 'punishment' doesn't work? How will the pupils react? What can you do? (Johnson *et al.*, 1991).

A personal concern is whether such an approach is conducive to the style of supportive, concerned and conciliatory ethos a school would wish to develop as part of its wider consideration of the problem. That is, a whole-school approach which is educative and not punitive.

In describing the use of 'victim support groups' Arora (1991) gives strong reasons why a school with its limited resources would be well advised to concentrate on helping the victim than trying to stop the behaviour of individual bullies. Firstly, because it is usually easier to teach new behaviours than to stop or change established behaviours. Thus, victims are taught new strategies to cope with bullying. Secondly, bullies get tacit support for their behaviour from various sources, such as parents and peers, who can provide active role models or encouragement. Moreover, bullies have learned that their actions bring rewards of personal satisfaction and social status, which makes their behaviour very resistant to change. There is also the danger that we may be holding the victim responsible for the bully's behaviour. But none of these points is meant to give the impression that bullying behaviour cannot be changed or to discourage schools from working to that end.

Helping the victims

General guidance is given by Besag (1989), who advocates that victims develop strategies to avoid being victimised, such as, staying with a group, not being last in a classroom, leaving valuables at home, and not showing anger or distress when being bullied, as this only encourages the bullies. More positively, victims should also be helped to develop their self-confidence and self-esteem. Improvement of friendship and social skills also reduces the likelihood that children may be isolated or rejected. Assertiveness training (see Chapter 4) can give individuals the ability to communicate their needs and desires in such a way that the rights of both parties are respected, that is, neither aggressively nor submissively. Herbert (1988) describes a social skills programme led by himself and a social worker. Eight pupils who were victimised took part and the programme included brainstorming to identify concerns and role playing to model alternative ways of dealing with bullying. Victims were taught social skills such as listening, holding a conversation, asking for help, coping with feelings, negotiating and responding to teasing.

■ Developing a whole-school response

Crisis-management approaches to bullying are essentially reactive, in that they respond to emergent problems. How much better for a school to create policies which are proactive, that is, they initiate practices which are anticipatory and so reduce the incidence of bullying throughout the school community. In working towards a whole-school response the aim must be to create an ethos of well-being which is supported by a management system of monitoring pupil behaviour. Ethos has both content and process (Purkey and Smith, 1982). Content refers to policy, structure and curriculum, and process refers to the school culture, quality of social relationships, and channels of communication.

Schools are caring communities and, as relatively closed communities, they have a measure of control over the internal factors discussed in this section. A preventative approach to bullying has to be school-wide, it must be integral to the ethos of the school, emanating from its structures and processes, and evident in the attitudes and behaviour of teachers and other adults. A whole-school approach to bullying is therefore predicted on the belief that a safe, secure learning environment is created when *all* members of staff accept responsibility for the behaviour of *all* pupils, not only in their own classrooms but as they move about the school.

■ Why is a whole-school approach preferable?

- ■ **To counter the view that bullying is an inevitable part of school life** – and so challenge teachers' and pupils' attitudes towards aggressive behaviour ~ examine their relationships with each other. A school has to decide whether it 'unintentionally' reinforces or discourages aggressive behaviour. (See Danielle Drouet's chapter on 'Adolescent female bullying and sexual harassment' for a discussion of this latter point.)

- **To move beyond a crisis-management approach** which only reacts to critical cases to a more preventative ethos.
- **To open up discussion at all levels.** In this way bullying will no longer be looked upon as a secret activity affecting the few. For it is this climate which discourages victims and those who witness bullying from speaking out and, also, encourages the bully to continue unashamed because the behaviour is not openly named in a climate which is critical.
- **To involve more people in the identification and condemnation of bullying.** In their 1982 survey Stephenson and Smith made a study of six primary schools with the highest incidence of bullying and six with the lowest. 'In all but one of the low bullying schools the teachers expressed articulate, considered and also purposeful views on bullying which emphasised the need for prevention whereas this was less apparent in the high bullying schools. The responses suggest that there was an agreed policy on bullying in the low bullying schools.' (Stephenson and Smith, 1988).
- **To draw up an agreed set of procedures for staff to follow when inquiring into a case of bullying.** For it is only when documented profiles are produced that a school will be able to isolate bullying individuals and break up bullying gangs.
- **To create a supportive ethos and break down the culture of secrecy.** When bullying is reported by pupils or their parents it must be taken seriously and acted upon in a way which discourages the bully without humiliating the victim. Children are reluctant to tell because they fear the consequences, not only from the bully but also from adults. Some adults are unwilling to listen or reluctant to believe, and dismiss the victim's allegations with counter-accusations of provocation or their parents as being over-protective.
- **To provide a safe, secure learning environment for all pupils.** This must be the ultimate aim, for it is the right of every child and young person attending our schools and colleges. Pupils cannot satisfactorily concentrate on their work if they are burdened with anxiety, humiliation and fear.

What are the elements of a whole-school approach?

These points are not discussed in the ensuing page but will emerge in the development of what is involved in a whole-school approach.

■ **A policy statement declaring the unacceptability of bullying**. It should be widely conceived and communicated.

■ **A multi-level approach involving a wide range of people**. The model 'Spheres of Involvement' (Tattum and Herbert, 1993) on page 74 illustrates the different people who can support a school in its anti-bullying programme.

■ **There is a need for short, medium and long-term strategies**. Discussion of these strategies is based on the model *Developing a whole-school response to bullying* (pages 68–69).

■ **A wide discussion of bullying to open up the issues and tackle what is a complex problem**. But discussion must progress to produce a set of procedures for teachers. The list in Figure 1 is from *Bullying: A Positive Response* (Tattum and Herbert, 1990).

Watch for early signs of distress in pupils – deterioration of work, spurious illness, isolation, the desire to remain with adults, erratic attendance. Whilst this behaviour may be symptomatic of other problems, it may be the early signs of bullying.

Listen carefully and record all incidents.

Offer the victim immediate support and help by putting the school's procedures into operation.

Make the unacceptable nature of the behaviour, and the consequences of any repetition, clear to the bully and his/her parents.

Ensure that all accessible areas of the school are patrolled at break, lunchtime, between lessons and at the end of the day.

Use all the pupils as a positive resource in countering bullying and discuss this with classes or tutorial group. Peer counselling groups may be used to resolve problems. Pupils can also be used to help shy children or newcomers feel welcome and accepted. Sexual and racial harassment also need to be discussed and dealt with.

The following steps may be followed in recording incidents of bullying and also as a means of conveying to all concerned how seriously the school regards bullying behaviour:

The bullied pupil should record the events *in writing*.

The bully should also record the events *in writing*.

The teacher and/or a senior colleague should record their discussions with both parties.

The parents/carers of the pupils involved should be sent copies of all reports, and the reports placed in the respective pupils' files for a *specified* period of time.

The parents/carers of the pupils should be asked to respond to the above *in writing*.

Figure 1 Advice and guidance for teachers

- **An anti-bullying campaign needs to be integrated within the school curriculum**. This means more than exhortations in morning assembly and one-off periods in a pastoral care or PSE programme. (Using the curriculum to change attitudes and behaviour is dealt with in detail in pages 71–73.)

A number of schools have already developed a whole-school response to bullying and several with whom I have worked have contributed to *Countering Bullying: Initiatives by Schools and Local Authorities* (Tattum and Herbert, 1993). Their different approaches are developed within five themes, namely, management strategies, using the curriculum, transition, educational and other agencies, and local education authority initiatives. These wide-ranging initiatives were developed to two local authorities and 16 schools from the maintained and non-maintained sectors. The schools cover the full age range, represent urban and rural schools, single sex and denominational schools, plus schools with large multi-ethnic communities. In their introduction to the management theme the editors observe that:

> 'The tackling of bullying in schools is rightly one of the functions of management. Put more simply, it is a management problem. There will always be those teachers who act individually to counter bullying whenever they come across it in the daily lives of their pupils. However, the work of an enthusiastic or committed teacher is insufficient to tackle the enormous problem of bullying in schools. If attempts to combat bullying are carried out on an occasional basis, reacting to the problem when it occurs, then we can guarantee that it will recur again and again, for it will be a matter of luck which child is with which member of staff, or who spots that bullying is happening' (Tattum and Herbert, 1993).

The different approaches developed by the 16 schools clearly show that countering bullying is a wide-ranging exercise and multi-dimensional. And, as Roland found in his Norwegian research, to be successful the programme has to be maintained and sustained. The model in Figure 2 (pages 68–9), 'Developing a whole-school response to bullying', presents a developmental 3 × 3 table offering short, medium and long term strategies. Short term may be thought of in weeks, medium term in months or terms, and long term as two to three years, thus maintained from one year to the next. The vertical elements represent what may be regarded as the overall tasks of school management, namely, administrative and organisational procedures, the delivery of the school curriculum, and the management of the wider school community – however conceived.

▨▨▨▨ Administrative and organisational procedures

It is neither possible nor necessary to discuss every item filling the nine cells of this chart, no more is every cell complete. Indeed schools may wish to draw up their own developmental plan using the model.

Initially, every school needs to review existing documents and procedures to see if they are adequate. Is bullying behaviour *named* in the school's handbook for new pupils, year handbooks and the general discipline policy statement, and hence presented as behaviour that is unacceptable? Some schools have produced leaflets on bullying, as part of their awareness raising exercise. In all cases pupils should be closely involved in the process so that they identify with the school's aims. Conspicuous reiteration and dissemination should be integral parts of any awareness raising programme.

Running concurrently with a school's awareness raising efforts should be work to achieve shared understanding about what constitutes bullying behaviour. A staff training day should include a wide spectrum of supportive adults, such as governors, support and ancillary staff – most especially midday supervisors. It is also advisable to carry out a survey to find out which children are involved in bullying according to age, sex, ability etc, and where, when, why and how children are bullied. This information will be of value in convincing sceptical adults, including teachers, that a whole-school approach is necessary.

▨▨▨▨ The importance of transition

Transition from home to school or to a new school or as part of the general migration from primary to secondary schools is a time of anxiety. In *Social Education and Personal Development* (Tattum and Tattum, 1992a) we discuss the 'survival skills' very young children need to assist their integration into a busy, active, social atmosphere of a nursery or reception classroom. But compared with rising-five children the pupils who transfer to secondary school have already spent mo re than six years, which is over half of their compulsory schooling, in a primary school. Therefore, they are familiar with many of the general features of schools and teachers. Nevertheless, this is still a major adjustment and they face it with a mixture of excitement and apprehension.

Good schools, that is, secondaries and their feeder primaries, are aware of the importance of this transition and in cooperation devise a preparatory and settling-in programme. The methods adopted will vary from school to school but in every case induction programmes should be directed towards alleviating the concerns commonly expressed in

	Short-Term Strategies	
Administrative Organisational Procedures	Raise awareness understanding Review current procedures. Examine existing Identify bullying 'hot-spots'. Set up working party.	
Using the curriculum	Raise issues in assemblies. Review provision pastoral care (PSE). Conduct curriculum audit on social education/bullying behaviour.	
Community and ethos	Place on governing body agenda. Invite parents to discuss issue. Create welcoming atmosphere. All adults to provide positive models. Reward good behaviour.	

Figure 2 Developing a whole-school response to bullying

Medium-Term Strategies	Long-Term Strategies
Look at school rules. Include bullying in 'code of conduct'. Include bullying in school handbook and other documents. Spell out sanctions. Review transition procedures. Develop skills to help bully/victim. Hold staff training day. Carry out school survey.	Draw up policy and statement. Disseminate to parents. Involve other agencies. Train midday supervisors.
Engage all areas of the curriculum in changing attitudes towards aggresive behaviour. Shadowing by staff. Consider assertiveness training and peer support. Appoint curriculum coordinator.	Ongoing review of short/ medium- term approaches. Project week. Playground landscaping etc.
Bullying box. Develop peer support. Involve pupils in defining behavioural expectations. Encourage parental support Use local celebrities to support anti-bullying campaign. Introduce non-bullying contracts.	Encourage community support, e.g., local councillors and businesses. Work with other agencies. Place school policy within current legislation.

research surveys into pupil transfer as illustrated in Table 1 (Tattum and Tattum, 1992a). We also discuss short and long-term measures, the former focusing on liaison between the receiving school and its primaries; and the latter resting mainly with secondary schools and their pastoral care staff.

Table 1 Anxieties about transfer

Galton and Willcocks (1986)	Hamblin (1978)	Youngman and Lunzer (1977)	Davies (1986)	Measor and Woods (1984)
Bullying Separation from friends	Homework Examination	Things stolen Losing things	Bullying Specific subjects	Size of school New work demands
Size of school	New teachers Bullying Size of school	School work Examination Bullying	Getting lost Homework	Losing friends Bullying New forms of discipline and authority

© Delwyn & Eva Tattum1992

Various measures are developed in detail in the section on the theme of transition in *Countering Bullying* (Tattum and Herbert, 1993). A primary school in Cardiff describes how, as part of its end of year anti-bullying project week, it invited three ex-pupils from the local comprehensive to talk to their Year 6 children about bullying. As the deputy head wrote,

'The staff chose Year 8 rather than Year 7 pupils for several reasons. They thought that Year 7 pupils would be the very ones most likely to be spreading the rumours about bullying. They might even be organising the initiation rituals on the basis that they wished to perpetuate the myth that 'It happened to us!'. In fact, the three pupils were reassuring and positive. The boy, David, advised: 'If you have any problems tell a teacher. That's the main message – If anything happens tell your form teacher or any other teacher and they will usually sort it out for you.'

In addition, two large comprehensives in the north of England present their transition initiatives. South Craven High School, West Yorkshire, wrote about their whole-cluster approach involving 10 official feeder schools, ranging from small village primary schools near the Pennine Way, to larger schools in the urban districts. A different way of including feeder schools in an anti-bullying programme can be seen in the contribution of Minsthorpe High School and Community College. As part of raising awareness a Pyramid INSET day on bullying was organised as an initiative towards strengthening the Pyramid links between Minsthorpe, the five feeder middle schools, and the seven first schools.

> 'The issue, initially seen as a whole school one is now seen as a whole Pyramid or even a whole community issue … . At a school level the continuing drive to establish set procedures adopted by all adults in the school and all the pupils is evidence of the effectiveness of the policy. At a community level, the preparations for a Community Day are testament to the determination of the community to tackle the problem' (Tattum and Herbert, 1993).

Finally, a prestigious independent school, Millfield School, elaborated on the particular problems of transition associated with boarding. They focused on transition into the senior school at age 13 years – 40% of their pupils transfer from Edgarley, their preparatory school for about 500 pupils, the rest arriving from schools throughout the UK and many countries across the world. The school conducted its own survey of pupils, to ascertain the extent and nature of bullying because 'A particular difficulty for pupils in boarding schools is that they cannot escape from those who bully them, by going home from school. This is why an effective pastoral and counselling programme is so important to encourage children to talk about their worries'. They found that dormitories are places where senior pupils, monitors and even prefects can be the ones who threaten and intimidate younger pupils. These are distressing features of bullying, as they leave the victims feeling that there is no safe place in the school. Schools in the maintained sector can learn from this finding and follow Millfield's scheme to educate senior pupils into their position of authority and responsibility.

Using the curriculum

The curriculum is more than the dissemination and mastery of a fixed set of facts, it is a vehicle for changing pupils' attitudes, values, beliefs and behaviour. In Chapter 7 Graham Herbert writes about using the total curriculum to influence children's attitudes towards aggressive behaviour. In an attempt to broaden our perception of how the curriculum may be used to combat bullying Tattum and Herbert (1993) divide it into two sections.

- The **cognitive section**, dealing with knowledge, understanding and necessary academic skills, classified by the National Curriculum Council (NCC) as study skills, communication skills, IT skills, problem-solving skills and numeracy skills.

- The **affective section**, dealing with attitudes and personal and social skills, which are built upon by considering the cross-curricular themes of the National Curriculum: Environmental Education, Guidance and Careers, Citizenship, Health Education and Education for Industrial Understanding.

Thus, to tackle bullying through the curriculum teachers must map not only the delivery of the cognitive curriculum but also the affective curriculum. In the primary school, where a teacher is predominantly responsible for the delivery of the National Curriculum to the class, an audit is not too complicated a task, but in a secondary school a curriculum coordinator may be necessary to draw together the contributions of all subject departments.

A curriculum approach could be tackled through a single subject or developed as part of a cross-curricular programme. A project week on the subject of bullying can provide a very good focus. English immediately lends itself to anti-bullying work through the reading of appropriate texts (see the resource list in Tattum and Herbert, 1990), prose and poetry writing, drama and role-playing. The work can extend into maths, in the form of a school survey, and design technology, by identifying 'hot spots' in the school – it can also be used to present graphically the survey data. Work can also extend into art, music, history, RE and PE. In the videos and resource materials developed by Tattum, Tattum and Herbert (1993), a curriculum approach is presented along the lines described in this section.

The importance of the playground

Many writers have pointed out the need for well-supervised playgrounds, as the short and midday breaks are times when bullying takes place. Schools need to identify bullying 'hot spots' and ensure that 'no-go' places do not exist. They may also consider segregating younger children into a particular sector of the playground, at least in the first term when transfer anxieties are at their height. But the most significant management changes to the playground would be to introduce a training programme for midday supervisors and to make play areas more creative and constructive social and physical environments, as described by Peter Blatchford in Chapter 8. For he broadens our perception of the affective curriculum as he points out that the playground is an important learning environment, for it is here that most children learn the social and personal skills necessary for smooth and effective interaction with their peers. He also argues that we should not be surprised that bullying takes place in such an impoverished environment.

In his observational investigation of children in a primary school play-ground Sluckin (1987) noted a pecking order – even in the pre-school playground, where there are rules, roles and rituals which pupils must learn if they are to negotiate successfully episodes of potential and actual conflict. Thus, entering the social world of the playground requires children to develop strategies

> '... to resolve all sorts of everyday social problems, such as joining in a game, excluding others, avoiding a role, starting and stopping fights, insulting, threatening, bribing, gaining a reputation' (Sluckin, 1987).

There is a growing realisation of the importance of midday supervisors to the general discipline and well-being of pupils. Unfortunately, they are under-paid, which limits a school's choice of suitable candidates, and under-trained. In Tattum and Herbert (1993) a primary school in Manchester describes how, after meetings with their lunchtime organisers, the school implemented their suggestions as to how the play area could be made less hazardous and more constructive. The recommendations included zoning the play area to separate quiet games from more robust chasing and ball games; an organiser was allocated a specific area to enable each one to come to know the pupils' interests, problems and fears; all the initiatives and purposes were openly discussed with the pupils, who responded positively. The headteacher commented, 'Perhaps the greatest benefit has been to raise the self-esteem of the lunchtime supervisors. They feel that their views are respected and are worth listening to.' North Manchester is one local authority which has produced a resource pack for the training of supervisors, which includes guidance on dealing with problem behaviour – including bullying.

▓▓▓ Community and ethos

We can define community at various levels. For example, Pepler and her colleagues (Chapter 6) maintain that, in order to bring about changes in attitudes, schools need to manage their communications and initiatives to involve individual pupils, the school as an organisation, families and the local community. They provide a useful model of 'what can be done' (page 90) at each level: victims, bullies, peers, parents, teachers and administrators. Pitts (Chapter 10) for his part, defines the community as the area immediately surrounding the school he worked with in London's East End. The school reflects the community it serves but it does not have to respond merely to external forces but be a force for change itself. Believing that, it must at times intervene even in the out-of-school behaviour of pupils to protect its more vulnerable members. This is very true about bullying, as children are daily presented with aggressive models at home, in the community and the wider society. Schools should set the standards of behaviour which others will follow and unequivocally declare their abhorrence of bullying wherever it happens.

In their widely used booklet *Bullying: A Positive Response, Advice for Parents, Governors and Staff in Schools* (1990) the authors, Tattum and Herbert, challenge other pupils who witness bullying to decide whether they are supporters or spectators, because onlookers are part of the problem. Some children do not enjoy their breaktimes because of what they see and hear. In Chapter 9, Rigby and Slee deal with ways of using peer group pressure as a resource to reduce bullying. In addition to involving pupils, it is important that schools engage teaching and non-teaching staff in the discussions and implementation of an anti-bullying programme. As bullying takes place in various locations about the school and at times when pupils are not closely supervised, it is essential that we draw on all adult resources as illustrated in the 'Spheres of Involvement' model in Figure 3 (Tattum and Tattum, 1992a).

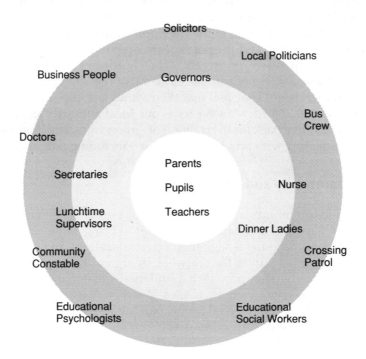

Figure 3 Spheres of Involvement

▨ Spheres of Involvement

In the inner circle are the three most involved persons, representing home and school. These parties must work together if the problem is to be resolved. The middle circle represents people who have direct association with a particular school. Secretaries, nurses and nursery nurses, dinner ladies and midday supervisors can be positively encouraged to discourage bullying. Specific advice for parents and governors can be found in Tattum and Herbert (1990) and we have already discussed the important part played by midday supervisors.

The outer circle represents a very wide range of people who, at different times, may be involved in cases of bullying. Bus crews and crossing persons can help a school identify bullies as they witness pupil behaviour to and from school. Police, doctors and solicitors are increasingly being brought in by families to handle the more extreme cases of bullying. Educational psychologists meet with individual cases but more and more look to have a positive role in working with a school on its anti-bullying programme. Finally, an important group of professionals are educational social workers who meet the problem when they visit families to enquire about absenteeism and its reasons. And it is because bullying is so widespread and persistent that we need to engage the support of all concerned persons to reduce its harmful effects on the communal life of the school.

A school-based anti-bullying intervention: preliminary evaluation

6

Debra Pepler, Wendy Craig, Suzanne Ziegler and
Alice Charach

Bullying is a pervasive phenomenon. Studies in Scandinavia, the United Kingdom, the United States, Japan and Canada have found that between 10% and 23% of children are involved in bullying interactions as either bullies or victims. The problem of bullying potentially affects all those involved: victims, bullies and peers. Firstly, the victims suffer physical and psychological abuse at the hands of their peers and may experience rejection, social isolation and anxiety. In extreme incidents, there have been suicides and violent deaths as a result of severe bullying by peers. Secondly, bullies are at risk of later maladjustment: longitudinal research indicates that childhood aggression is associated with adult anti-social behaviour and limited opportunities to attain socially desired objectives (Farrington, 1991; Huesmann *et al.*, 1984). Finally, bullying may also affect peers. Peers may be drawn into the aggressive interaction by group pressure and other social psychological factors (Olweus, 1992). Even if they do not participate in bullying, peers who observe the bullying experience distress as observing others in conflict raises anxiety (e.g., El-Sheik *et al*, 1989). The negative prognosis for the victims, aggressors and peers in bullying incidents necessitates further research to determine the nature of bully/victim interactions and the effectiveness of intervening in this problem.

'The Toronto Bullying Survey'

The impetus for the Toronto Board of Education anti-bullying project came from a survey conducted in 22 elementary schools within the Board (Ziegler, Charach and Pepler, 1992). Using questionnaires and discussion groups, this survey investigated the extent of bully/victim problems, students' ideas, attitudes, and experiences of bullying and victimisation, as well as parents' and teachers' perceptions of these problems. The student self-report questionnaire, based on the one used in schools in Scandinavia (Olweus, 1989), was administered to 211 children in 14 classrooms from Grades 3/4 to Grade 8 (ages 8–14). The qualitative method involved reading a story about bullying at school, followed by a class discussion and/or role-play activity related to bullying. A total of 457 students from Junior Kindergarten to Grade 8 were involved in this aspect of the study. We summarise the responses of students and school staff below as they provided an impetus and framework for the anti-bullying intervention.

What did the pupils say?

Bullying is a frequent occurrence according to Toronto students: 49% reported having been bullied at least once or twice during the term. Twenty percent of students reported being bullied more than once or twice during the term; 8% reported being victimised weekly or more often. The proportions of boys and girls who reported being victimised were essentially equivalent. Younger children were more likely to report being victimised than older children. When asked whether they had bullied other students, 24% of students admitted to bullying at least once or twice during the term and 15% of students reported bullying more than once or twice a term. Three times as many boys as girls acknowledged bullying others on a regular basis. Playgrounds and hallways were reported to be the locations where bullying was most likely to occur (by 81% and 57% of students, respectively). Supervised settings, such as classrooms and hallways, were cited by about twice as many students as a locale for bullying compared to unsupervised settings, such as on the way to and from school. There was a discrepancy between the perceptions of children and adults in estimates of the prevalence of bullying. In general, teachers and parents underestimated the amount of bullying that children experienced at school.

As preliminary work for the development of the anti-bullying programme, children were asked about interventions to stop bullying incidents. Thirty-two percent of the students reported that peers frequently try to stop bullying incidents at school and an additional 13% indicated that peers intervene at least occasionally. When asked how they personally responded to bullying, 43% of students reported that they tried to help; 33% reported that they did nothing, but should have done something; and 24% of students reported that they did nothing because it was not their business. Some children's responses to other questions were not as prosocial and revealed a potential social contagion effect: a third of the students indicated they could join in bullying a student they did not like. Nevertheless, the vast majority of students surveyed viewed bullying negatively. When asked how they felt when someone was being bullied, 61% of children reported that it was very unpleasant, 29% responded that it was somewhat unpleasant, and only 10% of the students reported that they didn't feel much when witnessing bullying.

Children were asked how often teachers directly tried to intervene in bullying to stop it. A quarter of the students indicated that teachers almost always intervened, 20% indicated that teachers occasionally intervened and 19% indicated that teachers almost never intervened. Compared to students, teachers saw themselves in a more positive light: 71% indicated that teachers almost always intervene, 14% indicated that teachers occasionally intervene, and none of the teachers reported that teachers almost never intervene. When asked what teachers can do to help, most students and staff indicated that teachers should talk to students (67% and 85%, respectively). About half the students and staff suggested that the teacher should punish the bully. Students were less likely than staff to suggest getting the bully and victim to talk to each other (48% and 71%, respectively).

▓▓▓ The anti-bullying intervention

Results of the Toronto board study provided direction for development of the school-based anti-bullying intervention. The behaviours of bullies, victims and peers unfold within the wider system of the school where adults are unaware of the extent of the problem and other children are unsure about whether or how to get involved. In particular, a whole-school intervention should build on the students' desire for bullying to stop and their inclinations to help victims. It is important to encourage children's tendency to intervene to help victims and discourage them from joining bullying episodes. The data from the Toronto survey confirm Olweus' (1991) contention that the optimal intervention must address bullying at the 'whole school', 'classroom' and 'individual' levels. The intervention must be a collaborative effort of teachers and parents and include the development of school rules against bullying and classroom discussions to influence the attitudes of 'neutral' students. The optimal intervention incorporates increased adult supervision of playgrounds. These components were incorporated into the intervention implemented throughout Norway which decreased the incidence of self-reported bully/victim problems by 50% over two years (Olweus, 1991 and Section I, Chapter 2).

In response to the results of the bullying survey, the Toronto Board of Education implemented a pilot anti-bullying intervention in four elementary schools. In was modelled on the Norwegian national intervention, which operates at the levels of the community (parents), the whole school, each classroom and individual students, with its most basic component the restructuring of the existing social environment of the school to create a climate which defines bullying as inappropriate and unacceptable behaviour (see Chapter 2).

During the summer of 1991, two team leaders were designated from each of the four schools involved in the Toronto pilot intervention. These team leaders met to learn about bullying and the Norwegian Intervention Programme and to consider the adaptation and implementation of an anti-bullying programme at each of the schools. One significant recognition from the planning meetings was that the anti-bullying intervention would not work without the motivation and support of administrators and teachers in the schools, hence this became a primary goal of the first year of implementation. We provide below a description of some specific programme components as part of the discussion of qualitative results.

How was the programme evaluated?

The anti-bullying project was implemented in four schools within the Toronto Board of Education. There were three schools with children from Kindergarten to Grade 8 (ages 5–14) and one senior school, with Grades 7 and 8 (ages 12–14). The schools were selected because of their interest in the problem of bullying and willingness to commit time, energy and resources to the intervention. A preliminary evaluation of the first six months of the anti-bullying pilot intervention was conducted with both a quantitative and a qualitative assessment. The quantitative assessment provided information on the reduction of bullying in the schools and behaviour change. This was complemented by the qualitative assessment which provided an evaluation of the process of implementing the anti-bullying programme.

Quantitative assessment

Self-report questionnaires. The quantitative assessment was conducted with the self-report questionnaire used in the bullying survey (Ziegler *et al.*, 1992), based very closely on the questionnaire developed by Olweus in 1989. The survey was administered by teachers to all 9- to 14-year-old students in the four schools. Due to the difficulties of reading and group administration, the survey was not suitable for students below Grade 3 (Roland, 1989). All questionnaires were completely anonymously. Data collection was conducted in October and May of the academic year during which the anti-bullying programme was implemented. The reference period for the questionnaire was the period of time since the beginning of term, approximately two months.

The self-report student questionnaire was completed in both the autumn and spring by 898 students (458 girls and 440 boys in Grades 4 to 8 in the four schools). Some Grade 3 students were included if they were part of a split Grade 3/4 classroom. The frequency of responses for different elements of a question were first calculated. A Z-test for proportions was used to calculate differences in frequencies of responses between the autumn and spring.

Frequency and type of bullying. Children were asked about the frequency of bullying at school since the beginning of term. There was no significant difference in the number of children who reported being bullied 'more than once or twice' comparing autumn to spring (12% and 13%, respectively). In contrast, there was a significant decrease in the reported incidents of bullying from autumn to spring (13% and 9%, respectively) when children were asked, 'How many times have you been bullied in the last five days?'

Analyses were conducted to examine whether there were significant decreases in certain types of bullying from autumn to spring (e.g., indirect and racial bullying). One form of indirect bullying is social exclusion. Significantly fewer children reported spending time alone at recess in the spring compared to the autumn (11% and 8%, respectively). A similar decrease was found in the numbers of children who reported spending time alone outside class time (such as at lunch) from the autumn to the spring (12% and 8%, respectively). There was no difference in the reported frequency of racial bullying over time.

Adult and peer intervention. A goal of the intervention programme was to heighten adults' and peers' awareness of bullying incidents and to enlist their support in targeting and intervening in these aggressive interactions. Children were asked how often adults tried to put a stop to bullying at school. They indicated that adults intervened in bullying episodes significantly more often in the autumn than in the spring (19% and 13%, respectively). This result is contrary to expectations and may indicate children's heightened awareness of bullying episodes as a consequence of discussions in the anti-bullying intervention. Children were asked whether their teachers and/or parents had talked to them about being bullied or bullying others. There were no differences between autumn and spring in children's reports of adults talking to them about being bullied or having bullied others.

Children were asked how often other students tried to stop bullying and what they would do if they saw another student being bullied. There were no significant differences in children's reports of the frequency of intervention by peers: 72% of children in the autumn and 67% of children in the spring indicated that peers 'sometimes' or 'almost always' intervened to stop bullying. When asked what they do when they see another child being bullied, 30% of the children in the autumn indicated they tried to help in one way or another. There was no change in the spring, when 29% of the children responded that they would help a victim.

Children's perceptions of bullying. It was hypothesised that the anti-bullying intervention would make children feel more uncomfortable about witnessing bullying and less likely to join in a bullying episode. Contrary to expectations, fewer children reported feeling uncomfortable when witnessing a bullying episode in the autumn than in the spring (90% and 86%, respectively). There was no significant difference in the number of children who reported that they could join in a bullying episode (even if it was someone they did not like) in the autumn compared to the spring (24% and 28%, respectively).

In summary, the quantitative analyses indicated some initial successes of the anti-bullying intervention, but these were limited. For example, fewer children reported being bullied 'in the last five days' and being excluded 'less frequently' in the spring than in the autumn. In contrast, adults' and peers' interventions to stop bullying episodes were relatively unaffected by the intervention. Finally, there was no decrease in the numbers of children reporting a willingness to join in bullying episodes.

Qualitative assessment

The processes and perceptions of success in the implementation of the anti-bullying intervention were assessed qualitatively. Interviews were conducted at the end of the school year with the anti-bullying team leaders in each of the four pilot schools. The format for the interview followed the Olweus Programme Follow-up Evaluation, with questions on inputs and outcomes at the community and school levels; questions on organisation at the community and school levels were also incorporated. Two of the co-investigators conducted the interviews, which each lasted approximately 90 minutes.

The responses to the interview questions were recorded and later analysed to determine the process of programme implementation, the successes and goals yet to be achieved, and plans for the following year. What was found?

The community level (outreach to parents)

Schools accomplished the goal of making parents aware of the anti-bullying project, mainly through presentations at Parent-Teacher Association meetings and through school newsletters. Schools communicated their awareness of and concern about bullying and encouraged parents to contact the school if they believed their child was involved in bullying. On the whole, parents indicated support and gratitude for this interest and focus. On the other hand, team members discussed the difficulty of disseminating information and enthusiasm about the programme beyond a small group of committed and interested parents. They believed that the broader community in some schools was not fully aware of the components of the anti-bullying intervention and the issues related to bullying. While some parents in at least one of the schools were reflecting supportive attitudes and using vocabulary modelled by the school staff, many parents in at least one other school still considered physical punishment as an appropriate solution to aggression and conflict problems.

Two schools indicated the need to work more with parents in the following year. In the senior school, the principal considered creating a parent group to focus on bullying. In this school, bullying generally occurred as name-calling and exclusion of students who did not conform.

The school level

In general, the goal of eliciting motivation and support for the intervention was met in all schools during the first year of implementation. Teaching staff in all schools participated in a school conference day on bullying and victimisation. In the three K–8 schools where children spend free play time in the playground, adult supervision was increased and the school bought more play equipment, providing more opportunities for constructive play. Staff from one school noted that the combination of painting hopscotch and other games on the playground and instruction in these games from the physical education teacher led to an increase in friendly, mixed-gender play.

Schools also focused on supervision in the halls, a prime location for bullying according to students' reports. In the Grade 7 and 8 school, the class schedule was altered for the following year so that fewer students were in the halls at any given time. Another school attempted to reduce the student traffic in halls to prevent bullying.

How did staff react?

The team members were questioned about the uniform and consistent handling of bullying by school staff. Three of the four schools had developed a school-wide code of behaviour. The behaviour codes prescribed positive rights and responsibilities, rather than establishing negative rules for behaviour. For example, the rule 'We shall not bully others' was recast as 'Every student has the right to a safe and orderly school environment'. Although these codes articulated the appropriate behaviours for students, they did not guarantee that staff were consistent in their responses to misdemeanours. It is clear that staff in all schools were initially informed of the problem of bullying and provided with guidelines for handling it. There is less evidence of regular staff discussions of how to handle bullying problems and concomitant behavioural change by the teaching staff. One school member noted that teachers were still uncertain about how and when to intervene in the playground and had difficulty distinguishing between rough-and-tumble play and aggression. This problem of detecting bullying in the playground was addressed in another of the schools by ruling out all rough-and-tumble play and play fighting. In response to bully/victim problems, staff seemed able to talk to students collectively, but the team leaders expressed concern that teachers were unable to move beyond lecturing students to create the climate for constructive, participatory discussion.

In more than one school, staff found it easier to deal with bullies than with victims. Some team leaders hypothesised that teachers were more aware of provocative victims – those who instigate aggressive interactions – than submissive victims. Some leaders indicated a tendency for teachers to think of victims as children who were difficult to like and who elicited bullying. The leaders identified a need to expose staff to the profile of a passive victim through literature, parents' descriptions and other illustrations of actual cases. This would sensitise teachers to recognise the victim who is innocent of provocation, evokes sympathy, but is difficult to identify.

Curriculum ideas

A number of curriculum units on bullying were introduced in the schools to change students' attitudes and behaviours related to bullying. For example, drama activities in the form of stories and role play were enthusiastically received. The primary teachers in one school developed units on fairy tales and on friendship relating to bullying and exclusion. Stories and novels were used across all grades to highlight bullying and stimulate discussions. Classroom discussions were also provided through the Learning Circle which is similar to the Quality Circle approach described in Chapter 4. This is a method to allow students to talk in a safe and structured way, without threat of judgement. Teachers implement Learning Circle as a means of improving interpersonal relationships in the classroom, teaching respect for others, and making peers more accepting. The process of listening respectfully to others may encourage tolerance and discourage interpersonal aggression. Social workers in two of the schools ran small group meetings several times over the year to talk about bullying, write about it, and make anti-bullying posters to increase awareness of the problem.

A mentoring programme was implemented in the senior grades (7 and 8) in two of the schools. Students were divided into small, mixed-age groups with a teacher who served in a non-academic, advisory capacity. Like Learning Circle, it provided an opportunity for students to address interpersonal, non-academic concerns in a comfortable and supportive climate.

Furthermore, many schools in Toronto have implemented a peer conflict mediation programme which trains children to intervene in conflicts in the playground and elsewhere. The conflict mediation does not exclusively target bullying but includes any interpersonal conflict which children need help in resolving. Mediators can initiate the intervention, or they can respond to a request from another child. Teacher support is always available to assist in mediating a conflict. An example of this type of intervention is the Peacemakers programme (Roderick, 1988).

■ What was achieved?

The results of the survey of bullying in Toronto schools indicate that bullying is a pervasive and stable problem. This chapter presents a preliminary analysis of the first six months of a pilot anti-bullying intervention within Toronto schools. The quantitative analyses of the effectiveness of the anti-bullying project indicated decreases in the number of children reporting being bullied 'in the last five days' and being excluded. There was, however, no significant change in children's reports of the prevalence of bullying in the last two months, racial bullying, peer intervention and in discussions about bullying with adults. Children reported significantly less adult intervention in the spring than in the previous autumn. Finally, fewer children reported being uncomfortable observing bullying in the spring than in the autumn. Together with the qualitative data, these findings highlight several important considerations in the implementation of a school-based anti-bullying programme. The implications of this preliminary evaluation will be discussed from a systems perspective comprising the school, classroom, teachers, peers, and individual bullies and victims.

Implications for intervention

School level

The prevalence of bullying is associated with the school environment, particularly with the attitudes and support of school staff (Stephenson and Smith, 1988). The limited change in the first year of the anti-bullying intervention illustrates the extensive time required to develop an awareness of the problems associated with bullying and a repertoire of skills to intervene. In the first year of the intervention, the schools identified the problem of bullying and started to develop specific interventions. For example, three of the four schools developed a general anti-violence policy. General policies, such as an anti-violence policy, may not comprise specific policies and initiatives regarding bullying and the consequences for this type of behaviour. The qualitative interviews with team leaders indicated that school staff had grown to recognise the problem of bullying. In order to intervene effectively in bullying problems, this recognition must be translated into attitudinal and behavioural changes by staff which in turn must be communicated to the students and their parents.

Under the anti-bullying intervention, some restructuring of the school environment had been started. For example, there was increased supervision of the halls and playground, and more structured activities, such as organised games, were being introduced in the playground. These initiatives are important in assisting teachers with the difficult task of supervising the playground and hallways, which are high risk areas for bullying and victimisation.

As head of the school, the principal has an essential role in providing leadership for an anti-bullying intervention. With school staff and parents, the principal can establish a policy of zero tolerance for bullying, an appropriate discipline programme and opportunities for professional development for teachers. The principal and school staff can work to develop a school ethos with the aims of changing attitudes towards bullying and creating a school climate that will not tolerate aggressive acts towards fellow students. An anti-bullying programme should extend to parents to incorporate them as partners in addressing the problem of bullying.

Classroom level

Teachers. All schools in the anti-bullying intervention conducted school conference days on bullying and victimisation. While this educational component is necessary, it is not sufficient. Team leaders indicated that the programme had been implemented to varying degrees across schools and classrooms. Schools expressed a need to increase communication with other schools participating in the anti-bullying programme. For a comprehensive implementation, teachers may require extensive resources, such as a specific curriculum, to facilitate their classroom discussions and teaching on bullying. An anti-bullying curriculum might contain suggestions of topics to be discussed in the Learning Circle time, role plays and activities to create an awareness of the problem and to develop respect, care, tolerance and empathy towards others in the classroom. Opportunities for classroom discussions and learning are a critical component in an anti-bullying intervention (see Herbert, Chapter 7).

Teachers play a critical role in children's lives and have an opportunity to provide a positive role model for children. To some extent, teachers need to see bullying from their own perspective, remembering their own experiences of bullying as a child and becoming sensitive to their own style of interaction with children. The fact that students indicated that adults intervened less often in bullying episodes in the spring than in the autumn may have been a function of children's increased awareness and identification of bullying episodes. On the other hand, teachers may not have clearly articulated their intentions and efforts to intervene. It is essential that teachers communicate to students that they will not tolerate bullying and that everyone must work together to make the school a safe and secure environment. To accomplish the goals of an anti-bullying intervention, teachers need strategies and resources about bullying and frequent opportunities to share them. What might these strategies be?

- As a preventative measure, teachers could provide opportunities for children to work together in mixed age, race and gender groups to increase positive social interactions, open communication, and to break down perceptions that may lead to bullying episodes.

■ Teachers may identify students who may be at risk for bullying and victimisation, and give these children additional individual support to address their problems associated with bullying.

The view of peers

The pattern of results of the preliminary evaluation suggests that students may have had a heightened awareness of bullying after six months of the anti-bullying intervention. The attitudinal change, however, was not in the expected direction. While the vast majority of students indicated discomfort, fewer students reported being uncomfortable observing bullying in the spring than in the previous autumn. Peers may play a critical role in bullying interactions. In an observational study of bullying in the playground, Craig and Pepler (1992) found that peers were involved as collaborators and observers in about 89% of bullying episodes. This result highlights the need to engage peers in an effort to decrease bullying in the playground (see Rigby and Slee, Chapter 9).

In the Toronto intervention, peer mentoring and conflict management programmes were implemented in order to engage peers and elicit their support. Peer programmes aimed at reducing bullying in the schools need to have two specific goals: firstly, to promote an attitude which disapproves of violence towards others; and secondly, to encourage peers to intervene to stop aggressive interactions. Within an anti-bullying intervention, students must develop an awareness of the problem, a willingness to report bullying, and a sense of security in the knowledge that protection and support are available from teachers and other peers.

Although a majority of children report that they feel uncomfortable watching bullying, a proactive approach is required to engage peers successfully in reducing bullying. An anti-bullying intervention must teach students about bullying, how to identify it and what they can do to stop it; it must convince students of the desirability and feasibility of intervention. Through activities such as role plays, drama and story-telling, students can begin to understand the perspectives of the victim. Once students begin to empathise with victims, they are more likely to support the victim and provide clear messages of disapproval to the bully. It is important that peers be made aware of the ways in which they may be inadvertently supporting and perhaps exacerbating bullying, through attention, joining in and lack of action to stop bullying episodes. Teachers can facilitate peers in turning their attention away from the bully and in providing positive support to the victim.

'Peacemakers'

As part of the anti-bullying intervention, one school implemented the Peacemaker peer conflict mediation programme (Roderick, 1988). Children were chosen as 'conflict managers' by their peers, and given extensive training in strategies to intervene in problems between children in the playground. A majority of playground conflicts can be readily handled by the conflict managers, with the knowledge that teachers are available for additional support.

The advantage of a programme of peer monitoring in the playground is that bullying is often hidden from adults. Observations of bullying in the playground indicate that peers intervene approximately three times as often as teachers to stop bullying (Craig and Pepler, 1992). While bullying may be difficult for teachers to detect, peers are present during bullying interactions and, therefore, can play a significant role in reducing the problem.

The Peacemaker programme is an excellent addition to an anti-bullying programme but not sufficient to reduce bullying significantly. Peer conflict managers intervene in visible physical conflict; however, they do not address problems of indirect, non-physical bullying. The burden of responsibility for stopping bullying at school must be shared by both the students and staff. Adult intervention and firm direction are essential. The adult plays a particularly important role in supporting victims and ensuring that the identification of a bullying problem does not accelerate their victimisation.

▬ Individual level

The view of victims

Inherent in a definition of bullying is the difficulty of victims to defend themselves. Once victimisation has been identified, it is important to support victims and ensure that they are protected from further abuse at the hands of bullies. The first step in assisting victims is to encourage them to report bullying incidents so that an adult can intervene. Once the bullying has been curtailed and the victim is safe, teachers can provide support for victims to help them develop skills and strategies to avoid further victimisation. These include teaching victims when and where to go for help and training victims in the skills of resisting and asserting themselves. Victims have been shown to have low self-esteem (Alasker, 1991; Roland, 1989); therefore, efforts should be made to enhance the self-image of victims, perhaps by providing opportunities for them to achieve attention and recognition within the peer group. Finally, many victims are excluded and isolated from the peer group (Craig and Pepler, 1992). In addition to enhancing victims' peer relation skills through social skills training, teachers can play a critical role in helping victims develop friendships with prosocial children at school.

Parents of victims should be contacted and encouraged to assist in supporting their children. Children may feel more comfortable disclosing victimisation experiences to their parents than to their teachers. With an awareness of the problems of bullying, parents may become increasingly sensitive in recognising signs of victimisation (e.g., headaches, stomach aches, school refusal or reticence, dropping grades). Although children may ask parents to remain silent about victimisation experiences, parents should be strongly encouraged to approach the school. Teachers may not be aware of individual children's victimisation experiences (Olweus, 1991; Ziegler *et al*, 1992); therefore, it is essential that parents initiate discussions with teachers as a first step in addressing the problems. In this way, parents and teachers can work together to protect victims and eliminate bullying experiences. When victims experience support from the home, school and peer systems, they may be able to break out of the cycle of an abusive bullying relationship.

The bullies

Bullying is a form of aggressive behaviour, hence interventions to stop bullying can be derived, to a certain extent, from our understanding of the treatment of aggressive behaviour problems (e.g., Kazdin, 1987). Firstly, there must be clear messages that bullying will not be tolerated and disciplinary action will be taken with anyone who bullies. It is important for school staff to be vigilant in monitoring bullies' behaviours and attitudes as they have a tendency to minimise their behaviours or blame others. Interventions with bullies should teach empathy, problem-solving, social skills and self-regulation. To redirect bullying behaviours, the bully might be provided with other means of experiencing leadership in the class and school. Bullies' problems often extend beyond the school: they tend to be aggressive towards their parents and siblings at home (Olweus, 1987). Hence, any intervention with bullies should seek parents' support to generalise improved behaviour and attitudes across contexts.

▆▆▆▆ Parent level

In the Toronto anti-bullying intervention, there was increased communication with parents about the problem of bullying. Within a school-based intervention support can be solicited from parents at two levels.

Firstly, all parents of children in the school should be provided with information about bullying and encouraged to attend meetings to discuss the problem and share in decisions regarding actions that the school should take to curb bullying. It is essential that the parent-teacher association of the school be firmly behind efforts to stop bullying. Parents can collaborate with school staff to develop a school policy and code of behaviours related to bullying. Parents can be engaged with school staff in developing strategies to address bullying problems in the school. For example, in some Toronto schools, parents shared in training children as conflict managers for the Peacemaker programme. In one of the intervention schools, as adults in the school environment, parents were encouraged to assist in playground supervision to reduce bullying. Despite reservations, this was reported to be a positive addition to the supervision of children.

The second level of parent involvement is initiated when individual children are identified as bullies or victims. Parents of these children should be contacted as soon as the problem is identified. Bullying surveys

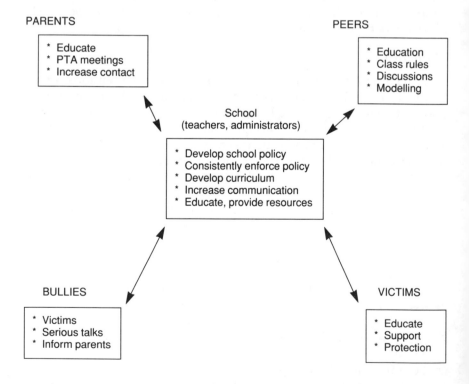

Figure 4 What can be done?

indicate that parents are often unaware of their children's involvement in bullying or victimisation (Olweus, 1991; Ziegler, *et al*, 1992). Hence, parents should be informed of the problem and provided with information about the consequences and sequels of bullying. It is important to have the parents' understanding and support in assisting bullies and victims change their behaviours and attitudes. Parents' involvement can be sought to work through the problem together with their children and teachers. The parents have a particularly important role in providing consistency in the approach to bullying problems across school and home contexts. With increased awareness of the problem, parents may recognise when bullying or victimisation occurs at home between siblings, between parents and children, or between the parents themselves. There is a current trend to include parents as partners in the educational process. This is a domain where their involvement provides a critical element in alleviating a major social concern.

To summarise

There is little doubt, based on the sampling of students in Toronto elementary schools, that bullying affects the lives of thousands of school children. To reduce bullying in schools, there is an urgent need for interventions which are ecological in design and comprehensive in scope as depicted in the figure, page 90. Bullying is a complex problem embedded in a number of systems that may inadvertently model, reinforce and maintain bullying interactions. In order to change behaviour patterns and cognitions that underlie bullying and victimisation, interventions must be extensive and address the problem with individual bullies and victims, the peer group and the school environment. The intervention must also encompass parents to enlist their support in developing appropriate attitudes and behaviours to reduce bullying beyond the school. Given the scope of the problem, the process of change is slow. The preliminary evaluation of the Toronto anti-bullying intervention suggests that a start has been made but considerably more work needs to be done to address the hidden violence of bullying in schools.

Acknowledgements: We are indebted to the team leaders, teachers, school staff and children in the four schools where the anti-bullying intervention was implemented. Their efforts and commitment are reflected throughout this chapter. This research was made possible, in part, by a grant from the Ontario Mental Health Foundation.

7 Changing children's attitudes through the curriculum

Graham Herbert

One of the major functions of managers in a school is to oversee the delivery of the curriculum. Part of this is to ensure effective timetabling, sufficient resources and appropriate levels of staffing to fulfil the stated aims of the school's curriculum and to deliver the National Curriculum. This process goes far beyond the narrow confines of the National Curriculum alone.

A further function of the school's managers is to ensure that the pupils in the school have access to all aspects of that curriculum. They must not be disentitled through any fault of the school's. One of the major causes of disentitlement is because a pupil does not feel safe in his or her environment. A pupil who feels threatened or worried about what will happen when the lesson has finished, is unlikely to learn effectively. This chapter is about all aspects of the process of providing a curriculum and an environment in which pupils can learn whether in the secondary or the primary sector of schooling.

Looking at the curriculum

The National Curriculum as presented to schools takes the form of discrete subjects. Defined for these separate subject areas are separate descriptors of what a child should know, understand and be able to do at each one of the four Key Stages of schooling. Major problems arise, however, if a school allows its teachers to retreat into subject specialisms and confuses the prescriptive, formal National Curriculum with the whole curriculum. The National Curriculum is only the minimum which should be delivered.

The National Curriculum Council is at pains to point out:

'The whole curriculum of a school, of course, goes far beyond the formal timetable. It involves a range of policies and practices to promote the personal and social development of pupils, to accommodate different teaching and learning styles, to develop positive attitudes and values and to forge an effective partnership with parents and the local community.' (NCC Circular No.6, 1989).

The school is legally bound to deliver the National Curriculum. To ensure that it is doing so, school managers need to audit what is being delivered. Broadly this can be called the *cognitive curriculum*, and is concerned with children's understanding, with a display and practice of skills and with the presentation of the knowledge they have learned.

However, if a school retreats into prescriptive and narrow subject specialism, how can managers know that 'positive attitudes and values' are being 'developed' or that 'an effective partnership with parents and the local community' is being 'forged'? The answer is of course that they cannot. By concentrating wholly on timetabled subjects, the school loses sight of the principal reason for its existence, namely *the education of children* and instead concentrates on the delivery and recording of the National Curriculum. The education of children and the delivery of the National Curriculum are not synonymous.

As well as considering what the school delivers, it is profitable to ask questions about what an individual child is learning. In this way we may come to understand something of the child's perspective of curriculum experiences rather than a teacher's or a school's manager's. We will also be in a better position to understand what the individual child knows, understands and can do. However, we will also be aware of what the individual child's attitudes are and how these can be influenced. This will be crucial when we wish to change an individual's or a group's attitudes towards bullying. Such a view of the *affective curriculum* must not be considered in an haphazard way, but must be audited as carefully as the formal, timetabled cognitive curriculum. Where can a school's managers begin to audit the affective as well as the cognitive curriculum?

Auditing the affective curriculum

A curriculum for personal development

The affective curriculum is often referred to as 'Personal and Social Education' (PSE). This is a starting point for introducing elements into the curriculum which will be effective in countering bullying.

In his book, *Personal and Social Education in the Curriculum* (1984), Richard Pring highlights a framework which can be used to audit the whole curriculum. The framework is as follows:

1 **Personal development**
   - *Intellectual competencies*: 'those skills and abilities of the mind that allow accurate observation, clear thought, hypothesis, logical argument and exposition.'
   - *Practical knowledge*: Those skills which are reflected in pupils' knowing how to achieve certain tasks.
   - *Theoretical knowledge*: Those abstractions which are necessary for the delivery of the National Curriculum.

Taken together, these three represent the cognitive aspects of the National Curriculum and relate to the attainment targets. They also relate to certain aspects of cross-curricular skills such as study skills, oracy and numeracy as well as the ability to apply IT skills. They can be recorded and quantified.

2 **Social development**

   - *Character traits*: Those qualities which reflect a pupil's determination or tolerance of others.
   - *Social competencies*: Those skills which allow a pupil to make use of the school as a resource, for example, the pupil's ability to understand organisations or understand the difference between 'banter' and 'cheek'.
   - *Personal values:* Those values which develop over time, for example, the way in which an individual pupil may decide to become a vegetarian, a devout Muslim or a Christian.
   - *Moral dispositions*: These are inclinations such as kindness or patience or generosity, those dispositions which govern the emotions.

The last four elements of the framework relate to those areas outside the National Curriculum but which we are asked to consider in the form of personal and social as well as moral and spiritual development. They represent the work outlined as personal and social skills, the content of RE and the cross-curricular themes such as Citizenship. It is important that these areas are recognised as well as the cognitive areas of the curriculum.

Taken together, these seven elements of personal development can act as an initial audit of work in the curriculum, and as a basis for monitoring personal development. Needless to say, not all of these elements will occur in any one lesson. What is important for teachers is that they are aware that all of these separate elements are interacting during their lessons and that the worth of the final four is recognised by both teacher and pupil. It is also important that teachers, particularly of specialist subjects, do not view these areas of the affective curriculum as someone else's job. As I said in 1988: 'To remove fear induced by bullying we must tackle it all day long.'

Such a framework of what makes each of us 'a person' must underpin this initial audit.

'What makes a pupil a developing person is the interaction of the seven aspects. The school as a whole will seek to develop all of them, help make the pupil conscious of them and better able to assess and develop them in the social context' (Marland 1989).

Once the affective curriculum is explicit a set of aims can be drawn up. Schemes of work, including work specifically designed to counter bullying, can then be designed to meet these aims. The effectiveness of the work suggested and the behaviour of pupils in a school can be monitored, both in the formal classroom setting and in the less formal playground setting.

To do this thoroughly, the school's managers must tackle the second part of the audit, namely, the social aspect. To help in achieving this aspect of the audit, a school's manager need to develop a form of analytical tool similar to that described above.

A curriculum for social development

In their book *Social Education and Personal Development* (1992a) Tattum and Tattum identify three ways in which the affective or 'social' curriculum can be delivered. These are:

- **The hidden social curriculum**. This 'creates the social context and social relationships in which the social curriculum is delivered'. It includes such things as the relationships between the school and home; dealing with pupils' behaviour and especially deviant behaviour; punishments and rewards; reacting to pupils' complaints, either about other pupils or staff; providing support for those pupils who are emotionally stressed; providing easy transition from one stage of schooling to the other; the use of the power which teachers wield over the pupils for whom they are responsible.

    This list must, however, be determined by the individual schools since the ethos which they wish to present will vary according to a variety of factors, such as the history of the school, the management structure and the community which the school serves. Members of the community need to be consulted and informed of such innovations as the school's behaviour policy, or how the school intends to tackle bullying and the ways in which the community can help the school to achieve its aims.

- **The formal social curriculum**. Those things which we are legally required to teach. 'The National Curriculum Council (NCC) presents personal and social development as a cross-curricular dimension' (Tattum and Tattum, 1992). This cannot be left to chance but must 'be co-ordinated as an explicit part of a school's whole curriculum policy, both inside and outside the formal timetable' (NCC, Circular No. 6, 1989). The NCC outlined five cross-curricular themes:

  1 Economic and industrial understanding
  2 Careers education and guidance
  3 Health education
  4 Environmental education
  5 Citizenship

  Again, the community needs to be involved through, for example, work experience; communications with local services; developing relations with the local health authority; using the local environment and its community as a stimulus for learning experiences; inviting parents into the school; allowing parents to take part in a curriculum workshop; ensuring there are clearly defined reception areas; displaying joint activities of both teachers and parents ...and so on.

- **The implicit social curriculum**. This is the area where so many schools fail because they do not take note of the practices which pervade the establishment. Many schools try to justify themselves with phrases such as 'This is a caring school' ... or 'We help pupils to realise their potential' ... or 'We encourage personal autonomy'. Laudable though these aims are, they do not help anyone to check if they are being achieved. Rather than offering such bland platitudes, a school's managers should determine the types of classroom methodologies which actively encourage the types of behaviour which they wish to promote. They should also determine the types of classroom practices which militate against the types of behaviour which they wish to remove from pupils, like bullying.

■ A policy for personal and social education

By making such concepts public and coming to a consensus about what the school means by personal and social development, a school manager is in a position to provide an effective framework in which staff can work and pupils learn. Within this framework, the school's curriculum can be experienced, work can be planned, the learning process monitored and assessed and the whole delivery evaluated on a regular basis, as can the types of behaviour which the school condemns.

The policy can begin by stating what the intentions of the school are: what does the school expect of its pupils at the end of each Key Stage in terms of personal development and social competencies?

Work can then be designed which will help pupils to develop towards agreed goals for the benefit of themselves, of others in the school, of the school environment and of society generally. Further, what an individual pupil is learning can be monitored effectively. Individual departments and teachers can plan to cover aspects of the social curriculum in the same way as they plan their coverage of the formal curriculum. The matrix shown in Figure 5 is one way of planning and recording all aspects of the curriculum during a series of science lessons at Key Stage three. The general principle can be transferred to all subject areas and all Key Stages.

School managers can now feel confident that 'positive attitudes and values' are being developed, since ways of achieving them are made explicit in the schemes of work and in the assessment processes. The school's intentions must also be made clear to members of the community. In this way they too will feel part of the process of helping to develop the curriculum, ensuring the 'forging of shared attitudes and values with parents and the community' (NCC, 1989).

The school will now have means of delivering the formal curriculum which is compatible with the personal and social development of each individual as well as limiting the amount of bullying which occurs in the school. Importantly, the values, attitudes and personal qualities which the school views as important will be in the public domain, open to scrutiny and critical analysis, thereby strengthening the ties with the community.

In this way we can fulfil the major aim of the education system, namely to educate people.

'If we concentrate on the cognitive and lose sight of the affective then we are in danger of delivering a worthless curriculum. Of course, we have to provide the scientists, the economists, the technicians of the future, but we must never forget that these are people; our aim is to educate people' (Tattum and Herbert, 1993).

SCHEME OF WORK FOR TOPIC

	Resources	Knowledge Covered	Understanding	Skills	Attitudes	Achievement
LESSON 1	Test tubes, racks, metal Cu, Zn, Mg, Acid	Metals react with acid to give H2	Make predictions based on the activity series	General lab. skills working safely Communications skills	Sharing ideas. Teamwork	Was able to complete experiments successfully and safely
LESSON 2						
LESSON 3						
LESSON 4						
LESSON 5						
LESSON 6						
LESSON 7						
LESSON 8						

Figure 5 Planning and recording matrix

By approaching our curriculum in the way outlined above we can be confident that we are educating 'people' and not merely fulfilling the limited and limiting requirements of the National Curriculum.

Developing a behaviour policy

To be effective a school must develop a social climate which is compatible with the desired and stated learning outcomes. Through an effective and workable behaviour policy, a school can create an appropriate environment in which individual pupils feel safe and bullying is not tolerated. Only if the school works consistently will the appropriate environment be created. Individual teachers may create an appropriate environment in their classrooms and deliver a coherent curriculum for personal and social development, but what happens to the pupils when they are no longer with this enthusiastic and committed teacher? What happens to them on the corridors, in the playground or on their way home? The likelihood is that they will be involved at some time in some kind of bullying behaviour, as a victim, or as an instigator of the behaviour, or as a spectator to it. When introducing a behaviour policy into the school the following questions need to be addressed if the whole school is to work in a consistent and coherent way.

- *Who else other than the school's staff should be involved in developing a behaviour policy?*
  - What store does the school attach to the views of others?
  - How can the school gather the opinions of other people?
  - Would putting this kind of development into the public domain result in a loss of respect or confidence within the community?
  - How interested and informed are these other people?
  - Who should collate, interpret and present as data the information which comes into school from outside?
- *What kinds of things should the behaviour policy contain?*
  - Should it be just a list of rules?
  - Should it include a list of sanctions?
  - Should it outline the responsibilities of all adults involved in the running of the school?
  - How much detail should there be in the drawing up of the policy? Should it contain a list of 'Do's and Don'ts'?
- *Having drawn up a policy, how should it then be implemented?*
  - How are the staff to be involved and what kind of INSET programme will be necessary? Who will pay for that INSET?

— How will the governing body become involved and at what stage should it be involved?

— How should the support services be used or consulted? Will the school's ancillary staff be a part of this process and how are they to be trained as well as consulted?

— How will the views of the children be canvassed?

— How can the parents of children be informed of what the school is attempting to achieve?

— How can the parents be recruited to help in the process?

■ *How can the behaviour policy be reviewed and evaluated?*
   — Will a record of all incidents be kept?
   — Will there be a written record of all the pleasant incidents which occur?
   — Is it unrealistic to look for measurable performance indicators?
   — What success criteria should the school realistically look for?

For a more detailed discussion of the issues raised here, as well as examples of how such systems and sets of procedures were introduced in schools see Tattum and Herbert (1993).

A number of things will have now been achieved:

■ There is a working definition of personal and social development in the school.

■ There is a planning and recording framework within which pupils and teachers can work.

■ The rules which govern social interactions in the school support that development.

■ The concepts surrounding these issues are in the public domain and open to criticism and review.

■ An environment exists in which both a curricular and an administrative approach can tackle the problems posed by bullying behaviour.

▨ Pupils and the community as a resource

Once pupils have begun work on the issue of bullying they can be encouraged to find their own ways to explore it. This can range from collecting poems, to analysing the use of areas of the school grounds, to drawing up data of different problem areas and presenting them in appropriate styles, to delivering an assembly for the year group or the school as a whole. This is an important step in the development of materials and particularly in the changing of attitudes.

La Fontane (1991) found that:

> 'Children considered a wide range of behaviour to be bullying, ranging from teasing to serious physical harm. There is, however, a common thread. While in the literature on bullying it is common to find bullying linked with aggressiveness, that is with the bullies' expression of feelings, many of these children also seemed to perceive it as an act conveying a message: one of hostility and rejection. . . . The bullied child feels isolated and lonely'.

She goes on to add that a reactive response

> 'may be inappropriate, because it does not alter the balance of power in the situation'.

By introducing attention to bullying into the curriculum in the way outlined here we can begin to change that balance of power. Importantly, it begins to give ownership of the curriculum back to those people who have never been consulted by the NCC – the children. David Pascall, when chairman of the NCC, insisted that: 'radical change can only be implemented with the support, commitment and ownership of those most affected.'

If those most affected by bullying in schools – the children – can have an input into the curriculum about this specific topic then we can begin to change those attitudes which make bullying such a problem in our schools and begin to shift the balance of power which presently so favours the bully.

Supporting the spectators

Those people who are not directly affected by the bully can also have a positive effect on what happens in the playground or wherever bullying occurs in the school environment. If the spectators to bullying, those thousands of pupils who are neither bullies nor victims, are brought into the attempts to limit the amount of bullying then the chances of achieving success are extended. If these other pupils feel confident that their reporting of incidents will have a positive effect on the situation, they are more likely to report any incidents which they witness. If their reports result in direct action by the staff and the pupils feel that something will be done about a problem, they are more likely to report the incidents. Such interventions will, of course, have a snowball effect: the more pupils report and feel confident in doing so, the more likely they are to do so and the more likely are such interventions to be successful.

It is not only the pupils who can intervene in bullying behaviour. If those adults who have been consulted about the behaviour and have been kept informed of the school's intentions are also encouraged to become involved in reporting incidents to the school, then they too are more likely to feel some measure of success at their own interventions. This will, of course, act as a form of deterrent to the bullies. If they are aware that their unpleasant behaviour is being monitored then they are less likely to become involved in it.

Monitoring the behaviour

Just as the cognitive curriculum needs to be monitored carefully to determine whether it is being delivered in an effective way, so too does the affective curriculum. However, there will need to be different success criteria. For example, do not expect an effective method of countering bullying to produce an immediate reduction in the number of bullying incidents reported to the staff. The opposite is true. If pupils lack confidence in the system the school has for tackling bullying, then they are unlikely to use that system. This will result in few, if any, reports of bullying incidents from the pupils. On the other hand, if the pupils have a trust in the approach which the school adopts, then they are likely to use it. This will result in an increase in the number of reports of bullying.

Methods of measuring and recording success

To monitor these numbers, the school must devise an easily administered method of recording bullying incidents, which provides anyone with the relevant information at a glance. A number of methods have been suggested to achieve this end.

- Surveys can be readministered after a period of time to measure in a quantifiable way the number of incidents taking place and the pupils' responses to them.
- Individuals can use 'post boxes' to inform adults about what is happening in the school. Obviously this system is open to abuse, but experience suggests that once operational it becomes trustworthy.
- A standard form of written record can be devised to inform the school's managers of who is involved in the behaviour, where it is

taking place, when it is taking place, what form the behaviour takes, how it manifests itself and, if possible, why it is happening. Such records can be completed by the pupils involved if they are old enough, or by the staff if the pupils are too young to complete a proforma.

(For a more detailed description of various methods of monitoring behaviour see *Countering Bullying*, Tattum and Herbert, 1993.)

- Attendance rates can be monitored. Research has suggested that if the school can counter bullying then there will indeed be a reduction in the rates of unacceptable absenteeism.

- The number of socially unacceptable petty incidents which occur in any school can be tracked. These can include such things as acts of petty vandalism, petty theft, minor disruption to lessons and social disruption which can affect the school's immediate vicinity from time to time.

A view of pupils' learning

In an article in *The Times Educational Supplement* (19 October 1992) Michael Armstrong argued that the presentation of the National Curriculum was, in essence, dull. It underestimated the nature and vitality of children's learning. By presenting the National Curriculum in the form of different subjects and measured by attainment targets, it has become too complex, too elaborate and too time-consuming. Crucially, it fails, he argued, to make any recognition of children's achievements.

The approach I have outlined puts the children's learning back into the centre of the curriculum itself and moves the prescriptive elements to the periphery. By concentrating on what pupils learn and how they learn, rather than on what ministers prescribe, we can help pupils to become creators of their own learning environment. The majority of pupils do not want to live in an atmosphere dominated by bullies and the fear they bring. By creating an environment in which all pupils learn effectively, a school can begin to tackle the problem of bullying, confident that the pupils will be an invaluable resource in helping them to achieve that.

By putting the individual pupil at the centre of the curriculum and concentrating on the development of 'self' in a social context, we are more likely to allow children to learn effectively. We can organise our classrooms to facilitate a 'diversity of experiences in a way which simultaneously acknowledges and ignores the boundaries between subjects' (Armstrong 1992). The delivery of the curriculum in such a way will allow teachers to challenge and influence children's attitudes not through an exhortation to change, but through the social interaction involved in the process of learning and developing as individuals.

8 Bullying in the playground

Peter Blatchford

Research on bullying, inspired by the pioneering work of Olweus in Scandinavia, had done much to focus attention on characteristics of bullies and victims. In Britain, Besag (1989) presented a helpful review of research on the personality, physical and family characteristics of bullies (e.g. aggressive, impulsive, strong, confident,had family problems) and victims (e.g. anxious, weaker and younger than bully, socially ineffective and shy, poor self-esteem, close relationships within the family). Interventions seeking to reduce the incidence of bullying have been influenced by this and other research, and have concentrated on the problems experienced by the bullies and victims. This work is obviously crucial but this chapter approaches bullying from a different direction. It looks at the situation within which bullying on school premises tends to take place. In other words, it looks away from individual characteristics of children and concentrates on features of school situations within which bullying occurs.

Where does bullying happen?

Olweus (1989) questions what he takes to be a widely held assumption that bullying takes place on the way to and from schools rather than at schools. He reports, on the contrary, that research in Norway and Sweden shows that almost twice as many pupils were bullied at school as on the way to and from school. Sharp and Smith (1991), in a survey of Sheffield schools, found that most bullying took place on school premises rather than during the journey to and from school. But does bullying occur anywhere in school or is it likely to take place in particular parts of the school or school grounds? And does it occur at any time during the school day or is likely to occur at particular times?

In a survey of the nature and extent of bullying in 17 junior/middle and 7 secondary schools, Whitney and Smith (1991) asked over 6000 pupils where they had been bullied in school. The playground was the most likely place, particularly in primary schools. For the primary pupils, 76% who said they were bullied reported that this was in the playground, with 30% identifying the classroom and 13% the corridors. For the secondary pupils, 45% identified the playground. Stephenson and Smith (1989) collected information from 143 children in the top two year groups in a primary school. They found that most bullying took place in the playground and the school field. They also report that sometimes pupils would identify a particular part of the playground as a likely setting for bullying.

Bullying, therefore, seems to occur on school premises and often takes place in the school playground, away from school classrooms and buildings. Why is this so? What is it about the playground and play/breaktime which lends itself to bullying? Do we need to consider what can be done to make the playground a more constructive place? Bullying does not occur in isolation, and an attempt will be made here to put it in the context of three dimensions of the school playground: physical, social and supervisory. In order to do this I concentrate on recent research on playground behaviour (Blatchford and Sharp, in press; Evans, 1989).

The school playground

The school playground and play/breaktime are often taken for granted. If asked to state their function, staff in schools will probably point to their role in allowing children (and staff) time to let off steam, relax and talk to friends. Many staff, of course, know about the problems that can arise at playtime, including bullying, but as I argued in my book *Playtime in the Primary School* (1989), playtime has a low priority. Over the decades we have done little to change the way it operates. Though there are signs of change, it would probably be still true to say that it attracts few resources beyond maintenance, and the main adult role adopted there is not an instructional but a supervisory one.

This is understandable. There are many competing demands, especially at present, on teaching time and school resources. However, it is a main theme of this chapter that play/breaktime has an important influence on school life and relationships, including bullying, and that improvements there may do much to affect the climate of relationships in the school and reduce unacceptable behaviour like bullying.

Play/breaktime certainly takes up a sizeable part of the school day. In a large-scale study of 33 inner London primary schools (Tizard *et al.*, 1988), it was found that it took up 28% – about the same time as was spent in the combined curricular areas of maths, writing, reading and oral language work. Interviews with pupils in the same schools, when aged 7 (reported in Tizard *et al.*, 1988) and 11 (reported in Blatchford, Creeser and Mooney, 1990; Mooney, Creeser and Blatchford, 1991) left us in no doubt that they considered breaktime a very important part of the school day. They seemed to have a highly charged and ambivalent attitude to playtime. They liked it but were also worried about fighting, teasing, not knowing what to do, being beaten up and bullying. This connection between attitudes to playtime and to bullying is revealed in Boulton and Underwood's (1992) finding that pupils who said they were bullied more often were also much less likely to like playtime.

▮ The effect of the playground environment

All of us have had experiences in a school playground. Some of the most powerful and enduring images of one's school life are centred there. Many of us may look back over our school life and have a very clear memory of the school playgrounds we have experienced – perhaps going back to infant and junior school days – and some of the activities that went on there. In contrast we may be hard pressed to bring the classrooms so clearly into focus.

School playgrounds have not changed much. If I can allude to a personal anecdote. My father who is now in his eighties went to a primary school in West Ham, East London. The school is still standing. Despite numerous conversations with me about education I have little doubt that he would find confusing much of what goes on in the primary classroom. In contrast, apart from a few markings, the school playground does not seem to have changed much at all. He would feel far more at home there.

The playground is often not a very interesting place. Many are little more than a hard area around the school buildings, with a few markings on the surface, and perhaps with an additional grassed area. Of course, this is something of an average. What is striking to a visitor to schools is the wide variation in the size and shape of outside areas. This variation seems arbitrary, in that some have inherited large playgrounds, perhaps with a field, while others have only a narrow space between school building and external wall. There is, though, a difference (in general) between rural and urban schools. The paradox has often been noted: rural areas have fewer people and yet more land. But this does not mean that a large field is any more interesting (or accessible in bad weather) than an urban playground. Both can be equally barren.

Given such an impoverished environment, it is little surprise if behaviour there can be unacceptable. The Opies, who are widely respected recorders of children's games, were scathing about what they called 'restricted environments', in which category they included school playgrounds.

> 'In the asphalt expanses of school playgrounds ... according to the closeness of the supervision they organise gangs, carry out vendettas, place people in Coventry, gamble, bribe, blackmail, squabble, bully and fight.'

And again:

> 'We have noticed that when children are herded together in the playground ... their play is markedly more aggressive than when they are in the street or the wild places' (Opie and Opie, 1969).

Evans makes a similar point:

> 'Children with little to do during their playtime may resort to seeking adventure through various forms of illicit play – for example, fighting, teasing and annoying other children' (Evans, 1989).

In one sense it is surprising that we expect pupils' behaviour to be anything other than unruly. A comparison with the classroom is instructive. What kind of behaviour would we expect if we sent large numbers of children into rooms within the school, without furniture or anything on the walls, without rules of conduct, and with only minimal supervision? (Actually there is a precedent – this sounds not unlike the situation during 'wet playtime' when the entire school are herded into the hall and head and supervisors try to keep order and their own sanity! A case of breaktime being brought into the school.)

More specifically, such an environment can be the breeding ground for bullying. It is relatively thinly supervised, and there are often hidden areas, corners, and nooks and crannies in the playground where pupils can retreat unseen by adults. It is also an arena within which large groups, especially of boys, can gather and where abuse of a victim by one or more children can go undetected.

▬▬ Improving the playground environment

It is now widely recognised that the school environs are a massively underused resource. Many schools are now involved in attempts to improve their playgrounds. There are many different kinds of initiatives. These include the installation of play equipment; the use at playtime of equipment and games; the 'zoning' of playgrounds, for example having specific and separate areas for quiet activities and dominant games like football; the introduction of alternative physical activities to football, like fitness circuits; making the playground more attractive with murals, plants etc.; all manner of 'green' initiatives, including the creation of ponds, 'wildlife' areas and other habitats.

There are a number of organisations that have conducted pioneering work, including Learning through Landscapes, and the National Playing Fields Association, and there are a number of texts which offer helpful advice (Brown, 1990; DES, 1990; Ross and Ryan, 1990; Young, (1990). Such improvements need not be merely cosmetic but can help the informal world of children's playground culture, and also offer possibilities for more formal activities in many curricular areas, at both primary and secondary levels.

▬▬ But is it really 'improved'?

Decisions concerning the playground environment involve difficult choices and complex issues. What might seem worthwhile to staff may seem irrelevant or constraining to pupils. Some schools have invested valuable money, often raised by parents, on expensive play equipment, yet play may not necessarily be improved, for example, one obvious and commonly considered improvement to the playground is the installation of one large piece of apparatus but it can create problems of access, supervision and restrictions on what play is possible. Careful preparatory work and extensive involvement of all in school, and on-going reviews, seem to be necessary precursors of successful schemes.

But it seems highly plausible that attempts to create a positive and constructive playground environment should help reduce anti-social and unacceptable behaviour there, including bullying. It would be one component of a whole-school approach towards bullying that worked at several levels. The assumption is that there are features of the school as an institution that affect bullying and the school environment is an important part of that institution.

Many have found that the involvement of pupils themselves in improvements to the playground is a particularly effective approach

(Sheat, in press). They are the main experts on life in the playground and the main users of it. They are likely to be more committed to improvements that they have been involved in designing.

Behaviour in the playground

There seem to be two main views about children's behaviour in school playgrounds. As I describe in more depth elsewhere (Blatchford, 1993), the first might be called the 'romantic' view because of the stress on what children learn and enjoy there. The Opies (1969) have been influential in the belief that if left to their own devices children will produce a rich and innovative repertoire of games. This theme was continued by Sluckin (1981) who illustrated with descriptions of playground behaviour ways in which children acquire social skills, like how to deal with and manipulate others. A second and contrasting view might be called the 'problem' view because emphasis is more on the harmful consequences of playground behaviours and the search for alternatives. It reflects the views of many teachers concerning the problems that can arise in the playground (Blatchford, 1989), and would include the recent awareness and growth of research on bullying.

These two views are both likely to be true – they are two sides of the same coin – but they do have different consequences for what is seen to be the appropriate role for adults in the playground. I come back to this point in the final section of this chapter.

But a common aspect shown by research in both traditions has been the complex and sophisticated nature of social relations between pupils in school, expressed at their most overt and distinctive in the playground. The study of playground behaviour can be a keyhole through which sight of 'children's culture' (Davies, 1982) can be obtained. In this context, bullying can be viewed not as an isolated behaviour but as one, albeit negative, expression of relationships in school.

Friendships

One area of interest has been children's friendships. This has been a research area of interest to developmental psychologists but several studies have looked at friendships in the school setting and in particular the playground (Davies, 1982; Goodnow and Burns, 1985). Developing and maintaining friendships requires skill and sensitivity, and there appear to be implications for the school progress and long-term social adjustment of those who have difficulties in making friends. The playground, of course, is a main forum where friends meet, especially when they are not in the same class. Davies and Goodnow and Burns show the many rituals and ordered features through which friendships are maintained.

The absence of friends can be important because they can help offset threats from others. The friendless or isolated child is particularly vulnerable to being bullied. Many studies (Besag, 1989) have shown the poor social skills and relative social isolation of victims of bullying. Boulton and Smith (Boulton and Underwood, 1992) found that victims of bullying experience extreme distress associated with peer relations at school. Apart from being less happy at playtime, victims were less likely to report having good friends in class, and more likely to report feeling lonely at school.

La Fontane (1991), in a report on over 2000 telephone calls to ChildLine, found that bullying can result from problems in relationships with schoolmates. This seemed to be more common with girls. In some cases bullying can result from friends having fallen out. It can be as punishment for a breach of loyalty, for example by informing staff about another child. Most importantly victims can perceive bullying as an act with a clear message of rejection and hostility.

> 'Bullying may serve to demonstrate to the victim that (s)he has no friends, while the instigator of the bullying can mobilise a group of supporters. The bullied child then feels isolated and lonely' (La Fontaine, 1991).

▓▓▓▓ Power relations between pupils

Another topic of research on playground behaviour, which also has relevance to bullying, is that on power relations between pupils. Sluckin (1981) has offered some compelling descriptions of children learning in the playground much about power relationships which will prepare them for values held in the wider, adult society.

Acquiring and maintaining status is a major feature of social relations in school. This can be expressed through, for example, athletic ability, but it can also be expressed through bullying weaker children. Being 'tough' is thought by pupils to command respect. Boulton and Underwood (1992) found that children who admitted to bullying said they did so because they were 'tough' or 'hard' – bullying therefore being a way they could display their power and dominance. Furthermore, bullying may be rationalised by the bully in order to make the aggression acceptable. Boulton and Underwood report that bullies were more likely to say they bullied because they were provoked – so they saw their behaviour as justified rather than gratuitous. Contrary to popular belief this may not mean the bully is unpopular with his or her peers – one reason being that bullies can form a sub-group with other aggressive pupils.

Boulton and Underwood also found that younger pupils in middle school could be bullied by older pupils, suggesting another way in which power relations can operate within school. It also suggests the value of approaches designed to encourage older pupils to take a responsibility for younger pupils.

These findings show the importance of seeing bullying in the context of other aggressive behaviours in school. Askew (1988) argues that bullying should be regarded as a continuum of behaviour which involves an attempt to gain power and dominance over another. She writes that 'all behaviour which involves power relationships and struggles between pupils will have negative consequences both for pupils' feelings of safety and for learning'. Askew goes on to argue that in order to explore the roots of bullying it is important to focus not only on the behaviour itself but on the ethos and organisation of the school. Stereotypes that equate masculinity with aggression are very deep rooted, both inside and outside school, and, in some schools at least, authoritarian relationships can reinforce and even cause the violence they seek to stop. Violence in the playground is not therefore a natural process – a case of boys learning to be boys (or men). As well as tackling bullying at the individual level one also needs to consider influences at the school level.

▰▰▰ Fighting

A playground behaviour with obvious connections with bullying is fighting. Evans (1989) makes the basic point that fighting is less likely to occur 'when children have the space, equipment and freedom to shape their own play.' But again research has indicated the surprisingly ordered position such seemingly anarchic behaviour has in social relations between pupils. Fighting can be a way of establishing who you are and what position you occupy in the status hierarchy. Davies (1982) illustrates how pupils have a keen sense of the appropriateness and inappropriateness of behaviours in different situations. Signs of weakness at being attacked put the victim at risk of unpleasant teasing and worse.

A sense of proportion is needed when considering fighting. Sutton-Smith (1981) in a fascinating historical overview of children's outside play makes the salutary point that play in the last century was far more

barbaric and physical than now, and that it now has 'neither the rough-
ness nor the fighting that there used to be'. Careful study of pupil
relationships also shows the constraint with which they can interact with
each other. Evans (1989) makes the point that given the close proximity
and absence of overt structure it is perhaps surprising how few fights
there are. And Sluckin (1981) showed how children commonly go to
great lengths to avoid fights, and show great skill in doing so.

Teasing and name-calling

If the popular view of bullying is of direct physical abuse of one child,
much research has shown that a common means of expression is through
verbal means – name-calling and teasing. Recent research has helped
understanding of its role in peer relations in schools (Kelly and Cohn,
1988; Mooney et al., 1991; Troyna and Hatcher, 1992). These researches
show that teasing and name-calling can be underestimated by adults
who may not realise how hurtful and cruel they can seem to the recipient. Sharp has recently found that three in four of a sample of 300 pupils
who had been called names found it unpleasant and hurtful, 6% of them
extremely so (personal communication). Mooney et al. (1991) found that
two thirds of a sample of 11-year-olds reported teasing and name-calling
taking place, a figure similar to that found by Kelly with a secondary age
sample. In the Mooney et al. study, insults were found to be mostly about
appearance, the recipient's family or were racist. The worst insults were
those directed at the one's family. (Interestingly, this form of insult was
never reported when the children were seven years.)

Significantly more black children said they had been subjected to
racist name-calling (27% as opposed to 9% of white children). In a study
of racism in mainly white primary schools, Troyna and Hatcher (1992)
show the variation in race-related incidents both between and within
schools. They show that racist views are not passively received, whether
from parents, school or media, but combine with other aspects of pupils'
everyday understandings and, in particular, 'the intricate web of social
relations within which children live their lives'. They also show ways in
which social processes of domination and conflict can become racialised.
In a sophisticated analysis these authors have done much to show ways
in which racism must be seen in the social context of peer relations.

Teacher versus playground

It has become customary to point to a distinction in schools between the
overt and the hidden curriculum. Both of these refer to messages

received by pupils from teachers. However, I have often been struck, after spending time in the playground, followed by time in the classroom, by the operation of a different distinction. This one is between two moral codes, the first being the teacher-dominated code of the classroom and the second being centred on the playground. The second governs relations between peers, and can include rules governing fighting and aggression. It can appear crude and largely based on retaliation and aggression but it seems likely that understanding of it will better inform attempts to deal with its more unacceptable face, as in bullying. Some attempts to affect pupils' behaviour seem to stem exclusively from the classroom-dominated code, as described in the Elton Report on *Discipline in Schools* (1989), leaving largely untouched the more powerful code that really seems to drive pupil relations. One needs to develop some understanding of it in order to go beyond just containing overt signs of misbehaviour.

Attempts to deal with the playground world of pupils are fraught with problems. The Opies had little doubt that the quality of children's play would suffer if adults became involved. It does seem likely that a heavy-handed approach will not be helpful. But some have tried a more sympathetic line, both learning from and also making suggestions to pupils. This can be seen in attempts to encourage discussion, perhaps between schools, of games played; projects on breaktime that involve work on games, markings or discussion on behaviour; the setting up of forums, e.g. children's councils, within which playground issues can be aired and action taken (Blatchford, 1989).

A number of recent schemes designed to combat bullying have worked directly on peer relations by giving extra attention to bullies and victims. Some, recognising the weak position of victims, have tried to empower them – by assertiveness training and social skills training. These are helpful, but to return to a theme of this chapter, one worry is that such approaches can isolate bullying behaviour and its consequences from its context in social relations. La Fontaine (1991) makes the point:

'The clear preponderance of group hostility over individual aggression suggests that more attention should be paid to the dynamics of children's social life, the exercise of power and the pressures to conform, rather than to searching for a cause in the individual characteristics of either bullies or victims.'

Supervision in the playground

Breaktime in British schools has two kinds of supervision. Teachers supervise during the short morning and afternoon breaks but for the longest length of time – that is at lunchtime – playground supervision is in the hands of ancillary staff.

Ancillary staff

In *Playtime in the Primary School* (1989) I reported on teachers' views that problems could arise at lunchtime, both because of its length and because lunchtime supervisors were not always able to supervise children in the way teachers might expect. I also argued that lunchtime supervisors should not be blamed. It is the inevitable outcome of a system that expects quality supervision for up to one-and-one-half hours from poorly paid staff who generally receive no training.

In fact, there is little research evidence on the kinds of interactions that take place in the playground between staff and pupils. This is surprising when one considers the wealth of information on interactions between teachers and pupils when they return to the classrooms. As Evans (1989) has argued, it is important to know what types of requests supervisors get, why pupils approach them, and what types of responses pupils get from supervisors. Evans feels that teachers were caught in a dilemma of wanting to be as inconspicuous and non-interventionalist as possible while at the same time having to respond with assistance to pupils. One consequence was that playground contacts between teachers and pupils tended to be officious and managerial.

Teachers and the playground

The quality of supervision can affect pupils' behaviour. Besag (1989) argues that 'some instances of bullying emerged or escalated as a result of staff being unpunctual or failing to be on duty or supervise carefully'. She also queries the adequacy of just observing playground behaviour: 'passive supervision is not always adequate to cover such problems as bullying' which because of its covert nature requires close attention and close supervision. Boulton and Underwood (1992) found that the suffering of victims was likely not to be noticed. Only about a quarter of victims said that teachers had spoken to them about being bullied and only one third of teachers were reported to 'sometimes or almost never' try to stop bullying. In the Thomas Coram Research Unit (TCRU) study some 11-year-olds felt one answer to fears about being beaten up and being bullied was the presence of more supervisors (Blatchford *et al.*, 1990).

On the other hand there is a danger that too heavy a hand can lead to an over-constrained environment and the possibility of a counter-reaction once the supervisor's back is turned – creating conditions when unacceptable and covert activities like bullying can flourish.

Evans reports that even experienced teachers were often unsure what role to adopt in the playground. Some were afraid to intervene. Some female teachers were intimidated by boys. Some felt it inappropriate to enter the child's world. And some held back because they felt that helping a child might compound the child's problems if they were unpopular or had low self-esteem.

There have been recently a number of schemes designed to train lunchtime supervisors (Fell, in press; Newcastle Education Committee, 1990; OPTIS, 1987). These schemes are reviewed in Sharp (in press). These are undoubtedly a good development, though they need to be handled sensitively in order to ensure that the concern with misbehaviour does not express itself only in attempts to control pupils, but also attempts to promote alternative ways of behaving. The schemes are also designed (like so much that is innovative in education) at a local level. With difficulties faced by LEAs, along with the growth of LMS, one worries that the general growth of supervisor training that is required will not easily be achieved.

Involving the pupils

Again there is a place for pupil involvement in playground supervision. This could express itself in participation in the supervision role itself (with older children having a supervisory role) and also in participation in discussions about rules of behaviour to be followed. Pupils are more likely to follow rules that they have a real stake in upholding.

General issues

One approach, given that most bullying in schools takes place in playground and at breaktime, would be to do away with breaktime altogether. A rather less extreme position would be to have a more flexible system within which classes do not all go out to the playground at the same time (Blatchford, 1989). These courses may be too extreme for most, who might be more inclined to try to improve conditions during the traditional breaktime.

▓▓▓▓ The whole-school approach

It seems likely that we need to approach bullying, not at one but at several levels at once. I take it as read that a 'whole-school' approach is required. One approach, within a whole-school approach, concerns the playground and breaktime, and I have suggested three levels: the playground environment, social relations at playtime and supervision at playtime. I have argued throughout that if the situational approach is followed it becomes helpful to view bullying not as an aberrant and isolated behaviour but in the context of the physical and interactive environment within which it occurs. There are many facets to such an analysis and only an overview has been attempted here.

Another theme has been the likely benefits of the involvement of pupils in approaches at all three levels, though there are likely to be benefits only as a result of a real involvement in decision making, not simply lip service to the idea (Blatchford, 1989).

▓▓▓▓ A *laissez-faire* or an interventionalist approach?

At a general level it is fairly easy to see how the playground and relationships there can be improved as one part of an approach to bullying but there are several difficult issues to be dealt with. One that seems to me to lie at the heart of dilemmas about how to approach pupils' non-curricular time in schools, including that in the playground, is the appropriate role of staff in the playground. I cannot resolve this debate here; I just want to cite what seem to be the competing positions: a 'hands off' approach or an interventionalist approach. When one observes life in the playground one is forced to say that the status quo is undoubtedly in favour of the former position. We seem to have little stomach for intervening in any fundamental way with pupil activities in the playground. We have little desire to change behaviour or attitudes, and are more likely to contain misbehaviour in the hope that nothing untoward happens until the bell goes.

It is not difficult to pick holes in this stance for the way in which expediency has superseded any coherent policy towards breaktimes during the school day. It is hoped that this chapter has gone some way towards showing that complaints about pupils' behaviour at breaktime rather miss the point. There are features about the situation itself which structure the kinds of behaviour which take place there. If we do not think through, and have a policy towards, breaktimes and the playground environment, then we largely have ourselves to blame.

But there are serious worries about the other, more interventionalist, position. It is quite conceivable that with the best of intentions we can rob children of one of the main arenas of peer culture. Surveys indicate that children spend much more time at home, for example, watching television and videos, and less time in unsupervised play out of doors. A recent Policy Studies Institute survey found that fewer than 1 in 10 junior school children go to school on their own compared with 8 in 10 two decades ago. Historical overviews suggest a major shift away from self-initiated play to more adult organised and supervised activities (Evans, 1992). Though this tendency can no doubt be exaggerated, it is probably true to say that for some children the school playground may be just about the *only* place where they play outside.

Listening to pupils

It is perhaps best to end with the pupils' eye view. Whatever adults may say about breaktime, and whatever the worries about bullying and other forms of aggression in the playground, the TCRU interviews with 11-year-olds showed very clearly that they like breaktime a great deal. In order to find out how much they liked the long lunchbreak they were shown five faces. The one on the left had a big smile and a bubble above it with the words, 'Great, I love it'. The next face had a less pronounced smile and the words, 'OK, I quite like it'. The middle face had a straight line for a mouth and the words, 'I don't feel one way or the other'. The fourth face had an upturned version of the mouth of the second face and the words, 'I don't like it very much'. And the last face had a very unhappy face and the words, 'Ugh, I hate it'. Over half (58%) of the children pointed to the first 'love it' face, and a further quarter (26%) pointed to the second 'like it' face. In all then 84% said they liked breaktime, a much higher figure than was found when the same question was asked about different curriculum areas (Blatchford, 1992). This massive vote of confidence is worth bearing in mind when adults consider problems that arise at breaktime.

9 Children's attitudes towards victims

Ken Rigby and *Phillip Slee*

Like other forms of children's social behaviour, bullying is influenced by how it is viewed by significant others. Prominent among these 'others' are, of course, the child's peer group. If sufficient numbers of children in a school approve of what bullies do, despise the victims of bullies or, for that matter, feel indifferent about whether their fellow students are bullied, we have a climate of opinion in which bullying is likely to flourish. Contrariwise, if children in a school are overwhelmingly opposed to the practice of bullying and are supportive of victims, we have a means by which pressure can be brought to bear upon bullies and potential bullies to prevent them from bullying others.

Previous work has suggested that social pressures within some schools strongly support the practice of bullying. Askew (1989) reported that in the course of conducting workshops with over 200 school teachers in England, many of them had 'talked about attitudes within the schools being uncritical of some forms of aggressive behaviour'. Askew went on to suggest that children in schools, especially boys, are socialised into accepting a very aggressive image of themselves, reinforced by the norms, rules and roles of the institution: 'bullying,' she wrote, 'is a major way in which boys are able to demonstrate their manliness'. And 'even though a boy might be physically weaker than another, to be able to 'take it like a man' is usually considered to be a second-best masculine quality.'

According to this view, it would appear that there is considerable peer-group pressure for a child to act as a bully (particularly if the child is a boy) and to despise children who are victimised, especially those who complain about it. We would expect this to be reflected in the attitudes of children towards bullies and victims: that is, children would generally be admiring of bullies and unsympathetic towards victims.

This is indeed a gloomy picture. It suggests a major obstacle to reducing bullying in schools, namely, the intransigent attitudes of the children themselves. If this is true we cannot really expect children to help to formulate policies and rules to reduce bullying; nor can we expect them to help in the implementation of policies to counter bullying and to protect the victims.

▓▓▓▓ But what do children think?

But is the pessimistic picture suggested by Askew really true? Until recently no study had focused directly on what children themselves were saying about bullying. We simply did not know whether, on the whole, children are sympathetic or unsympathetic towards the victims of bullies at school; whether they deplore or admire those who continually bully others.

The question of what children feel and think about bullies and victims is clearly an important one. Those who seek to manage bullying in schools need to know whether they can count on the support of school children themselves in assisting in this process, or whether they will be opposed by substantial numbers of children who have been socialised, as Askew suggests, into adopting stereotypically masculine or macho images of themselves which prevent them from being concerned about the problem.

We report here on the first study conducted in schools to discover the nature of the attitudes of children in both primary and secondary school towards victims and bullies, and examine the implications of our findings.

▓▓▓▓ Assessing children's attitudes to victims

It should surprise no one to hear that children, like adults, differ amongst themselves in the sympathy they feel for people who are victimised. We know from research, if not from experience, that some individuals are highly empathetic and others are not (Hoffman, 1977); and that, despite overwhelming evidence to the contrary, some individuals hold to the belief that this is 'a just world', and that victims deserve what is coming to them (Lerner, 1980). Fortunately there are others relatively free from this delusion. But what has not hitherto been known is the *proportion* of children who hold what might be called 'pro-victim' attitudes, that is, a readiness to give support, at least verbal support, to children who are victimised by bullies at school. We have had little idea, either, whether attitudes towards victims change with age, or, for that matter, whether girls and boys differ in such attitudes.

To provide answers to such questions required the development of a reliable and valid *attitude to victims scale* appropriate for school children. In order to achieve an adequate standard of reliability or internal consistency for such a scale, multiple questions were needed, each dealing with related aspects of the proposed construct. A demonstration that the answers to the various questions *are* empirically related is commonly expected of multi-item scales before claims of reliability can be made. Only then can one justify combining or aggregating scores allocated to item-responses to provide a score reflecting a coherent attitude. The first stage in the development of a possible scale was to provide a set of items which may be said to tap the construct of interest, namely, attitudes towards victims of school bullies.

We know, however, that respondents, whether children or adults, are often inclined to give an acquiescing response, to agree or say 'yes' to propositions regardless of content (Cloud and Vaughan, 1970). This tendency can, nevertheless, be taken into account by providing a balanced set of items, with one half worded in such a way that agreement signifies a positive attitude towards the object of interest, and the remaining half worded such that agreement signifies a negative attitude. In this study it was considered particularly important to avoid the possibility that the results would reflect little more than a general 'set' on the part of the children to agree or disagree with statements about which they had no strong opinion.

Finally, as a validity check, we asked this question: 'What do you think is the right thing for teachers and children to do about bullying: try to stop it or just ignore it?' For the scale to have validity we assumed that those who believed that teachers and children should try to stop it would have significantly higher scores on the Pro-Victim Scale.

The procedure for assessing children's attitudes began with the authors devising 20 items which in their view reflected pro- or anti-victim attitudes. These items were based largely on the authors' experiences of talking to children in schools about bullying. Half the items were expressed in the pro-victim direction, for example, 'weak kids need help', and half were worded in the opposite direction, for example, 'nobody likes a wimp'. Children could respond by circling one of three responses: 'agree', 'unsure' or 'disagree'.

▒▒▒▒ Whom did we ask?

The children who answered the questionnaire consisted of 325 boys and 360 girls, drawn from four mixed-sex schools, of which three were primary schools (two state and one Catholic) and the other a state high school. About half (55%) the children attended the high school. Ages ranged from 6 to 16 years. The schools were located in areas of similar socio-economic status (lower to middle class) in Adelaide, a major urban centre in Australia.

There were 667 questionnaires for which every one of the items on the Pro-Victim Scale was answered. Item scores were computed so that the most pro-victim response received a score of 3, 'unsure' 2, and the anti-victim score, 1. Hence maximum and minimum scores were 60 and 20 respectively. As a check on the validity of each item, correlations were computed between item scores and the sum of the scores for the remaining items. Each correlation was positive and significant. In other words, each item response contributed meaningfully to the total score. To discover whether the scale had good internal consistency, the alpha coefficient statistic (Cronbach, 1951) was also computed. The obtained value was .78. This provided evidence that the scale is a reliable one.

Did the pro-victim scores generally agree with the children's views on what should be done about bullying by teachers and children? Relatively few children thought bullying should be ignored, only 57 (about 10%). These children had significantly lower pro-victim scores (with a mean of 45) than the other children, who had a mean pro-victim score of 50. (Further details of the psychometric qualities of the scale are given in Rigby and Slee, 1991.) The Pro-Victim Scale is thus both reliable and valid as a measure of children's attitudes towards victims of school bullying.

▒▒▒▒ Aspects of attitudes to victims

Despite the demonstration that the scale was reliable and valid, it was none-the-less possible to distinguish between various sets of items, each set being closely related to different aspects of attitudes towards victims.

We were able to distinguish three components of the scale. These were:

1 Rejection of 'weak' children
2 Approval of bullying
3 Support for victims

1 *Rejection of 'weak' children*
The tendency to reject other children being bullied because of their supposed weakness was indicated by agreement with these items:

- I would not be friends with kids who let themselves be pushed around.
- Kids who are weak are just asking for trouble.
- Kids should not complain about being bullied.
- Soft kids make me sick.
- Nobody likes a wimp.

Children agreeing with these statements are clearly unlikely to provide support for victims. Indeed, expressing such views must contribute to the isolation of victims. They are seen as not worthy of friendship, as getting what they deserve; contemptible if they complain and generally despicable. What proportion of children have such attitudes?

Depending upon the precise question asked, between 10 and 30% of the children gave a 'rejecting' response. There was a tendency for males to be somewhat more rejecting of victims, but not in all cases. Boys and girls were similar in that one in four was dismissive of children they called 'wimps'. Perhaps the most telling statistic, however, refers to the one in five children who agree that they would *not* be friends with kids who let themselves be pushed around. We must bear in mind that such a sentiment, even if expressed in an anonymous questionnaire, is likely to seem 'socially undesirable'. The true proportion is likely to be larger. At all events, 20% represents a sizeable group, and sufficient to account for the fact that typically children who are continually bullied have relatively few, if any, friends at school (Olweus, 1984).

We should note, too, the comparatively large proportions of children who were 'unsure' about their response. From this it appears that a large number of children (about one in three) appear not to know whether children should or should not complain about being bullied at school. There is clearly a good deal of conflict on this issue; much uncertainty as to whether it is proper to 'tell tales' or, in the Australian idiom, to 'dob in' one's tormentor. We shall return to this important question later.

2 *Approval of bullying*
This is different from rejecting or despising victims. It is a more positive evil, as is indicated by the following items:

- It's OK to call some kids nasty names.
- It's funny to see kids get upset when they are teased.
- Kids who get picked on a lot usually deserve it.

Children who agree with these statements feel first that it is somehow legitimate for some children to be targets of abuse. Victims get what is coming to them. It's a just world. Name-calling is OK for these kids. Moreover, it is enjoyable to see children get upset as a result of teasing. However, approval of bullying behaviour appeared to be limited to a small minority of children: fewer than one in five; and less evident among girls than among boys. Nevertheless, it is this hard core of uncaring children who appear to identify with bullies, or at least provide encouragement for them, that constitute a major problem. We should note, too, again the large proportion of children who did not know how to respond to the question whether kids who get picked on usually deserve it. More than one child in three was unsure.

3 *Support for victims*
These statements reflect this tendency:

- I like it when someone stands up for kids who are being bullied.
- It's a good thing to help children who can't defend themselves.
- It makes me angry when a kid is picked on without reason.

Agreeing with these statements implies not only a sense of justice that is activated when 'a kid is picked on without reason', but also admiration for people who try to do something to help them (Table 2).

Table 2 Responses of boys and girls to items relating to expressed support for victims

| | Boys (percentages) | | | Girls (percentages) | | | Gender |
	Agree	Unsure	Disagree	Agree	Unsure	Disagree	difference
I like it when someone stands up for kids who are bullied	81	14	5	84	12	4	ns
It is a good thing to help children who can't defend themselves	66	22	12	60	31	9	*
It makes me angry when a kid is picked on without reason	78	16	6	86	12	2	*

Note: Gender differences indicated as follows:
* = .05 ns = non-significant. Where the differences are significant, girls are more supportive of victims.

Here the results were encouraging for those who believe that substantial numbers of children will approve of actions to provide assistance to children who are being bullied. Evidently four children out of five (in this sample) felt angry when a child is 'picked on without reason', although we should recall that about 50% of children did not disagree with the proposition that 'kids who get picked on usually deserve it'. Less ambiguously, about four out of five children appeared to admire those who intervene, who 'stand up' for kids who are bullied. Yet here again a qualification is needed. One third of the children could not agree that it was necessarily 'a good thing' to help children who can't defend themselves. Admiring those who take action to help may not extend to an acceptance of those who are 'helped'.

On balance, however, these results do suggest that teachers can depend upon a large majority of their students to support interventionist programmes. This is an important conclusion. The problem to which we shall return is how support can be mobilised.

What are the age and gender differences?

We had been prepared to expect that as children get older their capacity for empathy would increase and with it a corresponding concern for the victims of bullying. We were supported in this view by the observation of the developmental psychologist, William Damon, who had argued that between the ages of 6 and 9 years a child becomes,

> '. . . sensitive to the 'general plight' of life's chronic victims, the poor, the handicapped, the socially outcast. This opens the way for a new domain of pro-social activity: the concerted effort to aid those less fortunate than oneself' (Damon, 1983).

This was not, in fact, what we found. On the contrary, the trend for both boys and girls was towards a *decreasing* support for victims, at least between the ages of 8 and 15 years.

To reach this conclusion comparisons were made between sub-groups of students of each sex in four age categories: 8–9 years: boys 41, girls 42; 10–11 years: boys 71, girls 67; 12–13 years: boys 105, girls 137; 14–15 years: boys 86, girls 98. Although the data for the age comparisons included results for three different primary schools, the mean scores for the schools on the Pro-Victim Scale were not significantly different. A pooling of the results was therefore justified.

The results for age groups are presented graphically in Figure 1. The most striking feature of these results is that between 8 and 15 years pro-victim attitudes appear less positive with increasing age.

We were not surprised that girls were, in general, more pro-victim

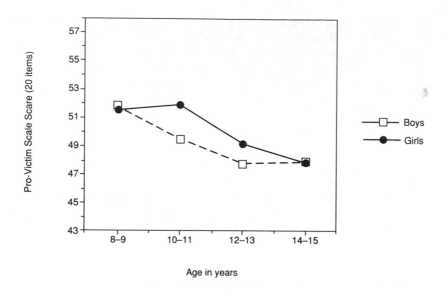

Figure 6 Results showing age trends for boys and girls on the 20-item Pro-victim Scale for children aged 8 to 15 years attending four schools, primary and secondary

than boys. This is consistent with what has previously been reported. According to Hoffman (1977) females are more empathetic than males, both in recognising the emotion someone else is feeling and in experiencing the same emotion themselves. It had also been claimed that females are generally more empathetic than males toward the victims of aggression (Frodi, Macawley and Thorne, 1977). Incidentally, it could not be claimed that the higher pro-victim scores of girls were due to their being victimised more than boys. For the sample of students assessed in this study boys reported being victimised more often than girls.

Despite the statistically significant gender differences in attitudes, it may be argued that in Figure 1 it is the similarities between boys and girls in their reactions to victims that are most evident. At the extremes of the age continuum, the differences are negligible. Moreover, for boys and girls the differences between the 8–9-year-olds and the 14–15-year-olds are equally marked, and, as we have argued, in the light of previous research in developmental psychology, surprising.

We cannot, however, dismiss the idea that among children there is generally a growth in the *capacity* for empathy with increasing age. Children do become increasingly less egocentric and more able to see things from another's point of view. This is too well established in the psychological literature to be seriously challenged (Damon, 1983). We therefore need to explain why it is that, despite a natural tendency for children to become more *able* to see events from a victim's point of view, *in the school environment* children evidently do not become more sympathetic to victims, and indeed become less.

One explanation is that as children grow older at school they are increasingly exposed to normative pressures that gradually induce more and more unsympathetic attitudes towards the victims of bullying. According to Askew (1989) the rules, norms and roles to be followed in schools are stereotypically male ones. It is seen as desirable to be dominant, independent, competitive, ambitious, aggressive, never to cry, and never to show emotional weakness. With increasing age it becomes more and more unacceptable to be a 'wimp'. In our experience, this is not an unfair description of the ethos or climate of many schools.

A second possible explanation is that as children get older, they see it as no longer a mature attitude to complain about what happens to them. It may be all right for an 8-year-old to be something of a cry-baby but 15-year-olds are old enough to look after themselves. Complaining about being bullied is not age-appropriate for older students. We may also add that reported bullying behaviour becomes less common with increasing age (Olweus, 1991; Rigby and Slee, 1991). This suggests that the proportion of children with justifiable complaints becomes less.

▓▓▓▓ What do older children think?

Both explanations were consistent with the data we had collected from children under the age of 16 years. We next asked what would be the case if we included more mature students in our sample. Would the trend towards weakening support for victims continue including the older age group?

In a further study we assessed school children from a large Adelaide co-educational high school between the age of 11 and 18 years. To do so we employed a shortened (10 item) measure of the Pro-Victim Scale. The reliability of this scale was found to be only slightly less than the longer scale. Mean scores on the new Pro-Victim Scale were computed for four age groups and for boys and girls separately.

It is worth noting that a consistent trend towards less sympathetic attitudes towards victims with age did not apply to older secondary students. In fact, for males beyond the age of 15, there was a significant change in the direction of the trend. The relationships between age and attitudes to victims for boys is curvilinear: becoming less sympathetic up to 15 or 16 and more sympathetic thereafter. Among girls, attitudes to victims at this school remained more or less the same throughout the age range, but, as in the case with the younger sample, girls were significantly more positive in their attitudes to victims than was the case for boys.

It appears from these results that the school climate increasingly promotes tough-minded, unsympathetic attitudes to victims in the lower and middle years of high schools only. Beyond that, in the top classes, the situation and also, perhaps, the nature of the children remaining at school make a difference. The remaining students, extending their schooling beyond the legal compulsory age of 16, will normally have ahead of them the prospects of higher education at a tertiary institution. The educational process will be viewed more as a co-operative venture; a higher level of intellectual maturity can be assumed. For the most senior students, particularly boys, peer pressure to reject victims and to admire school bullies appears to be relatively ineffective. Perhaps, too, many older males have so distanced themselves psychologically from the 'young kids' that they no longer feel that admitting one's vulnerability is a sign of immaturity.

▓▓ Summary of findings

At this point it may be useful to summarise the results from the studies on which we have reported.

1 Attitudes to victims of school bullying were assessed in a reliable and valid measure suitable for use with school children.

2 We were able to distinguish between three aspects of the attitude: (i) a tendency to reject weak children, (ii) an approval of bullying behaviour, and (iii) support for victims.

3 A substantial minority of school children (as much as 15 to 20% in the sample) do tend to reject children who may be labelled as 'weak'. A similar proportion of children are inclined to approve of bullying or at least to condone it. A somewhat larger group of school children are unsure of what they think about these matters.

4 Despite the above, school children are, for the most part, supportive of people who will stand up for children who are being bullied.

5 Between the ages of 8 and 15 years the attitudes of both boys and girls at school become less supportive of children who are victimised. At the same time girls tend to be slightly more supportive. Beyond the age of 15 years students were found to be more pro-victim than those somewhat younger than themselves.

▪ To complain or not to complain?

If a child were being badly bullied by a stronger person, or persons, would he or she, in fact, complain about it, and, if so, to whom? In one study in South Australia, we asked children between the ages of 11 and 16 years what they thought they would do if they were 'being bullied every day by someone bigger and stronger' than themselves.

In total 280 students answered this question (49% were boys and 51% girls). Less than one in three said they would 'probably' or 'definitely' see a school counsellor or teacher; about half said they would tell their parents; three out of five indicated that they would get their friends to help. There were no significant gender differences. It was evident that in the school environment, even under conditions of extreme harassment, only a minority of students (33%) would inform the school authorities about it, although a majority (60%) would get their friends to help them. We should add that this was a school in which a policy had recently been put into place to encourage children to tell if they were being bullied! We wondered what kinds of social pressures operated in the school environment that might account for this reluctance on the part of many children to seek help from the school.

▪ Assessing attitudes towards those who complain

In a subsequent study Rigby and Black (1992) used a projective, sentence completion test to explore how children felt about the 'complainers'. This enabled them to identify a range and quality of viewpoints on this question that could not be derived from attitude scales using forced choice alternatives.

The relevant item included in their questionnaire read, 'Children who complain about being bullied … '. Respondents were asked to write a completion. The subjects consisted of secondary students from a co-educational independent high school in a small urban centre in Victoria. Children attending this school are drawn mainly from families of middle socio-economic status. Questionnaires were completed anonymously by students in the first and third years of the secondary school; their ages ranged from 12 to 15. The sentence was completed by 93% of the students receiving the questionnaire; 82 boys and 82 girls.

The responses were classified according to whether they reflected positive, neutral (or mixed) or negative attitudes towards those who complain about being bullied. For example, a 'positive' sentence completion was '… are very sensible'; a negative one, '… are a pain'. Neutral responses consisted of those that could not be classified as above, either because they did not imply an evaluative judgement: '.... are smaller and not in the in-group', or involved 'mixed' content, e.g., '... are mostly right, but get a bit too complaining.'

Table 3 Attitudes towards children who complain about being bullied, as inferred from sentence completion

		Numbers of children Age groups	
Response:		12–13 years	14–15 years
Positive	boys	20	18
	girls	28	17
Neutral	boys	8	6
	girls	12	8
Negative	boys	14	16
	girls	6	11

The results (Table 3) showed that positive, supportive responses far outweighed negative ones for boys and girls in both age groups. As in the previous analysis for secondary students, there was a tendency for fewer positive and more negative responses to be made by students in the older age group.

Of further interest are the kinds of things the respondents evidently had in mind when they thought of children who complained of being bullied. What follows are selected quotations from the sentence completions, with males indicated by 'm' and females by 'f'; ages are given in years.

1. Negative content

It was possible to identify three kinds of responses which were essentially critical of the complainer. The first to be noted are simply *denigratory* remarks; the second deplore the complainer's behaviour on the grounds that it is actually *self-defeating*; the third imply that complaining is an inadequate way of behaving and suggest *better alternatives*.

(a) *Denigration:* Often sentence completions in this category involved short, hostile and insulting comment. Complainers were described as 'losers' (m,13), 'wimps' (f,12), 'poo dicks' (m,15), 'pussies' (m,15), 'stupid' (m,13), 'a pain' (f,12). They were also described as people who 'often complain too much' (m,12), 'have little self-respect' (f,14), 'little kids who don't know anything' (m,14), 'normally ask for it' (m,12), 'bring it on themselves usually' (f,15), 'are often wimps trying to get other people in trouble' (f,14), and people who 'should take it with a grain of salt' (m,14).

(b) *Self-defeating:* For some children, complaining was seen as simply counter-productive. According to one student, complainers were 'stupid because they just get bullied more' (m,14). Others added: 'they get bullied more for whingeing' (f,15); 'they get teased' (m,12), and 'often get into more trouble from the bullies' (m,13).

(c) *Better alternatives:* In castigating 'complainers', some respondents suggested by their responses that there were better alternatives to simply complaining and that complainers should learn to act independently. They should, for instance, 'look to themselves to see if they can do something to prevent it' (f,14), 'not tell the teacher but find another way to deal with it' (m,14), 'go to self-defence lessons' (m,15), 'at least do something about it than complain' (f,15). Some saw fighting back as clearly preferable. Complainers should: 'stick up for themselves and not let themselves be pushed around' (f,14), 'face up to the people bullying them' (m,14), 'bully the bullies back' (f,13).

2. Positive content

According to some, complainers were 'very sensible' (m,13); 'all right' (m,12); 'smart' (f,12); 'strong' (m,13); 'pretty courageous' (m,12); 'good' (f,13) and 'normally nice inside' (f,13). Their complaining was seen as justified: 'is fair enough because you would if you were being bullied' (f,12); 'is good or it will keep happening' (m,12); 'are usually telling the truth, I feel sorry for them' (f,13); 'are trying to protect themselves' (f,14); 'something should be done' (m,15); 'need to be helped to have their self-confidence restored' (m,14); 'should be listened to and believed by people who will do something about it' (f,14); 'should have the bully stopped' (5,12); 'should be helped by you' (f,13).

A number of those approving of 'complainers' insisted upon the rights of victims. 'they have a right to complain to people if they are bullied' (m,14) and 'shouldn't feel scared to do so' (f,14). Rights mentioned included 'the right to speak up' (f,13); 'the right to be listened to' (m,13; f,13) and the 'right to be protected' (f,14). 'Complaining', commented one, 'is not dobbing' (m,13). 'No child should be bullied' (f,14) added another.

Some provided positive advice: 'should go and tell someone to help stop bullying' (m,14); 'go and tell a teacher' (m,12); and 'should tell their parents or teachers and then they can deal with it' (f,13). Some expressed a personal readiness to help: 'I help as much as possible' (f,14); 'I would go and help them' (f,13).

3. Neutral or mixed content

Finally, there was a substantial minority of students whose sentence completions could not be classified as 'positive' or 'negative'. Some appeared detached or objective. Running through the things they wrote provided almost uncanny echoes of what research psychologists have been saying about bully/victim problems (Olweus, 1991; Besag, 1989; Smith and Thompson, 1991; Rigby and Slee, 1992). Those who complain were described as 'usually smaller and not in the in-group' (m,14); 'sometimes very quiet and don't like coming to school' (f,12); 'don't have much confidence' (f,14); 'usually used to warm, friendly people around them' (f,15); 'are people who should make more friends, get into a group of kids' (m,12); 'some bully other kids in return; some don't' (f,15); 'usually keep it [bullying] to themselves' (f,13).

Other students expressed mixed feelings. 'I feel sorry for them, but sometimes they deserve it' (f,12); 'sometimes they're over-reacting and want attention and maybe sometimes some kids need help with this' (f,14); 'are sometimes right and sometimes want to get other kids in trouble' (f,12); 'I pity them but laugh with everyone else' (m,12); 'are people I feel sorry for, although I hate to admit that sometimes I just don't care and I'm glad it's not me' (f,14). Other 'neutral' comments included straight advice: 'should stay away from bullies' (m,12); 'should move schools' (f,13); and pure detachment, 'I would not really care unless I was involved' (f,12).

We can see from the content analysis of the sentence completion what a wide range of judgements children make about those who complain of being bullied. If we had any doubt about the divided nature of the student population on this issue, here was strong evidence confirming the earlier indication of divisiveness evident in the results from the Pro-Victim Scale. Many school children were clearly divided in themselves, struggling with contradictory impulses – feeling sympathetic at times, but also derisory and cynical; sometimes wanting to help but equally determined to follow a self-preservatory impulse to steer clear and thank their stars they were not involved.

▇▇▇▇ What are the implications?

Attitudes of others affect the way people behave and this applies to bullying behaviour in schools, just as it applies to other forms of behaviour. We do not, however, claim that this is a total explanation of why children bully others. Some children appear to be innately more aggressive than others and remain so into adulthood (Farrington, 1993). We know that frustrating and negative experiences in the home may predispose some children to bully others and that some children who are bullied by others have been 'over-protected' by insecure parents (Olweus, 1980; Bowers, Smith and Binney, 1993). All this is granted. But in addition to these factors, what children think of bullies and victims is a powerful determinant of what happens in interactions between children at school.

Teachers need to know what these attitudes are. From our research there are grounds for supposing that children's attitudes towards victims are generally supportive, although we have to remember that there are substantial minorities of children who despise victims of bullying, abominate complainers and informers, or are indifferent to their plight. Schools differ in the extent to which children support victims and there are both age and gender differences of which we should be aware. For teachers who wish to mobilise children's pro-victim attitudes in a management plan, it is very desirable that they get to know the attitudes of children in their schools and the variations between sub-groups of children.

How teachers obtain this knowledge can vary. Some may prefer to use an anonymous questionnaire like ours. It has the advantage of demonstrated reliability and validity. It might usefully be supplemented by the sentence completion question discussed earlier. However, the use of questionnaires is by no means essential; certainly not for teachers who have established open and flexible lines of communication with their students, as many have. Teachers will know if they are simply hearing the socially desirable answer, designed to please. If there is any doubt, then written anonymous answers will be preferred.

Involving the children

Supposing a picture has been obtained, in a systematic way, of what the children think of bullies, victims and complainers. How can this knowledge be used? Our answer is that it should be shared with the students. They have a right to know what their peers think. At the same time, it is important that, if anonymous data collection has been used, care is taken not to embarrass anyone with quotations that may be recognised and individuals identified – whether these are positive or negative. Handled well, survey results become a springboard for informal class discussions and fruitful exchanges of points of view.

We are assuming that what emerges from the inquiry, formal or informal, is, as we have found, on the whole constructive. Whatever the balance of opinion, there will be some constructive results that can be highlighted, and there will be children who have remained neutral or are simply perplexed.

For some children the results will come as a surprise. They have taken it for granted that everyone, or nearly everyone, agrees in stigmatising victims of schools bullies and in ridiculing children who complain of being bullied. They will now have to adjust to a new view of their peers. Incidentally, to use the force of the majority blatantly to coerce the minority on such matters will be counter-productive, and succeed only in reinforcing the anti-victim attitudes they may be able to share with a sub-group of bullies.

It must be remembered that minority groups, however small, may exert disproportionate influence on individuals who have somehow identified with those groups. The admiration of some children is often sought much more readily than the admiration of others. For the teacher who is aware of the interpersonal dynamics and clique formations in a class, knowledge of who thinks what about bullying can be very valuable. In open discussions, readjustments of attitudes can occur and new behaviours foreshadowed.

Simply talking with children about what they think about bullying is useful in itself. No doubt it will raise awareness of the problem and result in some misconceptions being corrected. But this is not enough. Out of class discussions, we suggest, should come ideas and resolutions about how bullying can best be managed. If the inquiry ends up with the teacher or the principal enunciating unilaterally *the* policy, *the* rules and *the* sanctions that are to be followed, the outcome is likely to be of quite limited value, perhaps even counter-productive. Involvement of the students in the formulation (not determination, necessarily) of policy and procedures, deriving from a knowledge and a guided discussion of what the children think, is what should be aimed for.

■ In conclusion

It is now generally acknowledged that anti-bullying policies and interventions should be preceded by careful attempts to assess the extent and nature of bully/victim incidents in schools (Olweus, 1991; Smith and Thompson, 1991). What has not hitherto been recognised is the importance of gaining a close understanding of children's perceptions of the problem in particular schools as a preliminary step to developing an intervention strategy. We believe that interventions will work best when they are consistent with what most children think ought to be done about bullying. From the studies reported in this chapter, it is evident that we have no cause to feel pessimistic. As Askew (1989) had suggested, we may expect peer-group pressure in schools for macho, uncaring attitudes to victims to grow and form an impediment or obstacle to positive and effective action to counter bullying. But the overwhelming majority of children will be on the side of the victim. We must listen to what they have to say and mobilise this resource as an important aspect of any intervention strategy.

10 Developing school and community links to reduce bullying

John Pitts

Brunel School is a mixed comprehensive at the centre of the Brunel Estate, a post-war housing complex in the heart of London's East End. The East End has a reputation for crime and violence but it is a reputation which exists alongside a less celebrated legacy of tolerance for racial and cultural diversity and social solidarity. The legacy of violence is evident in the threat of a local primary school child to 'put' a classmate 'in hospital'. And it is there in the respect which is still expressed by some older residents for the notorious local gangsters of yesteryear, the Kray brothers. A member of the support staff of Brunel School, interviewed by David Downes (1990), said:

> 'There's an incredible rate of violence round here that never reaches police files', she offered examples of 'a 14 year-old girl who ran away with a 19 year-old man who had done time. Her family lured him up onto a balcony and threw him over. Nothing was ever done – he was not killed but very badly injured. ... One family was threatened by another for suspected grassing, quite wrongly, but the father had had an unusual job for the area, a Customs and Excise Inspector, retired, married to a much younger woman, an alcoholic. She was followed to the drink shop [and] viscously attacked. ... Later, they broke into the flat, hammering the door down, tied the wife up and threw the elderly man down the stairs. The youngest child was in such danger of attack by the children of the other family that support staff got him transferred right out of the area ...'

Downes points to 'a set of power relations on the estate' characterised by family feuds and reprisals 'that bears more than a passing resemblance to the era of the Krays'. On the other hand, the majority of families on the estate are law-abiding, non-violent and adhere to quite different values. The catchment area of the school is wider than the estate but a significant minority of its pupils are drawn from the estate and the areas surrounding it.

The Brunel Estate

In his report Downes emphasises the importance of the relative isolation of the estate. Bordered by an arterial road to the east, a railway to the north, an industrial estate to the west and a canal to the south, there is only one road in and out. This isolation has fostered both a strong sense of attachment to the estate, a 'community spirit', and a strong feeling of defensive territoriality. A prominent spray-canned warning which reads: 'Beware – you are now entering the Brunel Estate', dates back to a feud between the 'Brunel gang' and youths from a neighbouring area. The fighting continued, on- and- off, from the mid-1970s to the mid-1980s.

Bengali families on the estate

It was at this time that a crime prevention project in the area identified the harassment of Bengali tenants as a major problem. The harassment culminated, in 1984, in a near riot involving up to 40 young men, eight Bengali families and the police. The Bengali families were promptly transferred off the estate by the Housing Department.

In the late 1980s the Housing Department began, once again, to move Bengali families onto the estate. Although they constituted only 3% of the estate's population, by 1990 they made up 40% of the victims of the 82 assaults reported on the estate in that year. However, the official statistics significantly understate the problem. In 1990/91, of the 30 Bengali families visited by representatives of the local law centre, 23 of them had been victimised on a total of 136 occasions (Sampson and Phillips, 1992).

The suspects almost always attacked in groups. They were young; 19% were under 12 and 64% were aged between 13 and 18. They were both black and white; 54% were Caucasian and 30% Afro-Carribean; 84% of them were male and some of them attended Brunel School. Furthermore, many of the attacks coincided with Brunel School's breaktimes or the end of the school day.

The climate in the school – and out of it

At the inception of the project racial tension and general turbulence at Brunel School were high. For two years there had been a significant increase in the numbers and the proportion of Bengali students from outside the Brunel Estate entering Year 7. Whereas in some local schools Bengali pupils constituted over 80% of the school roll, for some years the Brunel figure had remained at around 40%. In consequence, it had become a 'white flight' school, popular with some influential white residents who saw it as 'their' school, to which, they believed, 'their' children should have a right of access. At the same time, there had been an increase in the proportion of students with 'behavioural problems' entering the school and an already overstretched staff group was beginning to feel the strain. These two factors were compounded by what Downes describes as the 'background culture of the area' which manifests itself in: 'very high physical contact at all times especially boy-to-boy and boy-to-girl, then girl-to-boy in reaction.'

These pressures had led to a feeling amongst staff that the school was no longer a 'safe place'. The most tangible expression of this 'threat' came from a group of adolescents who tended to 'hang around' the school entrance. Some of them were unemployed ex-pupils and others were pupils who had been permanently excluded for violent or uncontrollable behaviour. They were often drunk or 'stoned' and were intimidating to staff and pupils. They were almost certainly involved, and may well have been the prime movers, in many of the racial attacks and other violent incidents on the estate.

Whatever the reality, their presence as bearers of the culture of violence and as a symbol of divisions and antagonisms in the community, cast an aura of fatalism upon the school. Martin Gay, the facilitator of the Year 9 representatives involved in the Brunel School Anti-Bullying Initiative wrote, in November 1991:

> 'When we talked about racial bullying there was a lot of shoulder shrugging and a common acknowledgement that inter-racial fighting was part of the nature of the area and there was nothing anyone could do about it. They said that if there was a racial fight going on and you didn't support your own racial group then it could lead to further trouble from the leaders of the groups, many of whom were grown men outside of the school'.

Downes refers to an incident at the school in 1990 in which a fight between a white and a Bengali pupil erupted into an orchestrated 'theatre of violence'. The incident culminated in a battle in the local market but few of the axe and mallet-brandishing protagonists were from Brunel School. Pupils were aware that, increasingly, violence against the Bengali community was being met by reprisals from groups of young Bengalis known as 'the Rock Street Mafia'. Whether the Rock Street Mafia actually existed, or was simply 'shorthand' for a rising generation of local Bengali young people who fought back, is not clear. Whatever the reality, however, each 'side' demanded racial loyalty. Pupils of all races felt intimidated and under pressure to take sides, even though most of them wanted no part in the conflict.

Inevitably, these pressures from outside the school found expression in behaviour inside the school. Year 7 pupils, talking to Una and Naseem, their group facilitators, said: 'People bully mainly because of racist reasons. White boys beat up Bangladeshi boys for no reason other than their skin colour.'

The borough in which the Brunel Estate is located has the second highest unemployment rate in London. Practically, this has meant that a growing band of young people with little money, and without the status, constraints, prospects and incentives provided by a 'steady job', are spending a lot more time on the streets. The worsening prospects for school leavers threatens to undermine the motivation of pupils, posing yet another challenge to an already over-extended staff. The simultaneous influx of a larger number of Bengali pupils and pupils with behavioural problems served to heighten these tensions.

The Brunel School Anti-Bullying Initiative

The Anti-Bullying Initiative at Brunel School was part of a broader project initiated by the Home Office, which aimed to reduce the violent victimisation of women, children and young people, and Asian residents on the estate. Alice Sampson and Phillips (1992) write:

> 'The starting point for this project was that preventing repeat or multiple victimisation can be an effective crime reduction strategy and that victims should be protected by all appropriate means in the context of their locality.'

An organisational development approach

The Anti-Bullying Initiative adopted an organisational development (OD) approach. Organisational development proceeds from the assumption that the policy objectives of complex 'human service' organisations will be achieved only if those policies win the support and articulate the interests of the members of that organisation. This support is gained by a process of continual consultation at all levels and it is the 'process' which holds the key to the success of OD. As Diana Robbins (1989) suggests, the most important aspect of policy statements is the impact that the process of their formulation has on the culture and ethos of the organisation.

The initiative workers believed that OD offered a way of identifying and working with those features of the school which promoted, or inhibited, violent victimisation. Their beliefs about what these features were, derived from their experiences as workers in the justice and educational systems, and research evidence about the development and operation of violent subcultures in prisons, residential establishments and schools (Mathiesen, 1964; Hargreaves, 1967; Jones, 1968; Power *et al.*, 1982; Willis, 1977; Rutter *et al.*, 1978; Dennington and Pitts, 1991).

This work suggests that bullying and violent victimisation is most likely to occur in an organisation:

- Where there is an extensive and rigid hierarchy in which information flow from those at the bottom to those at the top of the hierarchy is poor.

- Where individual members of staff, who are the organisation's culture carriers, pursue incompatible goals and espouse or enact conflicting values.

- Where the deployment of rewards and punishments appears to be arbitrary and done without reference to a common standard or set of rules.

- Where staff appear to be indifferent to violent behaviour not directed at themselves.

- Where there is no expression of warmth between people at different levels of the organisation.

Conversely bullying and violent victimisation will be least likely to occur in an organisation:

- Where there is a relatively flat hierarchy in which information flow upwards and downwards is maximised and where that information affects decisions made by staff.

- Where staff, in consultation with other members of the organisation, have regular opportunities to discuss goals and values and participate in policy formulation.

- Where the deployment of rewards and punishments is seen to be fair and proportional and corresponds with standards or rules to which members of the organisation at all levels can subscribe.
- Where staff are actively concerned about violent behaviour.
- Where there are frequent, spontaneous expressions of warmth between people at different levels of the hierarchy.

The goal of OD is to facilitate the movement of the organisation along the continuum from the former type of organisational structure, towards the latter. While bullying and other anti-social behaviour in schools do not simply originate within the school, research suggests that the structure of a school and the culture it generates can either contain and reduce, or exacerbate, such behaviour (Hargreaves, 1967; Power et al., 1972; Rutter et al., 1978). The initiative at Brunel School aimed to contain and reduce this behaviour.

Introducing the initiative

This was attempted by introducing the initiative to the whole school in a series of year assemblies. At these assemblies, an initiative worker asked for two volunteers from each class to join a consultative group. The volunteers from each of the five classes, in each of the five years, met for three sessions with two social work students or lecturers, who acted as group facilitators and recorded participants' deliberations. Using case study material and other age-appropriate exercises, these groups discussed the problems of, and their preferred solutions to, bullying and violence in the school and in the local community. Alongside this, initiative workers undertook two 'problem finding' sessions with the whole staff group and a further three, 'problem-solving', sessions with 10 staff representatives. At the end of this process the Brunel School Student-Staff Anti-Bullying Working Party, composed of five pupils (one from each year), four members of the staff, the deputy head, and an initiative worker, who acted as secretary, was brought into being. Its job was to operationalise the anti-bullying policy and strategy adopted by the pupils and staff of Brunel School and to monitor its effectiveness.

Developments in the school

The consultation process within the school and the policies and strategies which flowed from it increased the reporting of bullying and violence dramatically. Breaktime supervision was reorganised in line with the findings of a survey of bullying 'hot spots' and 'safe areas' undertaken by the working party. Staff procedures for dealing with cases of reported bullying were reviewed and a new code of practice emphasising the rights and responsibilities of staff and pupils was presented at a half-day 'Bullying Conference'. This was backed up by a poster competition. A 'bully box', into which pupils could post 'bullying forms' requesting a confidential meeting with the member of staff of their choice, was also established.

However, it was the changed climate of communication, promoted in large part by the active and enthusiastic support of staff, which opened the floodgates and let the information flow.

▄▄▄▄ What came out of the initiative?

Staff were sometimes taken aback by the things they learned. In one case, they discovered that extortion, intimidation and violence perpetrated against most members of one class by a few pupils had been going on for over a year. Other pupils revealed that they had feigned sickness in order to stay away from school and so evade their tormentors. The intensive 'problematisation' of bullying at Brunel School yielded some other surprises. One girl posted a note in the 'bully box' asking if somebody could help her to stop bullying other pupils.

The greater openness, improved communication between pupils and staff, and the experience of participation in decision-making meant that other areas of school life came under the microscope. Pupils sought a meeting with the head to discuss the deterioration in the school dinner service since its privatisation. Unsatisfied by the outcome, they requested a further meeting with the contractors and the governors. The issue of equal opportunities for girls in sport was raised. The girls argued that they should not have to ask for football teams to be created but that these should exist as an option available to all pupils.

Others asked for timetabled opportunities in the school day to meet staff informally and share their concerns and ideas with them. This was an experience of managing different, competing and sometimes conflicting demands robustly, but non-violently, and actually bringing about change.

Pupils talked about the ways in which racism and violence, both within the school and beyond it, could be countered:

'. . . this led on to a discussion of what the school could do to help young people argue against becoming involved in racial conflict. They felt that they needed ammunition to use against bigots (some of them said that this included their parents). They said that it was all very well the school having an anti-racist policy that was read out in assembly after an incident had occurred, but what they needed was education about why various groups of people have come to this country and why they have a right to be here. The group concluded that if attitudes were to change, the issues of race and anti-racism must be part of the timetable, not just a policy document or a reaction to an incident' (Martin Gay, Year 9 Facilitator, November 1991).

An early casualty of this greater openness, were the taboos against 'grassing': informing on the perpetrators of bullying. Bullying in institutions thrives on secrecy and collusion. For its survival, it requires that those on the receiving end, either because of adherence to an 'unwritten code' or the threat of reprisals, keep quiet. The 'no grassing' taboo had, apparently, been blown apart.

The school-community relationship

But if the new openness was to be sustained, the school had to demonstrate a capacity to act decisively against persistent bullying, especially in cases where reprisals against victims and their families, in school and in the community, were threatened. The need to do this arose very soon. The relevant minute of the meeting of the Brunel School Student-Staff Anti-Bullying Working Party indicates how the issue was approached.

'Bullying Incident
The working party discussed what should be done about a situation, which has just come to light, in which two pupils have been bullying three others and had threatened them with weapons. It was felt that:

(a) This was the first big test of the anti-bullying strategy and that the whole school needed to see that something was done and that what was done was seen to be fair and effective.

(b) It was agreed that parents should be informed and that, as far as possible, they should be involved in the response.

(c) Pupil members of the working party repeated their belief that in cases of serious bullying, like this, suspension was neither adequate nor effective. It was agreed that the response should be school-based.

(d) The group discussed whether the responsibility should be put back onto the bullying students and whether they should be presented, by a senior member of staff, with a 'contract' which stated the kinds of behaviour, in and out of school, which would and would not be required of them. Any breach of this contract would mean that they would have to pursue a special programme in which they were separated from their class and placed under the supervision of a senior member of staff for a specified period.

(e) It was suggested that the bullying student could be offered the option of counselling and that people who need help to stop bullying could also fill in the bullying form.

(f) It was suggested that, since some of the bullying involved criminal offences, a further sanction would be the involvement of the police.

(g) It was also felt that if this were to happen, it would be much safer, in terms of future reprisals against the bullied students or their families, if the school initiated the contact with the police and pursued the prosecution. It may be that discussion with the police is needed on this point.

(h) It was also felt that the support of other students had been, and would be, crucial if behaviour of this kind was to continue to come to light (Brunel School Anti-Bullying Working Party minute, October 1992).

This incident threw up some of the key issues confronting a school which realises that if it is to protect its pupils, it must sometimes intervene in the out-of-school behaviour of other pupils, their friends and their families as well. It raises the question of where the authority of the school ends and that of other agencies and individuals begins. Beyond this lies the strategic question of how, and to what extent, in its dealings with these agencies and individuals, the school can influence the style and quality of their responses. These issues were raised at a subsequent meeting of the working party:

'Police Involvement
It was agreed to invite Anna and Katherine the crime prevention project workers and Inspector Nixon, of the local police station, who is responsible for organising patrols in the area, to the next meeting. However, the Working Party needs to think about what it wants the police to do, where and at what times. It also needs to consider the kinds of situations which are better handled by the police and where the authority of the school ends and the authority of the police begins. There is a question about the kind of consultation or co-operation that is most desirable and, presumably, the school needs to establish a policy and guidelines on these matters. Beyond this is the question of the role of the school in relation to pupils identified by them as being involved in crime and those who allege that they have been treated in racist, discriminatory or

illegal ways by the police' (Brunel School Anti-Bullying Working Party minute, November 1992).

This latter issue was a particular bone of contention at the school. A few months previously, the police were called to the nearby market because of a reported assault on a Bengali boy by some Afro-Carribean boys. The incident became very acrimonious and culminated in, what appeared to Brunel School pupils to be, a random round-up of Afro-Carribean boys with a lot of racial abuse thrown in. Clearly, this was not the kind of policing the working party wanted but, on the other hand, they could not simply prescribe a style of policing which would meet all eventualities.

▩ The actions taken

The working party decided that it needed to develop a dialogue rather than a prescription, and that this dialogue would be pursued via a meeting with the police and the production of two short video films.

At the meeting with the police the following agreements were reached.

1 That the sergeant who was present at the meeting would be the liaison officer between the working party and the police and would be invited to attend working party meetings as and when appropriate.
2 That police officers would enter the school, if requested to do so by the head, who was also at the meeting, and speak to individuals and groups about the legal status and possible consequences of their behaviour.
3 That police officers would only initiate action in the school if pupils were carrying offensive weapons or dangerous drugs but that this would always be done in consultation with the head.
4 That if there was concern that conflict in the school was going to spill over onto the estate and that pupils would therefore be in danger, the sergeant or inspector would be informed and the relevant home beat officer and other patrols alerted.
5 That any racist or oppressive behaviour directed against pupils by police officers would be reported to the inspector who would assist pupils to initiate a formal complaint.
6 That the bullying 'hot spots' in the community, identified by the working party in their research for the video, would be identified as priority areas for the relevant beat officers.

The video was to be produced in collaboration with the bullying initiative workers and the media development unit of a local university. The relevant working party minute reads:

'Bullying Video'

'It was agreed that the project workers and a member of the Media Development Staff of Walford University should make one, and possibly two, brief videos. They would help focus discussion of the responses that other agencies and individuals might make to the problem.

One video would concern the problems of bullying encountered by students going to and from school. This could begin with some of the changes in playground duty at Brunel School and then talk about the fact that people are at risk outside the school as well. It would consider who is in danger, where, why, and which individuals or organisations have the power to do something about it. The "target" audiences for the video would be: the staff of Brunel and other local schools and colleges, parents, other adults in the community, community/tenants associations, the governors, the education authority/ youth service, transport authorities, the police, and crime prevention workers. The object would be to stimulate these groups to think about the problem and identify their responsibilities and what they could do about it. It would also, ideally, prompt different groups and individuals to co-operate.

The other video would also remind adults of what bullying is like and what it means to children and young people. It could show it from the perspective of both bullying and bullied students. The video should show: where it is, what it is and what it feels like. This video would concentrate on initiatives taken in Brunel School and the kind of support needed from staff, parents, governors, and the education authority to sustain these changes.

Working party members would put the "script" together and conduct interviews but nobody has to participate if they did not want to. There was a question of permission and confidentiality to be overcome. The videos could be used for staff training. Accurate information from other students would be essential. Racist/sexist bullying must be dealt with.

It was agreed that the question of bullying on journeys to and from school could be raised in Year Assemblies and different coloured bullying slips could be used to record the problems encountered by pupils.'

These videos were not intended simply as vehicles for information about the problem of bullying to be carried beyond the school. The making of the video is also a means whereby a network of agencies and individuals, in the surrounding community, with the power to do something about the violent victimisation of children and young people can be brought into being. In opting for this approach to the school-community relationship the working party was attempting to generalise the greater openness created in the school to the community it serves. In doing this, its efforts were converging with those of the crime prevention workers concerned with racial attacks on the Brunel Estate.

The Brunel Estate Crime Prevention Project

Like the strategies developed in Brunel School, the central features of the Brunel Estate Crime Prevention Project are the co-ordination of the responses of statutory and voluntary organisations and the mobilisation of the 'silent majority' of law abiding non-victims and non-perpetrators.

In their report, Sampson and Phillips (1992) argued that:

> 'The rate of repeat racial victimisation suggests that no specific agency, or agencies in collaboration, were successfully carrying out the task of protecting multi-victims. Reasons for this included under-resourcing, a reluctance to become involved and working practices within the police, housing and victim support.'

Creating a shared response

On the basis of this analysis the project decided to appoint a Re-Victimisation Prevention Worker with responsibility for co-ordinating the information, practices and policies of statutory and voluntary organisations in the area. This was necessary because the development of services for victims of abuse and attack, like 24-hour telephone 'hotlines', will only work if the relevant agencies have devised, and are committed to, a shared response. As with the bully box, success is contingent on a rapid, predictable, sensitive response to the wishes of the caller, and a set of formal responses which are practicable and have 'teeth' – the capacity to invoke appropriate sanctions. The ultimate sanction the project deemed appropriate was prosecution by the police followed by the removal of the perpetrators from the estate by the Housing Department. Inter-agency co-ordination is undertaken by an Inter-Agency Project Management Group in which the voluntary and statutory agencies co-ordinate their anti-victimisation activities.

As in the school, the effective support of victims by their peers and neighbours holds the key to the prevention of re-victimisation in the community (Pease, 1991). As we have noted, the 'culture of violence' on the estate is overlaid on a less obvious but far more pervasive pattern of non-violence and, if only as a result of indifference, tolerance towards black and Asian families. The mobilisation of this decency and tolerance and its transformation into 'social solidarity' forms the basis of the strategy of 'cocooning'. Cocooning describes the process in which:

> 'A small number of sympathetic neighbours, as ethnically diverse as possible [are] encouraged to give active support and companionship to the victim[s] in the week or two after any assault or serious incident' (Downes, 1990).

As in the school, supporting white people who identify with the plight of victimised black people is of particular importance.

Another aspect of the re-victimisation worker's role which is analogous with, and linked to, the Anti-Bullying Initiative is that of encouraging the reporting of attacks and supporting the victims, emotionally and practically, throughout the process of prosecution. On the basis of the more complete information yielded by higher levels of reporting the worker is able to liaise with the police about protection for witnesses, if necessary, but also in order that they can target their foot patrols more accurately in terms of time and location.

Work undertaken by Pease (1991) indicated that the perceived isolation of a victim from the rest of the community increases the likelihood of victimisation. As a result, the re-victimisation worker on the Brunel Estate attempts to put victims in touch with language classes and crêches, and to provide escorts where necessary. Work with adult victims explores employment and training opportunities while initiatives with younger people emphasise sport and leisure pursuits. The priority for small children and their parents is the provision of safe, supervised play areas.

▰▰▰ Working with the bullies

The project has also appointed a Detached Offender Worker to work with the perpetrators of violence and abuse in an attempt to divert them from crime. He works with young people, including those who sometimes hang around outside Brunel School, who are suspected of being involved in racial abuse or violence but have so far evaded arrest. This is an attempt to divert them from crime by steering them towards work and training opportunities, if possible, or other legitimate sources of social status and self-esteem. While similar initiatives have proved to be successful in other areas, the lack of access to legitimate opportunities for young people in the area poses a formidable problem (Smith, Farrant and Marchant, 1972; Bright and Petterson, 1984; NACRO, 1988; Downes, 1990).

The problem of 'old boys'

Adolescence may be a period of transition but how long it lasts and when it ends depend upon whether a young person has the social and economic wherewithal to proceed to the next stage in the life cycle. In 1990, in an adjacent borough, black juvenile justice workers observed that the upper age limit of members of the local Afro-Carribean 'posse' had risen to over thirty. One of the consequences of this has been that the older members have introduced some of the younger ones, who are still at school, to more serious crime. These men cannot make the transition from adolescence to higher status adult roles because they lack the economic wherewithal to assume these roles (Pitts, 1993).

Horrific though the feuds, vendettas, intimidation and attacks with which we are concerned may be, they are also, overwhelmingly, acts committed by children and young people, not by adults. Yet many young people on the estate who, in a period of boom, would have cut their ties with the school and school-age friends and got on with adult life, are now condemned to seek such status as they can from a peer group, many of whose members are still at school. Thus, they are only semi-detached from the school, its social networks and its tensions.

The transition to adulthood enables young adults and school students to be separate and, quite literally, to 'mind their own business'. As it is, there are too many people competing for the same social space. Behind the apparent struggle between the races is another struggle between the generations. It would follow from this that if serious training or employment opportunities are not created in the area then, as this dispossessed group grows older and larger, the pressures on the school will also grow.

Looking to the future

The Repeat Victimisation Project and the Brunel School Anti-Bullying Initiative continue and as they do, they come to resemble one another more closely. This is hardly surprising because the multiplicity of behaviours which we describe as 'bullying' cannot be logically separated from other, similar, but differently designated behaviours, which occur in the community served by the school.

The school mirrors the community but, as we argue here, it can also be a force for change within it. Beyond this, it is evident that unless, like Brunel School, it attempts to effect such change, its internal anti-bullying strategy will have limited impact.

Acknowledgement: As secretary to the staff-student working party, it has been my job to write about the changes at Brunel School. The working party members, Carol, Danielle, Farid, Graham, Irene, Kerry, Louie, Mike and Peter, have brought these changes about.

Helping Vulnerable Children

Child, school and family

Delwyn Tattum

The language of bullying and 'victimology'

The importance of this section on vulnerable groups is that it challenges the misplaced, conventional wisdom that victims are in some way to blame for being bullied. In my introduction to Section II, I wrote about 'provocative victims', but they constitute less than one in five of victims. The majority are passive victims who in no way provoke the bully. Regrettably, some people find it easier to 'blame the victim' than to tackle the bully. This kind of response is evident in a school's recommendation that the best solution would be to transfer the 'problem' child to another school. But victims are *not* the problem and a displacement response is *not* a solution. The bullies remain in the school and if they are permitted to continue unchallenged they will find new targets on whom to direct their viciousness. It was also emphasised earlier that bullying behaviour must be named in policy documents, school handbooks and codes of conduct. The word 'bullying' must enter into the language of teachers as they name the behaviour and condemn the perpetrators.

In this section the word is used in an encompassing way to include racial abuse, sexual harassment and the humiliation of children with special needs. In the language of victimology we can ask ourselves three harsh but necessary questions:

- Are children who are from a different culture to be blamed for their ethnicity?
- Are girls to be accused because of their femininity?

■ Are special needs children to be made to account for their disabilities?

▬▬ Bullying and racism

The Elton Report (1989) links bullying with racial harassment:

'A positive school atmosphere involves a sense of community. This sense of community cannot be achieved if a school does not take seriously bad behaviour which mainly affects pupils rather than teachers. It should be clear to pupils that such behaviour is a serious offence against the school community which will be punished. We therefore recommend that headteachers and staff should:

66.1 be alert to signs of bullying and racial harassment;

66.2 deal firmly with all such behaviour; and

66.3 take action based on clear rules which are backed by appropriate sanctions and systems to protect and support victims.'

In 1984 the DES published *Race Relations in Schools* in which it commented on the widespread nature of racial harassment and the need for whole-school policies in order to improve the skills of teachers in dealing with incidents and in promoting genuine equality of opportunity in schools. The message was reinforced by the incumbent Secretary of State for Education, Sir Keith Joseph, in a speech on 'Racial Bullying in Schools', in which he said that effective learning could take place only when pupils had a feeling of self-confidence, well-being and security flourishing in conditions conducive to equality of opportunity, mutual respect and co-operation.

The wider implications of racial bullying were forcefully made in the Swann Report, *Education for All* (1985):

'We believe the essential difference between racist name-calling and other forms of name-calling is that whereas the latter may be related only to the individual characteristics of a child, the former is a reference not only to the child but also by extension to their family and indeed more broadly their ethnic community as a whole.'

Cohn (1988) reported on racist name-calling following a study of six schools (3 primary, 3 secondary) in an outer London borough. She maintained that teachers have to choose between being silent and acquiescent and speaking out. Ethnic origin is a convenient way of categorising, evaluating and reacting to one another, and children will treat others with respect or as inferior as they hear them described in complimentary terms in society in general and school in particular.

Bullying and sexual harassment

It is the youngster with racist attitudes who needs to change, and in sexual harassment it is male society that is to blame. As I write this piece the national news is full of the release of a 15-year-old youth who, during school time, had raped a 15-year-old girl. His justification for his behaviour was that it was his birthday and she had refused to give him a birthday kiss - no doubt as a male right! The judge in the case at Newport Crown Court ordered the boy to pay the girl £500 compensation to enable her to go on holiday to forget the ordeal. Upon her return to school the girl was subjected to inexcusable bullying. She was blamed for telling about the assault and, as Danielle Drouet (Chapter 13) writes, many girls and boys attacked her reputation by calling her names like slag and bitch. (The sentence was later reviewed and considerably increased.)

A major concern about sexual bullying was developed by Askew (1988), which is that in many schools, both single sex and co-educational, the masculine ethos portrays and hence encourages aggressiveness and sexual harassment. Boys are expected to be competitive, dominant, forceful and ambitious – an implicit code of toughness, not being afraid to fight, and being able to look after yourself is evident. 'Bluntly stated, some teachers are bullies and present aggressive models for pupils to learn that domination and intimidation is how to get your own way' (Tattum and Tattum, 1992).

Bullying and children with special needs

Children with special needs in mainstream schools are also vulnerable to the taunts of cruel schoolmates. The case of Rebecca was reported in *The Observer* (28 April 1991). She had suffered from cerebral palsy since birth. Her speech is slow and her movement laboured but her intelligence and determination are exceptional. In the summer of 1990 she took her GCSEs, in nine subjects, and gained A grades in them all. Becky was also a member of the school's popular steel band but a group of teenage girls made her life a misery because they thought that she did not fit in with the image they thought the band should present; Becky and her sister were forced to leave the band.

▨ The rights of children

In America the families of victims of bullying have taken out lawsuits against the school administrative district to put legal pressure on the school system itself. In the UK too, families are turning to litigation in cases where they believe a school has been negligent in its care of their child or a local authority has mismanaged their provision of education when a child has been subjected to excessive stress and hurt from bullying. Ruling in favour of a plaintiff a Californian judge cited the States' Victims' Bill of Rights and stated, 'Safe, secure and peaceful schools are constitutionally mandatory'. Unfortunately, in the UK we do not have a Bill of Rights and so we fail to identify adequately the 'rights', as opposed to entitlements, of children attending schools.

Interestingly, in June 1992 the Lothian Children's Family Charter was launched, so that young people in Lothian will have direct access to an independent adjudicator if they feel they are being mistreated by peers or adults – including teachers, social workers or health professionals (Tattum and Herbert, 1993). The 24-page document is based on the 1989 United National Convention on the Rights of the Child and covers everything from the right to play safely to the right to an education free from abuse and harassment. Some of the rights it is suggested children should have are:

- Appeal against all decisions regarding their welfare to an independent adjudicator.
- Give or withhold consent to their own adoption if aged 12 or over.
- Avoid punishment which diminishes their dignity; pupils should not be made to feel foolish or write repetitive lines.
- Freedom from racial, sexual and religious harassment.
- Access to information held on record concerning them.

These are far-reaching rights which above all challenge the perceptions and attitudes of adults – parents, teachers and others who are responsible for the well-being and care of children and young people. Before bullying can be stopped in schools teachers must examine their personal attitudes towards the basic right of a pupil not to be threatened, abused or intimidated by other members of the school community.

▇ Long-term consequences for bullies and victims

There is growing evidence which strongly indicates that bullying is an intergenerational problem, that is, that adult males who were known school bullies produce a new generation of school bullies. The model (Figure 7) 'Cycle of Violence' (Tattum, Tattum and Herbert, 1993) illustrates the cyclic progression from pre-teen bullying to juvenile delinquency to violent adult criminality and family abuse. Several studies show the continuity between aggression in childhood and adolescence and later violent crime – and supportive evidence of the final stage in the model, the intergenerational link, is provided by Farrington (1993) in a recent scholarly analysis of research into bullying.

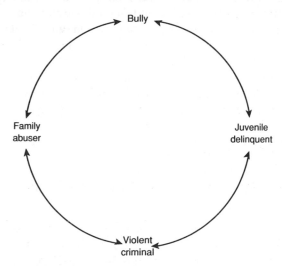

Figure 7 Bullying cycle of violence

▇ Bullies now ... criminals later?

Reviewing some of the research into violent careers we find that Stattin and Magnusson (1989) followed up 1027 children from Orebro, Sweden and found that teachers' rating of aggression at ages 10 and 13 years significantly predicted officially recorded offending – especially violent criminal acts, up to the age of 26 years. Teachers' ratings covered aggressiveness towards teachers and children, disturbing and quarrelling with other children, impertinence and obstructiveness.

In the UK a five-year study of 200 pupils from various secondary schools was made by David Lane (reported in Tattum, 1988). In his sample, 50 pupils were randomly sampled who were disruptive but *not* bullies and 50 who were *both* disruptive and bullies. In the first group, 17 (4 girls, 13 boys) received convictions totalling 33 offences of which four involved violence towards other persons, but in the second group, 31 (5 girls, 26 boys) received a total of 162 convictions of which 22% (36) involved violence. In his chapter in Tattum and Lane (1989) David Lane deals in detail with the subject of the violent personal histories of bullies.

A 22-year longitudinal study was carried out in the USA by Eron and his associates (1987). They found that young bullies have a one in four chance of having a criminal record by age 30, whilst other boys have a one in twenty chance of becoming adult criminals. The team studied 870 boys from age 8, when they had been identified as being aggressive by peer nomination. Of the 409 children traced through to age 30 most had delinquent records and tended to have children who displayed aggressive behaviour. They also abused their wives and children. In this study the researchers did not specifically name bullying but did contain items such as saying mean things, taking other children's things, pushing or shoving others, doing things that bother others, and starting a fight over nothing. The fact that the study did not name bullying is not surprising, as it started in the 1950s when the word was not used to describe peer-peer aggression. But the behaviours itemised would be recognised today as examples of bullying behaviour.

In Norway, Olweus (1989) also writes of bullying as a 'component of a more generally anti-social and rule-breaking behaviour pattern'. From his follow-up studies he found that:

> 'Approximately 60 per cent of boys who are characterised as bullies in grades 6–8 had at least one court conviction at the age of 24. Even more dramatically, as much as 35–40 per cent of the former bullies had three or more court convictions at this age whilst this was true of only 10 per cent of the control boys (those who were neither bullies nor victims in grades 6–9). Thus, as young adults the former bullies had a fourfold increase in the level of relatively serious, recidivist criminality' (Olweus, 1989).

Finally, Farrington (1993) presents new analyses of the Cambridge Study in Delinquent Development to investigate the intragenerational continuity and intergenerational transmission of bullying. As he claims, 'No other research project has ever followed up adolescent bullies to investigate whether their children became bullies' (Farrington, 1993). The project is a forward-looking, longitudinal survey of 411 London males from age 8 to age 32. The sample came from six primary schools, and was overwhelmingly white, working-class and of British origin. In addition to a series of tests, teacher and peer questionnaires, the boys engaged in eight face-to-face interviews over the study period of 24 years.

When interviewed at age 32 the study males were asked whether they had any children and the 259 who were parents reported a total 560 children. Several children were eliminated from the survey because they were either too young (under 3 years) or living elsewhere. But of the 323 eligible children 32 (7.1%) were reported by their fathers to be bullies and 52 (16.1%) victims of bullying. Bullying was most prevalent among boys age 11–15 and virtually absent among girls age 7 or over. When concentrating on the study males who were known bullies, as opposed to being generally aggressive (fighting, delinquency), Farrington reports that 'there was a significant tendency for study males who were bullies to have children who are bullies' and, most remarkably, there was a strong tendency for study males convicted of violent crimes to have children who were bullies. Seven (35%) out of 20 convicted violent men had child bullies, compared with 7.9% of the remaining 140 study males. Moreover, the continuity between the male's bullying and his child's bullying was statistically independent of any continuity between the male's general anti-social behaviour and his child's general problem behaviour. It is also evident that there was intergenerational transmission of bullying and that bullying by primary age children, and especially at age 14, significantly predicted bullying at 18 and at 32 (Farrington, 1993).

▄▄▄▄▄ A problem for the future

It is evident that bullying is a serious problem which we can no longer ignore or dismiss with adult clichés. It is a pattern of destructive behaviour which if not changed will have disastrous consequences for subsequent generations of children, their families and society at large. Aggressive behaviour is learned. Living with parents who abuse them teaches children that aggression and violence are effective and acceptable means to dominate others and get our own way.

'Violent incidents and ongoing intimidation in schools are more likely when the school itself fails to take the issue seriously. If a senior member of staff concurs with the view that:

This is a boys' school. You have to accept bullying. If a child can't take it, they should be in another school, then bullying is likely to flourish. Similarly, if the school felt unable to act in case it

'made the situation worse', then the situation became worse. . . .
These children cannot be hidden and will not go away, but will as
adults reap with destruction what we sow now with neglect'
(Lane, 1988).

Less is known about the long-term effects of bullying on victims. The short-term distress is obvious enough! Rutter (1987) and others have argued that the social isolation and anxiety of victims is bound to have an adverse effect on the development of self-image and self-esteem, which have been shown to be so important in protecting children from negative life experiences. If the bullying is experienced persistently and over a long period bullied children often feel isolated and wonder what is wrong with them that they should be singled out. They may even begin to feel that they deserve the taunts, abuse and harassment and can engage in acts of self-denigration. They can become withdrawn and less willing to take social, intellectual and vocational risks. In extreme cases they take these feelings of inadequacy into adult life. Tragically, for some the stress is so great that they cannot tolerate it any longer and commit suicide.

Racial violence
12 and bullying

David Gillborn

'On several occasions while on her way home from a school in the North-East, an 11-year-old Asian girl was confronted by a group of white youths from another school. They would wait for her on the bridge over the motorway, which she had to use to get home. On one occasion the youths grabbed her and dangled her over the railings, threatening to drop her. The girl's mother, worried about previous incidents, arrived to meet her and was able to rescue her. When she asked them why they had done it, the youths replied that it was because her daughter was a 'black bastard'.'

'A black African head of department in a medium-sized, comprehensive, co-educational school had to enlist the aid of his headteacher in resisting the torrent of racial abuse directed at him by pupils upon his appointment. An Indian teacher in a similar type of school had the experience of a girl's refusing to work for him because, she said, he was a 'Paki'.' (Commission for Racial Equality, 1988).

Any attempt to address issues of 'racial' and ethnic relations in schools must be understood within the wider social context. The UK is a racially structured society. It is no accident that, in terms of educational and occupational achievement, for example, black people are over-represented among those with the poorest life chances. Many people believe this fact reflects centuries of systematic exploitation and exclusion (Hall, 1992; see note 1 at end of chapter). Similarly, racism in schools – like racism in society more generally – is a dynamic part of social life that changes and has different consequences in different situations. Hence, a pupil who is actively racist in one context may count a black peer as a close friend in another setting. In such a politically charged arena, we should also be careful to avoid simplification and dogma: not every conflict between white and black children will have a racial meaning; it is not only black and Asian children who are victims – refugee children from Europe and Latin America are also potential targets in a society that defines such groups as an unwanted threat to (white) national culture and prosperity (Le Lohe, 1992).[2]

Racial violence and harassment often highlight (in the most disturbing and graphic ways) the relationship between life in individual schools and wider political and social forces. Solomos (1989) draws a direct parallel between a rise in popular nationalism and more frequent violence towards black and other ethnic minority communities. Similarly, during the Gulf War several schools reported increased attacks on Asian pupils. These were fuelled by a crude racism that equated a single political regime with the whole of the Islamic world and assumed all Asians to be Muslim (Runnymede Trust, 1991a, 1991b; Searle, 1992; Sivanandan, 1991).

Nevertheless, a recognition of the wider picture should not blind us to the possibility of change on a smaller scale. A concerted attempt to combat racial violence and harassment – even in a single school – has the potential to improve the experiences and life chances of all those involved in the institution (including pupils, teachers, parents and members of the wider community) and to contribute towards the deconstruction of racist structures on a larger scale.

In this chapter I examine how people have responded to, and combated, racial violence and harassment in schools.[3] My aim is to show that real progress can be made but also to explore some of the reasons why success is rarely easy and never complete. I hope that the chapter will encourage, and enable, more people to get involved in the struggle.

▉ Defining and quantifying racial violence and bullying

'One of the most common interactions we have in the playground, the most common, widely used, abuse is 'You dirty Paki' or 'Fuck off, Paki' (LEA officer).

'almost as British as the weather' (A victim of racial harassment, quoted in Skellington and Morris, 1992).

The field of 'race' and ethnic relations is littered with disputes over terminology. There is neither time nor need in this chapter to engage with such arguments at length. The most common definitions of racial violence and harassment include any act of bullying that appears to have a racial motivation or where there is an allegation of racist motives. Such behaviour covers an enormous range, from name-calling and jostling in corridors, to violent assault and murder (CRE, 1988; Macdonald *et al.*, 1989).

The involvement of a 'racist motivation' is more than a mere definitional nicety – the 'racial' element changes fundamentally both the meaning and the experience of bullying. Racist name-calling, for example, may degrade not only the individual victim but also his or her family, religion, culture and entire home community. In addition, the attack carries extra weight because of the prevalence of racist beliefs and ideologies throughout society. To be called 'fatty' is not the same as being called 'a dirty Paki'. This is not to imply that other forms of bullying are trivial, but to appreciate the 'extra-crippling dimension' brought to bullying by racism (CRE, 1988). Neither victim nor aggressor may be conscious of all the factors involved, but they are often fully aware of the consequences:

> 'If I call someone 'dickhead' it doesn't really hurt them, but if I call someone a 'black bastard', something like that, that would hurt them.' (A white primary school pupil quoted by Troyna and Hatcher, 1992a).

Contrary to popular belief, racial violence and harassment are not limited to the inner-city. Indeed, where there are few people of ethnic minority background – as in rural areas – the risk may be intensified because of their relative isolation (Gordon, 1992a; Swann, 1985).

Attempts to chart the frequency of racial incidents in the UK have fallen foul of definitional problems, bureaucratic indifference and variations in the proportion of incidents that are actually reported (Gordon, 1992a ; 1992b). The same problems have dogged survey-based studies of racial harassment in schools (Cohn, 1988; Kelly and Cohn, 1988) because they are unable to explore fully the part that racist language and acts routinely play in the lives of pupils and teachers (Troyna and Hatcher, 1992a). A survey of 18 multi-racial comprehensive schools in England, for example, found 'little hard evidence' of overt racism (Smith and Tomlinson, 1989). Yet a simultaneous qualitative (interview and observational) study of one of the same schools concluded that 'racist attacks (usually, but not always, verbal) were a regular fact of life for most Asian pupils' (Gillborn, 1990; see also Gillborn and Drew, 1992).

All that can be concluded with any certainty is that racial violence and bullying occurs (to some degree) in schools the length and breadth of the country: it is not limited to schools with a significant proportion of black pupils. Additionally, it should be noted that most qualitative studies, which penetrate institutional facades and give a voice to minority students, reveal racial bullying on a much wider scale than suggested by statistical approaches.

Responding to racial violence and bullying

'Children are frightened to tell and those that do come back with nothing ... If I say something to you once and if you say, 'Oh, go away, we'll deal with it next time ...' I may take the message once but if I come and say the same thing again and *you* reply the same thing I won't come to you a third time ... That's the situation the children are in because they come and nothing happens. 'Kitchoy na?', that's what the children say in Bengali which means 'Nothing happens', 'Nothing is done'. It's just a waste of time' (18-year-old student reflecting on life in school, quoted by Pitt, 1991).

Pupils are often ignored when they report incidents that they consider to be racist. Worse still, they are sometimes rebuked for 'telling tales'. They may even find themselves the victim of further abuse from the teacher; in one case, for example, a primary school pupil was 'forced by the teacher to stand up and spell out the word "golliwog" when the child refused to read it out in class because he found it offensive' (CRE, 1988). The most common response, according to pupils' accounts, is that teachers simply fail (or refuse) to recognise that racial bullying is different from playful boisterousness. In the eyes of both victim and aggressor, inaction by teachers usually looks like tacit approval:

'It was a poem about this black sailor and it had this picture of him kissing a white woman ... the boys went mad, 'Oh, they come over here, nicking our jobs, oh bloody Pakis, nick our girlfriends ... The teacher didn't say anything ... I was really embarrassed, you know. I mean it was as if I wasn't in that classroom. I didn't exist, you know, when all this was coming out ... All these people that I thought were my friends ... worked up about it. 'Blackies coming over here' ...' (Year 9 student, quoted by Pitt, 1991).

> 'When a black girl's mother complained to a school of racist name-calling she was told that 'she would have to produce twenty black pupils who had had similar experiences of racial abuse if the school was to take the matter seriously' (Commission for Racial Equality, 1988).

A lack of official action leaves few options open to the victim. One of the most obvious is a physical response that matches (or surpasses) the severity of the original attack. Clearly this is a dangerous situation; at the very least, the original 'victim' is likely to find him or herself in trouble with school authorities, at worst the violence may escalate further. While this course of action may or may not be encouraged by parents, the increasingly politicised youth cultures of some minority groups suggest that a violent response is both legitimate and unavoidable.

Schools, of course, cannot sanction violence, yet their response must be flexible enough to reflect a sense of justice that is valid in the eyes of pupils and the local community. At the school level, the best way to avoid such incidents is to establish a firm and practical policy on racial harassment – it is not simply that values of justice and democracy demand that action be taken, it is also the case that where racial violence and bullying are ignored, schools are fuelling the development of a potentially explosive situation.

Therefore, a purely reactive stance – where a school *responds* after the event – is not enough. What is needed is a shift of intent, away from attempts to contain/manage racial harassment, towards an actively anti-racist approach that *combats* racism and racial harassment.

Combating racial violence and bullying

The first task in dealing with racial incidents is to be clear about what kind of behaviour we mean. I prefaced my earlier remarks, on the incidence of racial violence and harassment, by adopting a general definition that reflects previous work in the field. Within individual institutions, however, more precise guidance may be necessary – otherwise uncertainty could led to inconsistent actions (or even inaction) by staff.

Coherent whole-school policies

Most successful policies on racial harassment and bullying, therefore, include a breakdown of particular types of offence, for example:

- Physical assault because of colour, ethnicity or nationality.
- Use of derogatory names, insults and racist jokes.
- Racist graffiti.
- Provocative behaviour such as wearing racist badges or insignia.
- Bringing racist materials into the school.
- Verbal abuse and threats.
- Incitement of others to behave in a racist way.
- Racist comments in the course of a discussion.
- Attempts to recruit others to racist organisations and groups.
- Ridicule of an individual for cultural differences, e.g. food, music, dress etc.
- Refusal to co-operate because of a person's colour, ethnic origin or nationality.

(Adapted from Hampshire County Council, 1991).

Whatever the specific guidance about identifying racial harassment, it is vital that all staff (including ancillary workers) have a chance to discuss how the policy should be put into operation. This should be managed to lead towards a clear statement of procedure to which everyone is bound. It should be emphasised that *all* staff are expected to act when they witness racial harassment and bullying, and that staff (just as much as pupils) are subject to the policy:

> 'A cleaner has just spent three hours cleaning and polishing the corridor floor. He has just finished when a young Sikh boy walks past and drops his empty crisp packet onto the floor ... he shouts at the boy 'Pick that up you dirty, little Paki!' ' (Case recorded in training materials prepared by the London Borough of Newham, 1991).

Although it is impossible to dictate in advance precisely how any single incident should be dealt with, it is vital that responses should be consistent: any apparent inconsistencies may be exploited – by pupils, parents and even other teachers – to discredit the entire system as 'unfair' (see Elton, 1989). Such cases undermine the position of those who *are* trying to apply the policy. Classroom teachers and their senior colleagues with managerial responsibilities frequently perceive the same incident in different ways (Gillborn, 1992a). To retain the confidence of all staff, it is essential that the school's policy on racial incidents is fully, and regularly, discussed.

■■■ The need for agreed guidelines

In order to support a consistent and serious response to racial harassment and bullying, therefore, staff should be aware of agreed guidelines that offer a structure for responding to each incident. These should include guidance that relates the severity of the incident to the range of staff who should be involved and the kinds of sanction that may be appropriate. Resource management should reflect the importance of these issues, for example, in-service time should be used to develop staff knowledge and confidence.

Because of the nature of racial violence and harassment all incidents must be recorded, along with a description of the action taken and its outcomes. No one should doubt the seriousness of racial harassment, and it must be understood that permanent exclusion and/or police involvement may be necessary.

In all cases it is crucial that both victim and aggressor have an opportunity to discuss their view of, and feelings about, the incident: how it came about, and what action is appropriate in response. Racism is a complex phenomenon: the same act may have different meanings in different circumstances. While maintaining a firm line, staff should be sensitive to the range of experiences and concerns that pupils bring to school; situations must be resolved in ways that remind both parties of the school's commitment to all its pupils.

I noted earlier that racial violence and harassment must not be subsumed within wider categories such as name-calling and general bullying; 'racial' harassment is qualitatively different. However, attempts to counter racial violence and harassment should not be developed in isolation. To single out racial incidents, without attention to related issues, may marginalise and devalue the work. Perhaps most importantly, policies on racial incidents must not give the impression to pupils that some are unduly favoured over others. When it comes to matters of 'fairness', pupils are remarkably perceptive – they will recognise when claims about equal rights are not sustained in practice (Woods, 1983). Similarly, as I have already shown, pupils are sophisticated enough to appreciate the unique nature of racial incidents. There is, therefore, no case for so-called 'colour blind' approaches, which simply ignore ethnic diversity (see Gillborn, 1990; 1992b). What is required are moves to include all pupils, their parents and the wider community in discussions about bullying and the special measures needed to deal with racial incidents.[6]

Stirring up trouble?

No matter how eloquent the policy statements, no matter how thorough the consultation with communities, pupils will soon work out for themselves whether a policy carries any weight in the day-to-day life of the school. At first pupils may be sceptical, but once they see that the policy is borne out in the actions of staff, this success will quickly encourage greater confidence in the system. As a result more pupils will be prepared to risk reporting incidents that they have suffered or witnessed. Initially, therefore, the implementation of a whole-school policy on harassment is likely to be accompanied by a marked increase in the number of reported incidents. In one inner-city school, for example, after the publication of the school's anti-racist policy, reported incidents of racial violence and harassment leapt from seven in one year to more than 90 in the next.

In the early stages of implementing a policy against racial violence and harassment, therefore, an apparent escalation in racial incidents should not be a cause for panic. If the policy has moved from the realm of rhetoric and into everyday school practice it is likely that an increase in reported incidents simply indicates that a greater proportion of such events are now being disclosed; the 'true' level may not have changed – indeed, it could have already begun to fall. It is vital, therefore, that schools persevere beyond the early stages of implementation.

It is almost certain that some people will assert that the policy has simply 'stirred up trouble' – a common cry among those who fear or resent any change in the status quo. Yet abandoning such a policy cannot be a realistic alternative; to do so would lend official weight to racist violence and harassment. This is not to say that once policies have been set up they should be immune to criticism and reappraisal. Indeed, it is essential that such issues be reviewed frequently, and amended where appropriate. However, we should always ensure that any changes reflect the best interests of all parties and are not expediencies adopted so as to hide (rather than address) a real problem.

 ## Towards an anti-racist school

Moves against racial violence and bullying should be a central element in every school's attempt to secure a safe and positive learning environment. Furthermore, such moves offer an excellent opportunity to start or extend a process of evaluation and change that encompasses both the formal curriculum (what the school teaches) and the 'hidden' curriculum (the messages conveyed in the everyday actions of teachers). A policy that espouses values of human equity and democracy will seem somewhat incongruous in a school whose curriculum remains steadfastly Anglo- or Eurocentric: rooted in the assumption that European history and society provide the only really important or valid form of knowledge and experience.

This is not to say that moves against racial violence must await a rigorous appraisal of the entire curriculum and operation of a school. What I am arguing is that a policy on racial harassment and bullying:

■ Provides a good vehicle for beginning such a process.

■ That broad changes in school ethos, pupil and teacher culture, are only likely as the result of such moves.

In isolation, even the most well-intentioned, clearly structured and consistently applied policy will only succeed within certain parameters – limiting the number of racial incidents and supporting the victims in school – but leaving wider attitudes and structures intact. As part of moves across the whole spectrum of school activities, however, such a policy can lead to real and important changes that extend beyond the walls of the school and into the community as a whole.

▰ The effects on pupils

The following excerpts, from interviews with pupils in a comprehensive school in the English Midlands, illustrate the far-reaching influence of changes that genuinely address anti-racist concerns as a *whole*-school issue. In this school, racial harassment draws a severe response from pupils that illustrates how anti-racist attitudes have become a key part of their own culture – their definition of what is acceptable. Here, racism between pupils is a serious offence, worthy of informal responses that isolate the aggressors.

> 'Sally (white pupil in year 9): 'there is some racism still … that's why we beat her up [she laughs]. Well, we didn't beat her up, we just mouthed off at her because of what she was doing. We didn't talk to her for *so* long.'
>
> Robina (South Asian pupil in year 10): 'We find if people are racist, for example, to an Asian girl, or a white person racist to a black girl or something. We find that that person is isolated. You know, even their *own* friends will isolate that person. Like if I'm racist to Karen [a white pupil] or something, everyone will go against me. We will isolate that person, that's the way we are … '

▉ The way ahead

'Differences between schools [in the amount and severity of racial harassment] seem to be mainly the consequence of the effectiveness of the stance that teachers, non-teaching staff, and in particular the headteacher, take towards racist incidents' (Troyna and Hatcher, 1992a).

Despite the long history of racism in this society, and the many complex factors that sustain it, schools and teachers are not powerless. In this chapter I have discussed some of the ways in which racial violence and harassment can be addressed within schools. There is no simple blueprint for change; whatever approaches are adopted there will be times of conflict and uncertainty.

Experience suggests that real progress can only be achieved through coherent whole-school approaches. These should involve as many groups as possible (including teachers, ancillary staff, parents, local communities and pupils). Clear guidelines must be available so that everyone knows the school's stance and the likely consequences of abuse.

Ideally, work on racial incidents should take place within a whole-school context that is supportive of all groups, not only 'racial' or ethnic minorities. Indeed, tragic events such as the playground murder of Ahmed Iqbal Ullah (Macdonald *et al.*, 1989) highlight both the need for action and the fact that all relevant groups must be included in the process. Narrow and essentialist views of white people as necessarily bad/racist are as damaging and unhelpful as the corresponding stereotypes of black people.

No one should think that change is easily won. Indeed, recent legislation in England and Wales makes progress even more difficult. A statutory curriculum now privileges European perspectives and languages, for example, while the law gives priority to 'freedom of choice' for white racist parents over the safeguards of the 1976 Race Relations Act (Runnymede Trust, 1992).

In this context the need for action at the school level is perhaps even more urgent. Mistakes will be made and the process will be difficult, but real change *is* possible: inaction is inexcusable.

Acknowledgements: I am indebted to the teachers and pupils who took part in my research, and especially to Tina Cartwright for all her help with the tapes. Thanks also to Eltaz Bodalbhai and Janet Pitt for sharing their expertise with me, and to Ian Massey for his comments on a previous draft.

Notes

1 Here 'black' refers to people of black African and Caribbean back-ground. The term 'race' also requires clarification: it is now generally accepted that, biologically, there are no meaningful subgroups within the human species, *Homo sapiens* (Demaine, 1989). However, the belief in separate races continues to flourish in certain societies; it is in this sense – as a socially constructed category – that I use the term 'race' in this chapter. For a useful discussion of the concept see Banton (1988) and van den Berghe (1988).

2 Where racism is defined with reference to the wider structures of power in society, some have argued that (by definition) only whites can be racist (Troyna and Hatcher, 1992a; 1992b). However, this view has been criticised for over-simplifying the complex nature of racism (Rattansi, 1992) and is difficult to sustain at the level of school practice, not least in the eyes of white pupils and parents – who must be included as an active part of attempts to eliminate racism (Macdonald *et al.*, 1989).

3 This chapter draws both on existing documentary sources and original data from my own research. The latter include work that was funded by the Department for Education (and jointly conducted with Jean Rudduck and Jon Nixon at Sheffield University) and a project on change in multi-ethnic schools sponsored by British Petroleum plc.

4 ' ... I am not against using violence in self-defense. I don't even call it violence when it's self-defense, I call it intelligence' (Malcolm X). Yunas Samad (1992) notes the part played by white racist attacks (both in the street and in print) in the mobilisation of Asian youth in Bradford.

5 Many practitioners are frightened by the term 'anti-racism'; aware of its stormy political history, they fear involvement in what could be a narrow and constraining ideology. Such fears reflect many factors, not least a political onslaught from the New Right (see Palmer, 1986), slanted media coverage (see Runnymede Trust, 1988) and infighting between different groups of multiculturalists, anti-racists and even multicultural anti-racists (see Gillborn, 1990; Massey, 1991). These debates are significant but they should not be allowed to stifle change at the school level. The Swann Report (1985), for example, argued that opposition to racism was an essential characteristic of any 'good' edu-cation – put simply, all schools should be *anti*-racist. How this is translated into practice cannot be assumed from outside – there is no anti-racist blueprint.

6 Again, there is no 'one correct way' of achieving pupil, parental or

community involvement. One school I have worked with used pupils' own ideas on fairness and respect as the starting point (literally) for their policy; another worked out a detailed policy among staff, then took this to pupils and community groups for comments and amendments. What matters is that everyone is given a voice and feels that they have genuinely played a part.

Adolescent female bullying and sexual harassment

13

Danielle Drouet

Sexual harassment is a problem which exists in co-ed and single-sex schools for girls and boys and has been described by many writers, teachers and researchers though more often as a 'by-product' of some other line of inquiry.

What is 'sexual harassment'?

Sexual harassment takes many different forms. For example:

- *Verbal sexual harassment*, that is, being called a 'slag', 'bitch' etc. or males commenting loudly on the size of a girl's breasts or what they would like to do to her.

- *Physical sexual harassment* includes boys standing unnecessarily close to girls, brushing up against them, grabbing breasts, 'pinging' bra-straps.

- *Visual sexual harassment* is manifested by boys teasing girls with pornography e.g. '*Playboy*' being used as a way of embarrassing and intimidating girls. Another example of visual sexual harassment is where pictures or posters containing images of women in the school corridors or classrooms are crudely defaced by male students. This may be extended to school text-books and library books. This type of visual sexual harassment affects both female teachers and pupils and female visitors to the school.

▉▉▉ Harassment of teachers

In schools it is not only girls who are subjected to sexual harassment. Nor is it only men who occupy positions of power who can sexually harass. Studies such as Whitbread (1980) and Jones (1985) identify unacceptable male behaviour between schoolboys and female teachers. Whitbread found that women teachers (especially younger ones and those with less status) were subjected to 'unidentifiable boys' milling around in a group, grabbing and making obscene comments and appraising remarks.

Askew (1989) studied women teachers' experiences of teaching in boys' schools and noticed that teachers were mostly concerned with the 'problem' of the boys. The problem was mainly a concern about the amount of aggression between boys and the demands made on teachers by boys. Askew argues that studying the education of boys has direct implications for girls' education because *all* schools perpetuate the values and ideologies of the dominant groups in society. Thus, the values of schools as institutions will reflect and reinforce masculine stereotypes, eg strong, competitive, dominant, aggressive. These stereotypes and values are consistent with, and underlie bullying and aggressive behaviour, and are more apparent in boys' schools but nevertheless exist in all educational establishments.

▉▉▉ The problem in boarding schools

A study by Newton (1993) revealed that bullying was a concern of many pupils at Malvern Girls' College – a single-sex independent boarding school. Through the use of a questionnaire and discussion with the girls it emerged that a wide range of activities which could be considered as bullying went unreported, e.g. verbal abuse such as criticism of clothes or physical features caused distress and affected victims' self-confidence.

Walford (1989) in his study of boys' public schools found that bullying was still present though more a matter of verbal and light physical abuse rather than the heavy physical oppression historically associated with boys' public schools, exemplified by the bully Flashman in *Tom Brown's Schooldays*. However, for some boys, the effects of such behaviour causes much unhappiness for the victims. This unhappiness is magnified in the closed environment of a boarding school because there is no escape home at the end of the day.

The reactions of the authorities

It is usually girls and women who suffer sexual harassment (verbal abuse, unwanted physical contact, etc.) in co-ed schools. Often victims do not complain because they fear that they will not be taken seriously. However, an extreme example such as the one which took place at the Bishop of Llandaff School, Cardiff (*The Times Educational Supplement*, March 15, 1991) highlights the issue. Three boys allegedly assaulted a girl in an empty classroom and conflict broke out between the teachers and the governors over the failure of governors to exclude the three boys. This case stresses the need for schools to educate pupils about the unacceptability of all types of sexist behaviour.

It must also be noted that some boys are ridiculed in co-ed schools, especially those who do not conform to masculine stereotypes of strength and aggression. Such boys are subjected to derogatory terms associated with feminity, e.g. 'cissy', 'soft' or associated with homosexuality, e.g. 'fairy', 'faggot', 'gay'.

Herbert (1989) points out that researchers found numerous examples of sexual harassment in schools and they also found that sexual harassment was accepted as part of the hidden curriculum for girls and one of the hazards of teaching for women staff.

> 'Sexual harassment was either ignored as a problem detrimental to women or it was regarded as 'normal' or 'typical' behaviour' (Herbert, 1989).

Some girls then experience verbal and physical abuse in the form of name-calling or being touched. They may also have their learning environment spoiled by defaced female images or by hearing abusive language in which females are described as 'slags', 'dogs' etc. Such experiences will provide unhappy, stressful environments which will affect their learning adversely. Some girls experience sexual harassment to the extent that they 'switch off' in lessons or become truants or modify their behaviour so that they come in for less abuse from the boys. The way in which some girls modified their behaviour was by joining in with the boys who were wasting time and this corresponds with Anyon's (1983) theory of accommodation and resistance.

Difficulties in recognising sexual harassment

One of the difficulties in recognising sexual harassment is that it includes behaviours that are regarded as 'normal' or 'typical' behaviour. Some male behaviour can be seen to be both 'sexual harassment' and 'normal male behaviour' depending on the context, the people involved and the way in which it is interpreted. This difficulty in identifying particular actions as sexual harassment results in confusion and often such behaviours are described as 'normal' or not spoken about. One example of this can be found in research conducted by Measor and Woods (1984). They describe an incident involving one male teacher and the way in which he speaks to and acts with particular girls:

> 'Mr. Hill [a teacher], always addressed one sixth form girl named Erica as 'Hey Erotica', and 'he would walk with his arm around the shoulders of a younger girl who was upset' (Measor and Woods, 1984).

Measor and Woods describe this behaviour as the teacher showing friendliness and fail to recognise that his actions may well have been sexual harassment. However, it must be remembered that in the male world of work gestures can signify power. For example, a boss may slap an employee on the back or put an arm on his shoulder but the reverse would be inappropriate.

What language can we use?

Another difficulty with recognising sexual harassment is the lack of language with which to describe it. Language is an important tool by which people describe their understandings of the world. The absence of a label makes it very difficult to discuss something which is unnamed.

This lack of language or namelessness is one of the ways in which discussions about sexual harassment are curtailed. Also, many girls and women lack political awareness either through lack of maturity or experience and find it difficult to articulate their experiences or discriminate incidents which, with hindsight, they can recognise as unacceptable or bizarre behaviour. Sexually harassing behaviour is often elusive to define, normal in its manifestation and often trivialised by others, e.g. giving 'friendly' birthday kisses, commenting on the size of a girls' breasts, lifting a girl's skirt with a ruler as she passes by. Such behaviour is often described as 'friendly' or 'appreciative of females' or 'just a joke', making it appear normal and therefore difficult for girls to define and so it is internalised by the victims and they remain silent.

Spender's (1980) analysis shows that language plays a crucial role in the continuation of male control and that naming the world is 'essential for the construction of reality'. Spender argued that all naming is of necessity biased because emphasis, selection and omission in naming forms the core of the process.

Similarly, Dworking (1976) argued that because men had constructed this culture and had named all the words, women had their values, perceptions and understandings defined for them. Behaviour which was not experienced by men would remain nameless or be made 'normal' and by default be deemed as unproblematic by the majority of both men and women. Until recently, because of this language deficiency many females who were 'sexually harassed' did not know what to call this unwanted behaviour. They were unable to express adequately their feelings or describe unwanted approaches.

If women are unable to describe or communicate the existence of such a problem then they are prevented from sharing the experience with others. Thus women are again made silent and left in an isolated and vulnerable position. Although since the 1970s sexual harassment has become an issue for some groups and has been labelled and defined, there are still many people who do not recognise it or if they do are unable or unwilling to deal with it.

■ Keeping quiet ... not telling

Girls and women who have experienced harassment often remain silent about their experiences. This silence can be compared with victims of other types of bullying, many of whom also keep quiet and do not tell. There is a code of secrecy surrounding victims of bullying behaviour and sexual harassment which must be broken. As Herbert (1989) points out, the reasons for this are varied and complex.

Some girls are silent because they believe they are *guilty* and therefore, in some way, they had 'asked for' the treatment and it was deserved. For example, an attack may have taken place somewhere their parents had forbidden them to go or at a 'wrong' time, such as being out of school during lessons.

Another factor ·is *fear*. Girls are sometimes frightened into silence because if they reveal that they have been attacked they may be open to further abuse and attack. Also it is important not to tell in order to retain a 'good' reputation. Fear of their parents' reaction may also keep them quiet: fear of anger towards the victim or threats of violence against the perpetrator if he is known to them. In some cultures where a girl's marriageability is dependent on her being a virgin then she may be frightened of the repercussions that 'telling' would have for the family.

Another reason for remaining silent is *protection*. A victim may feel sorry for the assailant because she believes that he has a difficult life or is rejected and wants to protect him from any more harm. Similarly, a victim may not tell her parents because she does not want them worried or upset. Girls also remain silent because they think that they might not be believed. The onus is often on the victim to prove that her version of an incident is correct and figures of authority (senior teachers, police officers etc. are not always sympathetic.

Unfortunately, many people still think that sexual harassment or assault is a trivial matter and this *trivialisation* also silences girls. Although a girl might be very upset by sexual harassment she may, nevertheless, feel that it is not important enough to report. Lack of knowledge or language resulting in an inability to name the attack as an attack also keeps some girls quiet.

Finally, *shame* further motivates girls to keep silent about sexual harassment. Like the guilt and concern about their reputation, many girls feel ashamed of what has happened to them and this can express itself in a reluctance to disclose details of an incident.

A consequence of this silence is that men are rarely challenged about sexually harassing behaviour.

> 'One of the outcomes of silence is that men and boys are not repeatedly challenged in any way about the inappropriateness of their behaviour. Thus we have a situation in which men do things for which they are then subsequently never challenged' (Herbert, 1989).

Ironically, the silence of the girls and women protects male behaviour which, in effect, means that men's perception of what they have done remains as behaviour which is acceptable and condoned or at least unremarkable.

▇▇ The problem in a girls' secondary school

In a study to explore girls' understandings of bullying and sexual harassment 51 girls in a single-sex school aged between 12 and 16 years of age were questioned about bullying and sexual harassment. Findings showed that verbal sexual abuse was the most common type of sexual harassment experienced and was also used extensively amongst pupils in the school. Names which most girls found offensive were those relating to their reputations rather than their sexuality. There were also differences among the girls in recognising some types of sexual harassment.

Details of the study

The study took place in a girls' secondary school in South East London and of the 51 pupils questioned 32 were in Year 10 (aged 15–16 years) and 19 in Year 8 (aged 12–13 years). Different age groups were chosen to see if differences existed in their understandings or experiences of bullying and sexual harassment. A questionnaire was used which allowed for both quantitative and qualitative responses, through ticking a box or by open-ended questions and the adding of further categories. The study was exploratory rather than built around specific, testable hypotheses. The objectives were:

- To see the extent to which the girls experienced sexual harassment inside and outside school.
- To classify different types of sexual harassment into bullying and non-bullying behaviour.
- To find out which abusive sexual terms girls find most offensive.
- To find the extent to which girls experience name-calling in school.
- To discover which behaviours the girls themselves considered to be sexual harassment.

The extent of sexual harassment

The first question contained five different behaviours which can be described as sexual harassment and girls were asked if they had experienced any of them. These were:

1. **Being physically touched in an unwanted way**, perhaps being touched on the bus or being grabbed at in the street.
2. **Sexual verbal abuse** as in being called a 'slag', 'bitch' or other sexually offensive names.
3. **Being made to perform a 'favour'** like lending money, giving food, doing homework for someone in return for their promising not to

spread gossip about you which would damage 'your name or reputation'.

4. **Being teased or embarrassed by being shown pictures of female pin-ups**, for example from *Playboy* or Page Three pin-ups.

5. **Avoiding going to places**, for example where there are often men/boys who shout out comments at girls.

Out of the total sample of 51 pupils 16 (31.3%) stated that they had been physically touched in an unwanted way (with 41% of the young girls saying that they had been physically touched compared with 25% of the Year 10 girls). Verbal abuse was experienced by the highest number of pupils with 80.3% of the total sample reporting that they had been called sexually abusive names. Again, there was a difference between the age groups: all 19 (100%) of the Year 8 girls said they had been called such names, compared with 22 (68.7%) of the Year 10 girls.

Performing 'favours' was the behaviour least experienced by the girls (5.8%), with no difference between the age groups. Being teased or shown pin-ups was reported by 17.6%, again with no difference between the age groups. After verbal sexual abuse most pupils avoided places where there are males who shout out comments – 37.2% of the total sample, with no significant difference between the age groups.

▰ Sexual harassment and bullying

Question 2 on the questionnaire listed the same five behaviours again. Pupils were asked to classify the behaviours as sexual harassment, bullying, neither or both. The aim was to see if the girls considered sexual harassment to be the same as or different from bullying.

Out of the total sample 74.5% thought that unwanted sexual contact was sexual harassment and 21.5% thought that it was both sexual harassment and bullying. However, there was a difference between the age groups. In Year 10 the majority of pupils – 31 (96.8%) – considered it to be sexual harassment and none of them thought unwanted sexual contact was bullying. In Year 8 fewer pupils (31.5%) stated it was sexual harassment and 52.6% thought it was both bullying and sexual harassment. This difference may be due in part to the fact that Years 7 and 8 had taken part in discussions about bullying during tutorial time and were more aware of the different forms bullying can take. It could also be that most Year 10 girls considered unwanted sexual contact to be sexual harassment because they are older and more conscious of their sexuality and had different experiences from the younger girls. They are perhaps more likely to regard unwanted physical contact as sexual harassment because their self-concept and sexual identity is more developed.

Again there was a difference between the age groups when considering verbal sexual terms. In Year 8, 68.4% of pupils thought name-calling was bullying and 5.2% thought it was sexual harassment. A larger number of girls in Year 10 thought that verbal sexual terms were sexual harassment (53.1%) and 34.3% thought that it was bullying.

Interestingly, none of the total sample considered performing 'favours' in order to protect one's name or reputation to be sexual harassment. The majority of Year 8 pupils (84.2%) and Year 10 pupils (78.1%) stated that it was bullying and 15.6% of Year 10 pupils thought that it was both bullying and sexual harassment. Mahoney (1985) documents incidents of 'servicing' which she argues is a form of sexual harassment resulting in humiliation and oppression for the girls. Here, the boys control the girls whilst extracting a service from them. Girls provide services such as homework, 'lending' money, providing food or school equipment. In return for these 'services' the girls have a 'good name or reputation'.

The majority of the total sample (52.9%) thought that being teased or embarrassed by female pin-ups was neither sexual harassment nor bullying, but more Year 8 pupils (31.5%) stated that it was sexual harassment than Year 10 pupils (21.8%).

The last question referred to unwanted comments about female sexuality. Here, pupils were more divided. Out of the total sample, 33.3% said it was sexual harassment, 21.5% bullying, 23.5% both and 21.5% neither. Between the age groups more Year 10 pupils (25%) thought it was bullying compared with 15.7% of Year 8 pupils.

▰▰ Is it? … or isn't it?

The results indicate that there is some confusion in recognising sexual harassment. Some girls do not name the behaviour as unwanted because they have become inured to it, e.g. being shown pin-ups, comments about their sexuality. This is perhaps because some people consider such behaviour as 'normal' male behaviour – sexual comments, wolf-whistles, touches, are men/boys just showing their appreciation of females. However, such behaviour is learned through socialisation and consequently it is possible to change attitudes and for men to behave differently and understand that for many women such attention is unwanted.

Roles for women and men are defined through socialisation. Social conditioning creates an artificial division between women and men.

'Typical' masculine and feminine traits often fall into stereotyped categories. For example, some 'typical' female characteristics include being submissive, gentle, emotional, sensitive, attractive, caring. On the other hand, 'typical' male characteristics include being sexually interested, aggressive, strong, unemotional, ambitious and rational. Although these stereotypical traits may not be true they become embedded in society and regarded as normal or typical.

These gender characteristics and behaviours are learned from role-models and from constant reinforcement, in the media and elsewhere. These are the images which young girls and boys aspire to and by learning to display the appropriate characteristics they feel a sense of belonging to and identification with their gender group. Failure to conform to assigned gender characteristics often results in being thought of as 'unnatural'.

◼ Offensive sexual terms

Question 3 asked girls to state which sexual terms (e.g. 'slag', 'bitch') they found most offensive and why. Many of the girls listed more than one term stating that they found them equally offensive. Responses to this question suggested that the names which pupils found most offensive were names which referred to their sexual reputations, like slag, whore, lezzie and were therefore very personal, rather than names which referred to their sexuality, like cunt, bitch. More of the younger pupils found being called a lesbian more offensive than the older pupils. This may be because many pubescent girls are very conscious about their appearance and developing bodies and do not wish to appear different sexually from other girls.

When girls are faced with sexual abuse they react by denying the accusation rather than objecting to the use of the category – it is important for a girl to prove that she is not a slag or a prostitute or a lesbian. As Lees (1987) points out, the language of 'slag' forms part of a discourse on sexuality that is characterised by a double standard. It is natural for boys to be after one thing in their relationships with girls – sex. A boy needs sex and it is acceptable for him to harass a girl – this is seen as 'natural' behaviour for a boy. Yet if a girl initiates sex or is seen to want sex then she is regarded as cheap or dirty. This double standard was recognised by some of the girls in the study who were angry at the way some men treat women but nevertheless do not question categories such as 'slag', 'bitch' etc.

■ Victims of sexual harassment

Question 4 asked the girls if they had repeatedly been called offensive names such as slag or bitch in school. Out of the total sample 68.6% reported that they had been victims of verbal abuse, with no difference between Year 8 (68.4%) and Year 10 (68.7%). Of the five examples of sexual harassment given in the questionnaire, verbal abuse was the one experienced by most pupils. Not surprisingly, in a single-sex school none of the girls reported having been embarrassed by female pin-ups or avoided places where boys gather. Two girls reported having been harassed by unwanted male physical contact in school and one girl reported having to perform a 'favour' in order to keep her reputation.

These results would suggest that verbal abuse was the most common form of sexual harassment in the school and that girls in single-sex schools use these terms extensively. As mentioned earlier, language plays a crucial role in male control and harassment is another way of exerting power. Harassment is a way of making girls feel inferior and of curtailing their power. Arnot (1987) argues that one way in which boys maintain the superiority of masculinity is by devaluing the female world and constructing gender categories which seek to do this, e.g. slags, lezzies, too tight. As Lees (1987) points out:

> 'This language is used by boys about girls and by girls about one another. Everyone is caught up in it. It determines how sexuality is talked about and displayed as a central feature of the social life of adolescents. It is reproduced as much by the social relations of the classroom as those of the disco.'

■ What did pupils consider sexual harassment?

Finally, the girls were asked to write down acts which they considered to be sexual harassment. Many wrote down several different behaviours. Most of the sample, 37 pupils (72.5%), thought that unwanted physical contact was sexual harassment, with 32.2% listing verbal abuse. Some pupils (21.5%) included rape in their answers. Four pupils answered that sexual harassment was being repeatedly asked or 'hassled' for sex. Thus for some pupils sexual harassment was regarded as falling into only one or two of the categories mentioned above whilst others regarded most or all of them to be sexual harassment.

Herbert (1989), draws attention to the fact that the criteria for sexual harassment have not been adequately clarified or recognised. Even by the mid–1980s researchers were describing behaviours which were clearly sexual harassment (e.g. demoralising statements from men teachers, sexually orientated remarks and aggressive male behaviour in the form of annoying touches) yet the term sexual harassment was not used. Thus there is confusion because the literature describes behaviours which clearly describe sexual harassment yet these are often ignored or described as 'typical' or acceptable male behaviour:

> 'Whilst definitions of sexual harassment remain uncontested or contradictory, gaps occur through which sexual harassers or sexually harassing behaviour may pass unnoticed or uncontested. Unclear definitions enable the practice to continue, for specific cases go unrecognised or unremarked.' (Herbert, 1989).

It is also important to recognise that although sexual harassment is an experience of which most girls are aware it does affect them in different ways depending on their class, race and sexuality. The confusion which arises from sexual harassment not being clearly defined and its effects on different girls is echoed in the responses of one of the pupils: 'Wolf whistles can be complimentary but when comments such as "I want to fuck you" are expressed then they become harassment.'

▉ What does this study tell us?

These findings reveal that sexual harassment, especially in the form of verbal abuse, is a serious problem for many girls. Many feminist writers have documented the experiences of girls in mixed-sex classrooms (Spender, 1982; Arnot, 1987) and point out that harassment is a means of acquiring power. One disturbing aspect of boys' harassment of girls is the effect this has on girls' self-esteem and academic attainment. However, it is becoming apparent that bullying is a feature in all-girls schools although it is different and may not be as physically aggressive as male bullying. Writers have long since pointed to an educational system which is not only middle class but also patriarchal, promoting male culture and male values and geared to the labour market. The verbal denigration and sexual subordination of girls is attributed to an educational system in which

> 'Mixed schools serve to support boys as they practise their sexual domination over girls and it attempts to teach girls that it is

"natural" for them to be tyrannised by men into a subordinate position' (Jones, 1985).

Although the sample in this study was limited there is no reason to believe that the school is atypical and the findings suggest that boys' attempts to assert their power over girls by the construction of gender categories and verbal abuse are not confined to mixed-sex schooling. These strategies are so pervasive that they are promoted by girls in single-sex schools who use them to acquire power and status with their classmates. Thus there are some groups of girls within single-sex schools who are victims of bullying in the form of sexual harassment in much the same way as girls attending mixed schools.

What might be the response?

Clearly then the answer to this type of bullying does not lie in single-sex schools as findings suggest that girls in an all-female environment are not protected from abuse and harassment. Arnot (1987) points out that notions of masculinity in this society need to be challenged but the answer does not lie in either mixed-sex or single-sex schools. She suggests that in the short term there should be programmes produced for reducing sexism in both types of schools and removing gender as an organising variable in the long term. Similarly, Keise (1992), found that all-girls schools were not necessarily a 'safe haven'.

> 'Whilst single-sex schools are generally far "safer" environments for girls in terms of avoiding sexual harassment from male students, girls-only schools can be just as unsafe for certain groups of girls in terms of behavioural problems and particularly bullying and harassment.'

Of course, to take on patriarchy and change education requires radical changes and such challenges to the existing power will undoubtedly meet resistance. However, one of the ways this will be achieved in schools is to empower girls through increased self-esteem, motivation and respect for members of their own sex – then they will be better able to challenge successfully prevailing attitudes.

Another finding from the study indicated that there is some confusion, firstly, in recognising sexual harassment and, secondly, in naming it. Often the distinction between sexual harassment and general unacceptable behaviour is not clear and the invisibility of sexual harassment will continue unless girls can name it and challenge it directly. The problem is compounded further because girls respond differently to sexual harassment depending on their race, class and sexuality.

What can teachers do?

Teacher intervention is an important factor in helping to eliminate sexual harassment in schools. Verbal sexual abuse whether directed at girls by boys or between girls needs to be challenged directly.

In previous research (Drouet, 1991) I compared pupils' and teachers' understandings of bullying behaviour and found that there were differences in how various bullying behaviours were rated. The study also looked at male and female teachers' understandings of bullying behaviour and found that male teachers tended to rate the more psychological types of behaviour described as more typically 'female' bullying (e.g. exclusion, spreading rumours, sent to Coventry) as being less serious than physical aggression or racist name-calling. Having taught in several schools (both mixed and single-sex) I have noticed that some incidents of bullying (e.g. racist abuse and racist name-calling or demanding money) are dealt with swiftly. But, often, pupils' complaints of verbal sexual abuse do not receive as much attention. Therefore, raising teachers' awareness is important if sexual harassment and verbal sexual abuse is to be challenged and victims feel that they will be supported.

A whole-school approach

Studies have shown that sexual harassment is a problem for many girls whether in mixed-sex schools or all-girls schools though it may take different forms. It is now widely accepted that schools can be effective in promoting good work and behaviour and where schools recognise that sexual harassment is a problem they can do something about it. If a school is serious in addressing the problem of sexual harassment and developing a whole-school approach there are several things to be considered.

Identifying the problem

It is important to find out *which kinds of sexual harassment* are causing most concern, e.g. intimidation by physical, verbal or written insults. This can be done through discussion and/or questionnaires to both staff and pupils. This study has shown that there is some confusion in identifying different types of sexual harassment and differences in categorising the behaviours into sexual harassment or bullying. Therefore it is up to individual schools to distinguish between the different types of sexist behaviour in their schools and clearly identify them in their policy so that everyone is aware which behaviours are unacceptable.

This raises other questions. For example, a sexual attack or assault may occur only once and therefore can be considered as bullying as many definitions of bullying require the attack – whether physical, verbal or psychological to be *repeated* attacks? The perception of the victim is important here. There is always the fear that it might happen again and the same is true of other types of sexual harassment, such as verbal abuse. Bullying and sexual harassment should be regarded as a continuum of behaviour which attempts to gain power. Consequently *all* behaviour which involves boys and girls seeking to dominate others will have negative consequences and should be dealt with. I think that sexual harassment should be included in schools' anti-bullying policies firstly because:

- Regardless of the context, it is characterised by the powerful seeking dominance over the powerless.

- Even if an attack only happens once there is the ever-present fear for the victim that it might happen again.

- Written statements on sexual harassment have mainly been included in equal opportunities policies which in themselves are not often radical in their intent. Reluctant Masters (1989) notes that equal opportunities policies usually focus on equality of access, become an end in themselves or are often not enforced. They often contain what Hoffman (1986) calls 'sex neutral language' which appeals to the lowest common denominator. Thus they are not policies that involve radical change and issues contained within them can become marginalised.

How to respond

- Raising the awareness of staff is crucial. Staff need to clarify their own views if they are to deal confidently with these issues. This could be achieved through in-service training and would serve the purpose not only of raising awareness but reinforcing existing positive attitudes or changing attitudes if need be.

- The school must establish a procedure for monitoring and evaluation so that the policy remains dynamic, in perpetuation and avoids stagnation.

- The school must create a climate in which pupils feel secure enough to report incidents in the knowledge that action will be taken.

- The school needs to deal with sexual harassment whenever it occurs and deal with taken-for-granted assumptions about sexuality and the structure of sexual relations in the curriculum.

- The school must commit to paper the philosophy and practice through which its policy will be effected and in a form which is easily understood by parents and pupils.

Thus there should be a bottom-up approach with leadership and support and a policy which has clear aims.

The notion of clear aims is not as straightforward as it may first appear. Hoffman (in *Reluctant Masters*, 1989) argues that we should be clear about what we are aiming for. Is the aim to eliminate the sexual harassment behaviour itself or to eliminate the inequality between men and women which gives rise to it?

> 'If inequality is the central concern what effects on status and power differences can be expected from elimination of sexual harassment? If the aim is to eliminate sexual harassment, are prohibitions on behaviour of individuals or protective procedures likely to produce the desired results or are there structural changes which would be more effective?' (Open University ILEA, 1989).

Clearly, the aim of a school policy on sexual harassment is to eliminate the behaviour and that is why it is important that the policy remains dynamic and avoids stagnation because in the absence of any real structural change, sexual harassment and bullying will continue to be present in our schools and it needs to be reduced to a minimum.

14 Bullying and children with special educational needs

Dabie Nabuzoka, Irene Whitney, Peter K. Smith and
David Thompson

Who are children with special needs and how may they be more vulnerable to bullying than other children? Some children, those who have been given a formal statement of special needs by the LEA, are clearly identifiable. These would probably constitute about 2% of the total school population of an LEA, though there is likely to be fewer than this proportion in a 'typical' school in a 'typical' LEA, as a number of these children will be educated in segregated provision elsewhere.

Many of these 'statemented' children, however, would be only slightly different from a number of other children in school – those others in the 18% identified by the Warnock Report as likely to need some special help at some point in their school career. In this sense the ideas and procedures developed for the 2% of statemented children will probably be very helpful for the other children who do not have a statement but behave similarly, and who claim similar concern from the adults around them.

One potential complication in considering the interaction between possessing SEN and being involved in bullying incidents is that a large minority of the 2% statemented children will have special needs primarily in the emotional and behavioural areas, that is, they are likely to show disturbed and disturbing behaviours. These children presumably will be involved in conflict situations, some of which may be bullying, often to a greater degree than other children. The main studies discussed here, however, did *not* involve many children with such types of statement, they were concerned with children who primarily had learning difficulties of one sort or another. This needs to be remembered when interpreting the findings. If the samples *had* included many children with emotional and behavioural needs, incidences of bully/victim problems reported would almost certainly have been higher.

▓▓▓ Children with special educational needs and school bullying

There are at least three likely factors which may enhance the risk of an SEN child being a victim of school bullying:

- Particular characteristics such as clumsiness, dyslexia or other disability, may be used as a pretext for bullying.

- An SEN child in an integrated setting may be less well integrated socially and lack the protection against bullying which friendship gives.

- Some children with behavioural problems may act out in an aggressive way and become 'provocative victims'. These last might also contribute to a raised incidence of bullying in children with SEN, since 'provocative victims' are often also seen as bullies by classmates.

Rather little research has been carried out specifically to examine whether this is the case, but two earlier studies suggest cause for concern. In a study of four Dublin schools, O'Moore and Hillery (1989) gave questionnaires on bullying to 783 pupils. Of these, 35 were attending special classes full time and 109 were attending remedial classes. They found that children in the special and remedial classes were more likely to be victims of bullying; this was especially true of frequent bullying ('once a week or more'), which was reported by 12% of special and remedial class children compared to 7% of non-remedial children. Differences in being a bully were not so obvious or consistent.

Martlew and Hodson (1991) compared 10 children with mild learning difficulties with 10 mainstream children matched for age and sex, in a mainstream school with an integrated resource unit for children with mild learning difficulties (MLD). Observations were made on children in the playground in both schools. Mainstream children interacted with each other, both in pairs and in groups, rather than with the children with learning difficulties. When the children with learning difficulties were with a group they tended to remain on the periphery. The MLD children were further compared with 17 children with mild learning difficulties from a special school; no difference in the patterns of interaction of the children with learning difficulties in the mainstream and in the special school were observed.

Generally, research suggests that being alone at playtime or not having many friends is a risk factor for being a victim of bullying. In this study, self reports on teasing, bullying and friendships were obtained from the children in the mainstream school; these showed that the children with learning difficulties were teased significantly more than mainstream children, and also formed fewer friendships.

▓▓▓ The Sheffield experience

As part of the ongoing research programme into bullying in Sheffield, we decided to look more closely at the probable increased risk of involvement of SEN children. Visits to five special schools within the Sheffield area, discussing the survey service and bully/victim problems, showed that this concern was likely to be justified. The head of one school for children with moderate learning difficulties indicated that children who had come to the school and had been bullied in mainstream schools, tended to retaliate first by bullying other children. In addition, these children were seen as victims of bullying usually because of their learning difficulties, or as a result of their social or emotional problems.

At a centre for young people classified as having 'school phobia' the head was of the view that although a phobia such as school phobia is classified as an irrational fear, there are many aspects of schooling where a fear reaction is not at all an irrational response. Such fear-inducing experiences included what was seen as bullying, intimidation and ridicule which some of their pupils had experienced. Children who were vulnerable in some way because of learning difficulties, lack of social skills or had some kind of illness, were regarded as especially at risk.

In this chapter we report some results from two more detailed studies. One, by Dabie Nabuzoka, used nominations from peers and teachers. The other, by Irene Whitney, Peter Smith and David Thompson, used in-depth semi-structured interviews. In both cases, we can report on the incidence of bully/victim problems in children with or without SEN, and relate to teacher perceptions.

▓▓▓ Are SEN children at greater risk of involvement in bully/victim problems?

The study by Dabie Nabuzoka looked at social relationships of children in two schools with integrated resources in Sheffield. These children were aged 8:0 to 11:8 years. Of 179 children interviewed, 36 had been statemented as having special educational needs defined as moderate learning difficulties. No other disabilities were involved in this particular SEN sample.

Each child was interviewed individually, and a technique known as 'peer nominations' was used. Each child was asked to name individuals from their class who they felt best fitted eight behavioural descriptions, including that of a bully and a victim. A 'bully' was described as 'someone who often picks on other children, or hits them, or teases them, or does other nasty things to them for no good reason', and a 'victim' as 'someone who often gets picked on, or hit, or teased, or has nasty things done to them by other children for no good reason'. The other behavioural nominations were of children who are 'shy', 'start fights', 'seek help', 'co-operate', 'disrupt', or are a 'leader'.

▄▄▄ What was found?

Taking children who were one standard deviation above the mean for nominations by classmates as a 'bully', Nabuzoka found 8 out of 36 children with special needs and 18 out of 143 children without special needs selected as bullies. The percentage is higher for special needs children (22% compared to 13%) but the difference is not statistically reliable.

Taking children one standard deviation above the mean for nominations as a 'victim', he found 12 out of 36 children with special needs and 11 out of 143 children without special needs selected as victims. Children with special needs (33%) were highly significantly more likely to be selected as victims than were those without any special needs (8%).

Two other findings were of interest. Although in the non-SEN sample boys were more likely to be bullies but boys and girls about equally likely to be victims (similar to what was found in the large Sheffield survey, Whitney and Smith, 1993) the indications from the SEN sample were that girls were as likely to be bullies as boys and more likely to be victims; that is, girls with SEN were over-represented in bully/victim problems in comparison to the normal gender difference. Secondly, Dabie Nabuzoka looked at 'bully/victims' – children one standard deviation above the mean for both 'bully' and 'victim'. These are likely to be children who are provocative and aggressive, being perceived as bullies and also getting victimised. Of the six children in his sample who fitted this category, four were in his SEN group.

▰▰▰ What do other children think?

Are bullies and victims seen differently by other children, in the case of children with SEN? It seems probably not. The correlations, or degree of association, between bully and victim nominations, and the other behavioural nominations, were calculated separately for the children with, and without, special needs. The picture is very similar for both groups. Bullies were seen as being disruptive and starting fights; victims as being shy and needing help.

Although correlation does not necessarily imply a causal relationship, the findings show that those children regarded as 'shy' and/or 'often in need of help' also tend to be victims of bullying. The similarity in the strength of relationship of being a victim and either 'shy' or/and one who 'often seeks help', between the sample of SEN children and the rest, probably means that the same criterion of vulnerability (implied by shyness and needing help) tends to be used to victimise other children whether they have special needs or not. On the other hand, these SEN children were more likely to be selected as victims of bullying than non-statemented children. A common factor here may be lack of friendships and protective peer relationships, which are generally found to be less in SEN children. Indeed, Nabuzoka found SEN children to be less popular and more rejected than non-SEN peers, a finding similar to that of Martlew and Hodson (1991).

Given this background of increased risk, it seemed important to consider children with SEN as part of the larger DFE-funded Sheffield Bullying Project (see Sharp and Smith, Chapter 4). With a grant from the Economic and Social Research Council, we examined whether the increased risks associated with SEN would be confirmed when SEN and non-SEN children were closely matched for age, gender and ethnicity. In addition, with a larger sample, we could see whether the risk was associated with different kinds of special educational needs. Finally, the effectiveness of intervention strategies against bullying, used for mainstream children, could be evaluated for SEN children.

▰▰▰ Work within the Sheffield Bullying Project

This research was carried out with children from eight schools participating in the DFE project, which have integrated resources for statemented children. The five secondary schools have integrated resources for special educational needs (1), moderate learning difficulties (2), hearing impaired children (1) and visually impaired children (1).

The three junior/middle schools have integrated resources for moderate learning difficulties (1), children with mild learning difficulties (1) and children with hearing impairments (1).

A sample of 93 children with SEN, and 93 children without SEN matched closely for age, ethnicity and gender, were interviewed in October/November 1991. The teacher at each school who knew each child best was also interviewed. The interviews were semi-structured, designed to explore both the child's perception of their relationships with peers, their feelings about the school, and whether or not they were involved in bullying or were being bullied. In the case of the teacher, the interview followed a similar format but primarily exploring what they thought the child was experiencing.

A second set of interviews was carried out with the children with SEN only and their teachers in May/June 1992. During the year there were planned interventions designed to reduce bullying problems within these schools (via the DFE-funded project). These second interviews focused on how these interventions had affected the child (as perceived by the child, and by their teacher), as well as whether any involvement in bully/victim problems had been reduced. These results are currently being analysed. Here, we report some findings from the first set of interviews.

Some of the findings

One of our findings was very clear; this study again confirmed that children with SEN were significantly more likely to bullied than mainstream children (MS). In response to a query about whether there was anyone at school who bullied them or was nasty to them, 65% of the SEN children who were interviewed said 'yes', compared to 30% of the MS children. The difference was particularly great for children in secondary schools; although the risk of being a victim generally is less in secondary schools than in junior/middle schools (Whitney and Smith, 1993), this decrease is rather small in the case of children with SEN.

SEN children were more likely to bully others than MS children but this was only appreciable for boys in secondary schools. These children tended to comment that they only bullied others in retaliation for being bullied. However, we found that this was also true of MS children who admitted to bullying others. Thus, with only a couple of exceptions, all children who admitted to bullying others also claimed to have been bullied by others. This may of course reveal some distortion in the self-report data (children who bully others justifying themselves); or it may reflect some truth of the situation in these classrooms. In any event, this data on 'bully/victims' could not be compared on the same basis as that obtained by Nabuzoka from peer nominations.

It was also interesting to note that at junior/middle school girls with SEN have a relatively greater risk of involvement in both bully and victim problems compared with girls with no SEN; that is, the usual gender difference is less in the case of children with SEN. This confirmed Nabuzoka's findings, which were carried out at different schools and used a different method of data collection. However, this trend was not observed at secondary schools.

As before, we found that children with SEN had fewer friends in school than other children. In general, most children in our samples reported having 'many' friends; but children with SEN were more likely to report having only 'two or three' friends, and nine children with SEN reported having only 'one' or 'none' compared with one matched MS child.

What can be done?

These studies show that SEN children are at greater risk for being bullied, if not for bullying others. It can also be said that being bullied, and indeed bullying others, is indicative of some lack of social skills. Almost everyone has been treated, or treated others, harshly. But different individuals have different capacities for coping with it so that some reactions may in fact reinforce the behaviour of the bully. For the bully, it becomes an easy way of fulfilling their desires without the rigours of interpersonal negotiation.

Teaching assertiveness and other social skills is one way of overcoming the problem for both the victim and the bully. The former can be taught things like how to say 'no', how to get help and also not be afraid to do what they want to do. The bullies can also be taught how to cope with their frustrations and to appreciate the needs of others in the same way they would like their needs to be appreciated.

However, in order to target specific intervention programmes at particular children, the need for such targeting needs to be identified. School teachers need to be able to identify which children are at particular risk for bullying others and which are at risk for victimisation. Children with special needs seem to be particularly at risk for victimisation. There are also some indications that they may be over-represented as bullies and bully-victims.

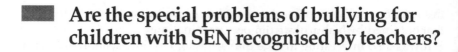

Are the special problems of bullying for children with SEN recognised by teachers?

This question is tied in with that of the general recognition of bullying. In the past, an unfortunately common reaction by school authorities has been to deny the existence of bullying in their school or to downplay its significance. Also, it may be difficult for teachers to be fully aware of the extent of bullying. Much occurs in school playgrounds, during mid-morning and lunchtime breaks (Whitney and Smith, 1993); since teachers normally do not supervise these, they may remain unaware of a lot of bullying which is going on there.

Yet, a child who is preoccupied with being bullied is often unable to concentrate on his or her lessons. For children with, for example, learning disabilities this places an additional burden on an already difficult task. Being able to recognise a problem of bullying for a particular child can therefore help the teacher to have a clearer picture as to the factors contributing to a child's overall learning difficulties. There may be a special need to help SEN children initiate and maintain relationships, and develop coping strategies against teasing and bullying.

Looking at teachers' perceptions

Both our studies yielded comparisons of teacher perceptions of bullying with those of peers. Nabuzoka asked the class teachers to rate 112 of the original 179 children (92 mainstream, 20 with special needs) whose peer nominations had been collected on bully and victim descriptions and six other behaviour descriptions. The same descriptions used by peers were given to the teachers to determine whether teacher perceptions differed from those of the children. As with peer nominations, the correlations, or degree of association, between bully and victim ratings, and the other behavioural nominations, were calculated.

Comparing teachers with peers, the picture was fairly similar for children involved in bullying. Those children scoring high as bullies also scored high as disruptive and starting fights, but low on shyness (especially for teachers). However, there were some marked differences with regards to children perceived as victims. Whereas peers regarded victims as 'shy', as well as 'seeking help', teachers did not. Instead, they tended to see victims as 'starting fights' (which peers did not). Separate calculations showed that the teachers did (like peers), significantly rate children with SEN as more 'shy' and 'seeking help' than children without SEN. The lack of association between being a victim of bullying and these behavioural characteristics of being 'shy' and 'seeking help' by teachers may either indicate that teachers are not aware of some factors putting certain children at risk for victimisation, or that in some ways they tend to 'blame' victims more than peers do for their predicament.

Whereas peers provided very similar correlations for non-SEN and SEN children (as regards bullies and victims), teachers did not always do so. Teachers saw children involved either as bullies or as victims as uncooperative, *except* for children with SEN. They also saw children with SEN who were victims as not being shy. Whether these differences lie in the teachers' perceptions or the realities of the situation are difficult to say but they were not perceived by peers; this does suggest it is influenced by the labelling of a child as SEN, which the teachers would be more aware of than the pupils.

Comparing teacher and peer perceptions

The study by Whitney, Smith and Thompson yielded a very direct comparison of teacher and peer perceptions; the interview with each child with SEN could be matched with an interview by the teacher who knew that child best. The teacher's perceptions of the extent to which children with SEN were being bullied and the children's own perceptions, differed significantly. Teachers tended to underestimate how often children with SEN were being bullied. However, the difference was only marked for children who are bullied in junior/middle schools; teachers in secondary schools were relatively accurate at estimating the extent of bullying for children with SEN. Teachers in both sectors were also relatively accurate as regards the incidence of bullying others but, as we have seen, this is not so much of a special risk factor for children with SEN.

Teachers also tended to underestimate how many friends SEN children had in school. Whereas most children with SEN reported having two or more friends, teachers often reported them having one or no friends (27 teachers reported this, compared with 9 children). The teachers usually thought that those children with SEN who had friends mainly tended to choose other SEN children, for about two thirds of children in junior/middle schools and about half in secondary schools.

Why were children bullied?

Teachers were also asked if they thought that the children were bullied as a direct result of their SEN. The majority thought this was the case; for about 67% of such children in junior/middle schools and about 82% in secondary schools. For example the teachers commented that children were bullied because of their disability, because they were deaf, because they had a low IQ, or because they lacked social skills and were unable to mix with other children appropriately which made them victims. When the children with SEN were interviewed they were not asked if they were bullied because of any special educational needs they had, so a direct comparison could not be made here. However, the children were asked, if they had been bullied, what kind of bullying it was. Some of the children's comments did reveal that their bullying was related to the SEN. For example (pseudonyms are used throughout):

Jane: 'They used to call me names like cabbage. My spelling is not too good and when they're handing out work they'll have a quick look at mine but they don't look at other people and my writing because they know I have special needs. I don't mind but I don't like it if they laugh at me and start talking about me and play tricks on me.'

John: 'They call me a spastic.'

Elizabeth: 'In class they say "look Elizabeth's here" and they tease me and call me names all the time. Or they stand up and do impressions of me walking up and down the classroom. They also call my friend names too, because she's well built they call her "whale". Linda gets called "maggot" because she's thin but because of my disability they can't call me maggot, they can call me other names that they know would hurt me, so it's worser, but it's not just me, it's not all me.'

Playground bullying

As remarked earlier, much bullying goes on in the playground. This was true of children both with and without SEN. Three secondary schools in our sample provided a room where children with SEN could go at lunchtimes to provide a more sheltered environment; this was something we asked about specifically. One school provided a purpose-built room for children with physical disabilities to use at lunchtimes. These children were allowed to take one friend with them into this room, a child with or without SEN. Children who had SEN that were not classed as physically disabling were not allowed to use this room unless as a friend of a disabled child. The second school provided a room for all children with SEN to use at lunchtimes. These children also were allowed to take one friend, with or without SEN, in with them. The third school provided a recreational room which all children, with or without SEN, could use at lunchtimes.

Some of the children's comments as to why they used the room revealed that they did see it is a safe haven from bullying. For example:

Elizabeth: 'I use the room every dinner time. It's a place where disabled people can come in without getting knocked down outside and they can play with their friends without people pushing you and shoving and calling names.'

Sally: 'I talk to people, my friends. You sometimes get bullied in the playground but you don't get bullied in that room.'

▰ Bad news and good news

This project, together with the linked DFE project, was to give much more detailed information on categories of SEN children at particular risk, and how well interventions can be expected to work. However, even from the earlier data, it is clear that children with special needs of a learning disability type are much more likely to be involved in bullying situations at schools than matched mainstream children.

The good news is that because of the prominence of their special needs, knowledge of these children and their difficulties by the special needs staff is generally greater than might be expected for the bulk of mainstream children, and schools are beginning to provide 'extra' services and resources for them. These are primarily intended to meet their special needs but also impinge on the bullying processes in ways which can be helpful, though they could sometimes make the children more exposed. Children with emotional and behavioural difficulties are also likely to be similarly clearly identified by special needs staff.

In many respects, teachers can give an accurate report of the difficulties faced by special needs pupils. However, we have obtained evidence that teachers in junior school may underestimate the extent of bullying which children with SEN are experiencing (as teachers may do for most children – Whitney and Smith, 1993). Furthermore, teachers may also – perhaps through the very process of statementing which is designed to help such children – regard those involved in bully/victim problems as less sociable (having fewer friends) and more liable to start fights than peers perceive them. If we take peer perceptions as more veridical (and they are probably the most knowledgeable witnesses), this does suggest a need for teachers not to use the 'statemented' or 'special needs' label in ways which might prejudice their views of a particular child and his or her potential in this respect.

Two general questions remain, both crucial for schools:

- How far is the knowledge of the difficulties faced by special needs children shared by those staff with no special needs brief?
- How many of the non-statemented children who have more minor or temporary special needs are also more highly vulnerable to bullying?

Answers to these questions still need to be sought.

Dabie Nabuzoka's research has been supported by a Beit scholarship from the University of Zambia. Irene Whitney, Peter Smith and David Thompson's research has been supported by a grant from the Economic and Social Research Council.

Bibliography

ACE (1990) 'Governors and bullying', *Bulletin 34*, ACE, London

Ahmad, Y. and Smith, P.K. (1990) 'Bully/victim problems among school-children', poster paper presented at Conference of the Developmental Section of the BPS, Guildford

Ahmad, Y., Whitney, I. and Smith, P.K. (1991) 'A survey service for schools on bully/victim problems', in P.K. Smith and D.A. Thompson (eds.), *Practical Approaches to Bullying*, David Fulton

Alsaker, F. D. (1991) 'Self-degrodation as a consequence of victimisation', paper to 11th Biennial Meeting for the International Society for the Study of Behavioural Development

Alschuler, A.S. (1980) *School Discipline: A Socially Literate Solution*, McGraw-Hill, New York

Anyon, J. (1983) 'Gender, resistance and power', in S. Walker, and L. Barton (eds.) *Gender, Class and Education,* Flamer

Arbeitsgruppe Schulforschung (1980) *Leistung und versagen: alltagstheorien von Schulern und Lehern*, Juventa, Munich

Armstrong, M. (1992) 'Dull, dull, dull … ', *The Times Educational Supplement*, October

Arnot, M. and Weiner, G. (eds.) (1987) *Gender and the Politics of Schooling*, Hutchinson

Arora, T. (1991) 'The use of victim support groups', in P.K. Smith and D.A. Thompson (eds.) *Practical Approaches to Bullying*, David Fulton

Askew, S. (1988) 'Aggressive behaviour in boys: to what extent is it institutionalised?' in D. Tattum and D. Lane (eds.) *Bullying in Schools*, Trentham Books

Banton, M. (1988) 'Race', in E.E. Cashmore (ed.) *Dictionary of Race and Ethnic Relations*, 2nd edition, Routledge

Bayh, B. (1975) *Our Nation's Schools – A Report Card. 'A' in School Violence and Vandalism*, US Government Printing Office, Washington DC

Beirn, R., Kindey, D.C. and McGinn, N.F. (1972) 'Antecedents and consequences of early school leaving', *Educational Documentation and Information*, 46, 182, pp. 1–116

Besag, V. (1989) *Bullies and Victims in Schools*, Open University Press

Besag, V. (1991) 'Parents and teachers working together' in M. Elliot (ed.) *Bullying: A Practical Guide to Coping for Schools*, Longman

Bjorkvist, K., Ekman, K. and Lagerspetz, K. (1982) 'Bullies and victims: their ego picture, ideal ego picture and normative ego picture', *Scandinavian Journal of Psychology* , 23, pp. 307–313.

Blatchford, P. (1989) *Playtime in the Primary School: Problems and Improvements*, NFER-Nelson

Blatchford, P. (1992) 'Children's views on work in junior schools', *Educational Studies*, 18, 1, pp. 107–118

Blatchford, P. (in press) 'Research on children's behaviour in the UK: a review', in P. Blatchford and S. Sharp (eds.) *Breaktime in the School; Understanding and Changing Playground Behaviour*, Routledge

Blatchford, P., Cresser, R. and Mooney, A. (1990) 'Playground games and playtime: the children's view', *Educational Research*, 32, 3, pp. 163–174

Boulton, M. and Underwood, K. (1992) 'Bully/victim problems among middle school children', *British Journal of Educational Psychology*, 62, pp. 73–87

Bowers, L., Smith, P.K. and Binney, V. (1993) 'Cohesion and power in the families of children involved in bully/victim problems at schools', *Journal of Family Therapy*

Bowles, S. and Gintis, H. (1976) *Schooling in Capitalist America: Educational Reform and the Contradictions of Economic Life*, Routledge & Kegan Paul

Brier, J, and Ahmed, Y. (1991) 'Developing a school court as a means of addressing bullying in schools', in P.K. Smith and D. Thompson (eds.) *Practical Approaches to Bullying*, David Fulton

Bright, J. and Petterson, G. (1984) *The Safe Neighbourhoods Unit*, NACRO, London

Brown, F. (1990) *School playgrounds*, National Playing Fields Association

Brusten, M. and Hurrelmann, K. (1973) *Abweichendes Verhalten in der Schule: Eine Undersuchung zu Processen der Stigmatisierung*, Juventa, Munich

Chazan, M. (1988) 'Bullying in the infant school', in D. Tattum and D. Lane (eds.) *Bullying in Schools*, Trentham

Cloud, J. and Vaughan, G.M. (1970) 'Using balanced scales to control for aquiescence', *Sociometry*, 33, 2, pp. 193–202

Cohn, T. (1988) 'Sambo: a study in name calling', in E. Kelly and T. Cohn (eds.) *Racism in Schools: New Research Evidence*, Trentham Books

Commission for Racial Equality (1988) *Learning in Terror: A Survey of Racial Harassment in Schools and Colleges*, CRE

Cowie, H., Sharp, S. and Smith, P.K. (1992) 'Tackling bullying in schools: the Method of Common Concern', *Education Section Review*, 16, pp. 55–57

Craig, W.M. and Pepler, D.J. (1992) 'Contextual factors in bullying and victimization', paper presented at the Canadian Psychological Association Conference

Cronbach, L.J. (1951) 'Coefficient alpha and internal structure of tests', *Psychometrika*, 10, pp. 191–198

Damon, W. (1983) *Social and Personality Development*, Norton & Company, New York

Davies, B. (1985) *Life in the Classroom and Playground: the Accounts of Primary School Children*, Routledge & Kegan Paul

Demaine, J. (1989) 'Race, categorisation and educational achievement', *British Journal of Sociology of Education*, 10, 2, p. 195–214

Dennington, J. and Pitt, J. (1991) *Developing Services for Young People in Crisis*, Longman

DES (1990) 'The outdoor classroom: educational use, landscape design and management of school designs', *Building Bulletin 71*, HMSO

Downes, D. (1990) 'Public violence on two estates', Home Office (unpublished)

Drouet, D. (1991) 'Understandings of bullying among pupils and teachers in an inner London secondary school for girls' (unpublished M.Sc. dissertation, South Bank University, London)

Dworking, A. (1976) *Our blood*, The Women's Press

Ekman, K. (1977) *Skolemobbing (School Bullying)*, Abo Akademi, Norway

Elliott, M. (1991) *Bullying: A Practical Guide to Coping for Schools*, Longman

El-Sheik, M., Cummings, E.M. and Goetch, V.L. (1989) 'Coping with adults' angry behaviour: behavioural, physiological and verbal responses in preschoolers', *Development Psychology*, 25, pp.490–498

Elton Report (1989) *Discipline in Schools*, HMSO

Eron, L.D., Huesmann, L.R., Dubow, E., Romanoff, R. and Yarmel, P.W. (1987) 'Aggression and its correlates over 22 years', in D. Growell, I.

Evans and C. O'Donnell (eds.) *Childhood Aggression and Violence*, Plenum Press, New York

Evans, J. (1989) *Children at Play: Life in the School Playground*, Deakin Universty Press, Australia

Evans, J. (1992) 'Children's leisure patterns: the shift to organised recreation', *Recreation Australia*, 4, 4, pp. 19–28

Farrington, D.P. (1991) 'Childhood aggression and adult violence: early precursors and later-life outcomes', in D. Pelper and K. Rubin (eds.) *The Development and Treatment of Childhood Aggression*, Erlbaum, Hillsdale, N.J.

Farrington, D.P. (1993) 'Understanding and preventing bullying', in M. Tonry and N. Morris (eds.) *Crime and Justice*, Vol. 17, University of Chicago Press

Fell, G. (in press) 'The Manchester lunchtime staff project', in P. Blatchford and S. Sharp (eds.) *Breaktime in the School; Understanding and Changing Playground Behaviour*, Routledge

Fox, M., Pratt, G. and Roberts, S. (1991) 'Developing the educational psychologist's work in the secondary school: a process model in change', *Educational Psychology in Practice*, 6, pp. 163–164

Frodi, A., Macawley, J. and Thorne, P.R. (1977) 'Are women less aggressive than men? A review of the experimental literature', *Psychological Bulletin*, 84, pp. 634–660

Frost, L. (1991) 'A primary school approach – what can be done about the bully?' in M. Elliot (ed.) *Bullying: A Practical Guide to Coping for Schools*, Longman

Gillborn, D. (1990) *Race, Ethnicity and Education: Teaching and Learning in Multi-Ethnic Schools*, Unwin Hyman/Routledge

Gillborn, D. (1992a) 'Management and teachers – discipline and support', in N. Jones and E.B. Jones (eds.) *Learning to Behave, Curriculum and Whole School Management Approaches to Discipline*, Kogan Page

Gillborn, D. (1992b) 'Citizenship, "race" and the hidden curriculum', *International Studies in Sociology of Education*, 2, 1, pp. 57–73

Gillborn, D. and Drew, D. (1992) ' "Race", class and school effects', *New Community*, 18, 4, pp. 551–556

Gobey, F. (1991) 'A practical approach through drama and workshops', in P.K. Smith and D.A. Thompson (eds.) *Practical Approaches to Bullying*, David Fulton

Goldstein, H. (1987) *Multilevel Models in Education and Social Research*, Griffin

Goodnow, J. and Burns, A. (1985) *Home and School: A Child's Eye View*, Allen & Unwin, Sydney

Gordon, P. (1992a) 'Racial incidents in Britain 1988–90: a survey', *Runnymede Bulletin*, no. 254, April, pp. 7–9

Gordon, P. (1992b) 'The racialisation of statistics', in R. Skellington and P. Morris (eds.) *Race in Britain Today*, Sage

Hall, S. (1992) 'The West and the rest: discourse and power', in S. Hall and B. Gieben (eds.) *Formations of Modernity*, Polity Press

Hampshire County Council Education (1991) *Combating Racial Harassment: County Guidelines for Schools, Colleges and other Educational Establishments*, Hampshire Council

Hargreaves, D. (1967) *Social Relations in the Secondary School*, Routledge & Kegan Paul

Haselager, G.J.T. and Lieshout, C.F.M. van (1992a) 'Social and affective adjustment of self and peer-reported victims and bullies', paper presented to the fifth European Conference on Developmental Psychology

Haselager, G.J.T. and Lieshout, C.F.M. van (1992b) *Enkele voorlopige resultaten van het Nijmeegse pestproject*, Katholieke Universiteit, Vakgroep Ontwikkelingspsychologie, Nijmegan

Heinemann, P.P. (1969) 'Apartheid', *Liberal Debatt*, nr. 2., Norway

Heinemann, P.P. (1973) *Mobbing: gruppevold blant barn og voksne (Bullying: Group-Violence among Children and Adults)*, Gyldendal, Oslo

Herbert, G. (1988) 'A whole curriculum approach to bullying', in D. Tattum and D. Lane (eds.) *Bullying in Schools*, Trentham Books

Herbert, G. (1989) *Talking of Silence: The Sexual Harassment of Schoolgirls*, Falmer

Hoffman, M.L. (1977) 'Sex differences in empathy and related behaviours', *Psychological Bulletin*, 84, pp. 712–722

Hoffman, M.L. (1986) 'Sexual harassment in academia', *Harvard University Review*, 56, 2

Hohr, H. (1983) 'Mobbing – skisse til en struktur – og bevissthetsteoretisk tilnaerming (Bullying: sketch of a structural and conscious theoretical approach)', *Norsk Pedagogisk tidsskrift.*, nr. 8, Norway

Horton, A.M. (1991), "The Heartstone Odyssey": exploring the heart of bullying', in P.K. Smith and D.A. Thompson (eds.) *Practical Approaches to Bullying*, David Fulton

Huesmann, R., Eron, L., Lefkowitz, M. and Walder, L. (1984) 'Stability of aggression over time and generation', *Developmental Psychology*, 20, pp. 1120–1134

Johnson, M., Munn, P. and Edwards, L. (1991) *Action Against Bullying: a Support Pack for Schools*, The Scottish Council for Research in Education, Edinburgh

Jones, M. (1968) *The Therapeutic Community*, Penguin

Jones, C. (1985) 'Sexual tyranny: male violence in a mixed school', in G. Weiner (ed.) *Just a Bunch of Girls*, Open University

Karabel, J. and Halsey, J. (eds.) (1977) *Power and Ideology in Education*, Oxford University Press, New York

Kazdin, A.E. (1987) 'Treatment of antisocial behaviour in children: current status and future directions', *Psychological Bulletin*, 102, pp. 187–203

Keise, C. (1992) *Sugar and Spice? Bullying in Single-Sex Schools'*, Trentham Books

Kelly, E. and Cohn, T. (1988) *Racism in Schools: New Research Evidence*, Trentham Books

Knox, P. (1988) *Troubled Children: A Fresh Look at School Phobia*, Pat Knox, Holyhead

La Fontaine, J. (1991) *Bullying: A Child's View*, Calouste Gulberkian Foundation, London

Landelijk Centrum GVO (1992) *Pesten op school aangepakt. Overzicht van lesmateriaal en achtergronginformatie*, Utrecht

Lane, D.A. (1988) 'Violent histories: bullying and criminality', in D. Tattum and D. Lane (eds.) *Bullying in Schools*, Trentham Books

Lagerspetz, K.M., Bjorkqvist, K., Berts, M. and King, E. (1982) 'Group aggression among school children in three schools', *Scandinavian Journal of Psychology*, 23, pp. 45–52

Laslett, R. (1980) 'Bullies: a children's court in a day school for maladjusted children', *British Columbia Journal of Special Education*, 4, pp. 391–397

Laslett, R. (1982) 'A children's court for bullies' *Special Education*, 9, 1, pp. 9–11

Lees, S. (1987) 'The structure of sexual relations in schools', in M. Arnot and G. Weiner (eds.) *Gender and the Politics of Schooling*, Hutchinson

Le Lohe, M.J. (1992) 'Political issues: the asylum bill: the role of tabloids', *New Community*, 18, 3, pp. 469–474

Lerner, M.J. (1980) *Belief in a Just World: A Fundamental Decision*, Plenum Press, New York

Lewin, K., Lippitt, R. and White, R.K. (1939) 'Patterns of aggressive behaviour in experimentally created social climates', *Journal of Social Psychology*, 10, pp. 271–299

Lowenstein, L.F. (1991) 'The study, diagnosis and treatment of bullying in a therapeutic community' in M. Elliott (ed.) *Bullying: A Practical Guide to Coping for Schools*, Longman

MacDonald, I., Bhavnani, R., Kahn, L. and John, G. (1989) *Murder in the Playground: the Report of the MacDonald Inquiry into Racism and Racist Violence in Manchester Schools*, Longsight Press

Mahoney, P. (1985) *Schools for the Boys*, Hutchinson

Marland, M. (1989) *The Tutor and the Tutor Group*, Longman

Marsh, P., Rosser, E. and Herre´, R. (1978) *The Rules of Disorder*, Routledge & Kegan Paul

Martlew, M. and Hodson, J. (1991) 'Children with mild learning difficulties in an integrated and in a special school: comparisons of behaviour, teasing and teachers' attitudes', *British Journal of Educational Psychology*, 61, pp. 355–372

Massey, I. (1991) *More than skin deep: Developing Anti-Racist Multicultural Education in Schools*, Hodder & Stoughton

Mathiesen, T. (1964) *The Defences of the Weak*, Tavistock Press

Measor, L. and Woods, P. (1984) *Changing Schools: Pupil Perspectives on Transfer to a Comprehensive*, Open University Press

Meer, B. van der (1988) *De zondebok in de klas*, Den Bosch/Nijmegan: KPC/Berkhout

Mellor, A. (1990) 'Bullying in Scottish secondary schools', *Spotlights*, No. 23, Scottish Council for Research in Education

Mooij, T. (1979) *Probleemanalyse van het voortijdig schoolverlaten in het ibo, mavo, havo en vwo*, Instituut voor Toegepaste Sociologie, Nijmegen

Mooij, T. (1980) 'Schoolproblemen en uitva in het voortgezet onderwijs', *Pedagogische Studien*, 57, pp. 369–382

Mooij, T. (1982) 'Onderwijsleersituatie en lesondergravend gedrag van lto-leerlingen', in E. Diekerhof (ed.) *Leren, wat moet je ermee?* Coutinho, Muiderberg

Mooij, T. (1987) *Interactional Multi-Level Investigation into Pupil Behaviour, Achievement, Competence and Orientation in Educational Situations*, SVO, 's-Gravenhage

Mooij, T. (1992a) *Pesten in het onderwijs*, Katholieke Universiteit, Instituut voor Toegepaste Sociale wetenschappen, Nijmegen

Mooij, T. (1992b) 'Predicting (under)achievement of gifted children', *European Journal for High Ability*, 3, pp. 59–74

Mooij, T. (1992c) *Geweld in het voortgezet onderwijs (onderzoeksvoorstel)*, Katholieke Universiteit, Instituut voor Toegepaste Sociale wetenschappen, Nijmegen

Mooney, A., Cresser, R. and Blatchford, P. (1991) 'Children's views on teasing and fighting in junior schools, *Educational Research*, 33, 2, pp. 103–112

Mulder, M. (1977) *Omgaan met macht*, Elsevier, Amsterdam

Mykletun, R.J. (1979) *Plaging i skolen (Bullying in School)*, Rogalandsforskning, Stavanger

NACRO (1988) *The Gold Links Project*, NACRO, London

National Curriculum Council (1989) 'The National Curriculum and whole curriculum planning', *Circular No. 6*, NCC

Newcastle Education Committee (1990) *Newcastle upon Tyne Midday Supervision Training Package*, Newcastle upon Tyne Education Department

Newham Council Education (1991) *In-Service Training Pack: Responding to Racial Harassment for Primary and Secondary Teachers*, Newham Council, London

Newson, J. and Newson, E. (1984) 'Parent's perspectives on children's behaviour in school', in N. Frude and H. Gault (eds.) *Disruptive Behaviour in Schools*, Wiley

Newton, P. (1993) 'Malvern Girls College', in D. Tattum and G. Herbert (eds.) *Countering Bullying: Initiatives by Schools and Local Authorities*, Trentham Books

Olweus, D. (1978) *Aggression in the Schools: Bullies and Whipping Boys*, Hempishere Press, Washington DC

Olweus, D. (1980) 'Familial and tempermental determinants of aggressive behaviour in adolescent boys: a causal analysis', *Development Psychology*, 16, pp. 644–660

Olweus, D. (1981) 'Bullying among school-boys', in N. Cantwell (ed.) *Children and Violence*. Akademilitteratur, Stockholm

Olweus, D. (1984) 'Aggressors and their victims: bullying at school', in N. Frude and H. Gault (eds.) *Disruptive Behaviour in Schools*, Wiley, New York

Olweus, D. (1985) '80,000 elever innblandet i mobbing (80,000 pupils involved in bullying)', *Norsk Skoleblad*, nr. 2, Norway

Olweus, D. (1987a) 'Bully/victim problems among school children in Scandinavia', in J.P. Myklebust and R. Ommundsen (eds.) *Psykologprofesjonen mot ar 2000*, pp. 395–413, Universitetsforlaget, Oslo

Olweus, D. (1987b) 'Schoolyard bullying: grounds for intervention', *School Safety*, 6, pp. 4–11

Olweus, D. (1989a) 'Bully/victim problems among school children: basic facts and effects of a school-based intervention program', in K. Rubin and D. Pepler (eds.) *The Development and Treatment of Childhood Aggression*. Erlbaum, Hillsdale, N.J.

Olweus, D. (1989b) 'Questionnaire for students' (Junior and senior versions. Unpublished manuscript)

Olweus, D. (1990) 'Bullying among school children', in K. Hurrelmann and F. Losel (eds.) *Health Hazards in Adolescence*, De Gruyter, Berlin

Olweus, D. (1992) 'Bullying at school: What we know and what we can do' (unpublished manuscript)

Olweus, D. and Roland, E. (1983) *Mobbing – bakgrunn og tiltak. (Bullying: Background and Management)* Kirke-og undervisningsdepartmentet, Oslo

O'Moore, A.M. and Hillery, B. (1989) 'Bullying in Dublin schools', *The Irish Journal of Psychology*, 10, 3, pp. 426–441

O'Moore, A.M. and Hillery, B. (1991) 'What do teachers need to know', in M. Elliot (ed.) *Bullying: A Practical Guide to Coping for Schools*, Longman

Open University ILEA (1989) 'Reluctant masters: Can't we find a better word?' London, Reprographics Service

Opie, I. and Opie, P. (1969) *Children's Games in Street and Playground*, Oxford University Press

OPTIS (Oxford Programme to Training, Instruction and Supervision) (1987) *Lunchtime Supervision*, OPTIS

Osborn, A.F., Butler, N.R. and Morris, A.C. (1984) *The Social Life of Britain's Five-Year-Olds*, Routledge & Kegan Paul

Palmer, F. (ed.) (1986) *Anti-Racism: An Assult on Education and Value*, Sherwood Press

Pease, K. (1991) 'The Kirkholt Project: preventing burglary on a British public housing estate', *Security Journal*, 2, 2

Perry, D.G., Kusel, S.J. and Perry, L.C. (1988) 'Victims of peer aggression', *Developmental Psychology*, 24, 6, pp. 807–814

Pikas, A. (1976) *Slik stopper vi mobbing (The Way to Stop Bullying)*, Gyldendal, Oslo

Pikas, A. (1989) 'The common concern method for the treatment of mobbing', in E. Roland and E. Munthe (eds.) *Bullying: An International Perspective*. David Fulton

Pitt, J. (1991) 'Action research on racial harassment in Portsmouth schools', *South East Hampshire Intercultural Support Group Newsletter*, no. 3, pp. 9–13

Pitt, J. (1993) 'Thereotyping: anti-racism, criminology and black young people', in D. Cook and B. Hudson (eds.) *Racism and Criminology*

Power, M.J., Benn, R.T. and Norris, J.N. (1982) 'Neighbourhood, school and juveniles before the courts', *British Journal*, 12, pp. 111–132

Pring, R. (1984) *Personal and Social Education in the Curriculum*, Hodder & Stoughton

Purkey, C.S. and Smith, M.S. (1982) 'Too soon to cheer? Synthesis of research of effective schools', *Educational Leadership*, December, pp. 64–69

Rattansi, A. (1992) 'Changing the subject? Racism, culture and education', in J. Donald and A. Rattansi (eds.) *Race and Immigration: Culture and Difference*, Sage

Reich, C. and Young, V. (1975) 'Patterns of dropping out', *Interchange*, 6,4, pp. 6–15

Reid, K. (1988) 'Bullying and persistent school absenteeism', in D. Tattum and D. Lane (eds.) *Bullying in Schools*, Trentham Books

Rigby, K. and Black, G. (1992) 'Students' attitudes to children who complain about being bullied', (unpublished manuscript)

Rigby, K. and Slee, P.T. (1990) 'Victims and bullies in school communities', *Journal of the Australian Society of Criminology*, 1, 2, pp. 23–28

Rigby, K. and Slee, P.T. (1991) 'Bullying among Australian school children: reported behaviour and attitudes to victims', *Journal of Social Psychology*, 131,5, pp. 615–627

Rigby, K. and Slee, P.T. (1992) 'Dimensions of interpersonal relations among Australian school children: implications for psychological well-being', *Journal of Social Psychology*

Robbins, D. (1989) *Child Care Policy: Putting it in Writing*, HMSO

Roderick, T. (1988) 'Johnny can learn to negotiate', *Educational Leadership*, 45,4, pp. 86–90

Roland, E. (1980) *Terror i skolen (Terror in School)*, Rogalandsforskning, Stavanger

Roland, E. (1983) *Strategi mot mobbing (Strategy against Bullying)* Universiteetsforlaget, Stavanger

Roland, E. (1988) 'Bullying: the Scandinavian research tradition', in D.P. Tattum and D.A. Lane (eds.) *Bullying in Schools*, Trentham Books

Roland, E. (1989b) 'A system orientated strategy against bullying', in E. Roland and E. Munthe (eds.) *Bullying: An International Perspective*, David Fulton

Roland, E. and Munthe, E. (1989) *Bullying: An International Perspective*, David Fulton

Ross, C. and Ryan, A. (1990) *'Can I Stay Today, Miss?; Improving the School Playground*, Trentham Books

Runnymede Trust (1988) 'Manchester school murder report', *Race and Immigration: Runnymede Trust Bulletin*, 216, June, pp. 1–5

Runnymede Trust (1991a) 'War in the Gulf – violence and tensions at home', *Race and Immigration: Runnymede Trust Bulletin*, 243, March, pp. 1–4

Runnymede Trust (1991b) 'Gulf war impact update', *Race and Immigration: Runnymede Trust Bulletin*, 244, March, pp. 9–10

Runnymede Trust (1992) 'Education round up', *Runneymede Bulletin*, 258, September, p. 6

Rutter, M. (1987) 'Psychological resilience and protective mechanisms', *Americal Journal of Orthnopsychiatry*, 57, pp. 317–331

Rutter, M., Maughan, B., Mortimore, P., Ouston, J. and Smith, A. (1978) *Fifteen Thousand Hours*, Open Books

Samad, Y. (1992) 'Book burning and race relations: political mobilisation of Bradford Muslims', *New Community*, 18, 4, pp. 507–519

Sampson, A. and Phillips, C. (1992) *Multiple Victimisation: Racial Attacks on an East London Estate*, Police Research Group, Home Office

Searle, C. (1992) 'The Guld between: a school and a war', *Race and Class*, 33, 4, pp. 1–14

Sharp, S. (in press) 'Lunchtime supervisor training in the UK: an overview', in P. Blatchford and S. Sharp (eds.) *Breaktime in the School; Understanding and Changing Playground Behaviour*, Routledge & Kegan Paul

Sharp, S. and Smith, P. (1991) 'Bullying in UK schools: the DES Sheffield Bullying Project', *Early Child Development and Care*, 77, pp. 47–55

Sheat, L. (in press) 'Pupil participation in school grounds design', in P. Blatchford and S. Sharp (eds.) *Breaktimes in the School; Understanding and Changing Playground Behaviour*, Routledge & Kegan Paul

Sivanandan, A. (1991) 'A black perspective on the war', *Race and Class*, 32, 4, pp.83–88

Skellington, R. with Morris, P. (eds.) (1992) *Race in Britain Today*, Sage

Sluckin, A. (1987) 'The culture of the primary school playground', in A. Pollard (ed.) *Children and their Primary Schools*, Routledge & Kegan Paul

Sluckin, A. (1981) *Growing up in the Playground: The Social Development of Children*, Routledge & Kegan Paul

Smith, C., Farrant, M. and Marchant, H. (1972) *The Wincroft Youth Project*, Tavistock

Smith, D.J. and Tomlinson, S. (1989) *The School Effect: A Study of Multi-Racial Comprehensives*, Policy Studies Institute, London

Smith, P.K. and Thompson, D. (eds.) (1991) *Practical Approaches to Bullying*, David Fulton

Solomos, J. (1989) *Race and Racism in Contemporary Britain*, Macmillan

Spender, D. (1980) *Man Made Language*, Routledge & Kegan Paul

Spender, D. (1982) 'Invisible women, the schooling scandal', Writers and Readers Co-operative

Stattin, H. and Magnusson, D. (1989) 'The role of early aggressive behaviour in the frequency, seriousness and types of later crime', *Journal of Consulting and Clinical Psychology*, 57, pp. 710–718

Stephenson, P. and Smith, D. (1988) 'Bullying in the junior school', in D. Tattum and D. Lane (eds.) *Bullying in Schools*, Trentham Books

Strand, A.E., Huseklepp, P., Buberg, A., Skomsvold, J.F. and Fure, O. (1983) *Til aksjon mot mobbing (Take Action Against Bullying)*, Universitetsforlaget, Oslo

Sutton-Smith, B. (1981) *A History of Children's Play: New Zealand 1840–1950*, University of Pennsylvania Press, Philadelphia

Swann Report (1985) *Education for All: The Report of the Committee of Inquiry into the Education of Children from Ethnic Minority Groups*, Cmnd 9453, HMSO, London

Tattum, D.P. (1988) 'Violence and aggression in schools', in D. Tattum and D. Lane (eds) *Bullying in Schools*, Trentham Books

Tattum, D.P. and Herbert, G. (1990) *Bullying: A Positive Response. Advice for Parents, Governors and Staff in Schools*, Cardiff Institute of Higher Education

Tattum, D.P. and Herbert, G. (1993) *Countering Bullying: Initiatives in Schools and Local Authorities*, Trentham Books

Tattum, D.P. and Lane, D.A. (1989) *Bullying in Schools*, Trentham Books

Tattum, D.P. and Tattum, E. (1992a) *Social Education and Personal Development*, David Fulton

Tattum, D.P. and Tattum, E. (1992b) 'Bullying: A whole-school response', in N. Jones and E. Baglin Jones (eds.) *Learning to Behave*, Kogan Page

Tattum, D.P., Tattum, E. and Herbert, G. (1993) *Bullying in Secondary Schools* (video and resource pack), Drake Educational Associates, Cardiff

Tizzard, B., Blatchford, P., Burke, J., Farquhar, C. and Plewis, I. (1988) *Young Children at School in the Inner City*, Lawrence Erlbaum Associates

Troyna, B. and Hatcher, R. (1992a) *Racism in Children's Lives: A Study of Mainly White Primary Schools*, Routledge

Troyna, B. and Hatcher, R. (1992b) 'It's only words: understanding "racial" and racist incidents', *New Community*, 18, 3, pp. 493–496

US Department of Health, Education and Welfare (1973) *Positive Approaches to Dropout Prevention*, Washington DC

van den Berghe, P.L. (1988) 'Race', in E.E. Cashmore (ed.) *Dictionary of Race and Ethnic Relations* (2nd edition), Routledge

Walford, G. (1988) 'Bullying in public schools: myth and reality', in D. Tattum and D. Lane (eds.) *Bullying in Schools*, Trentham Books

Walker, J. (1989) 'Resolving classroom conflicts non-violently', in E. Roland and E. Munthe (eds.) *Bullying: An International Perspective*, David Fulton

Whitbread, A. (1980) 'Female teachers are women first: sexual harassment at work', in D. Spender and E. Sarah (eds.) *Learning to Lose*, The Women's Press

Whitney, I. and Smith, P.K. (1993) 'A survey of the nature and extent of bullying in junior/middle and secondary schools', *Educational Research*

Willis, P.E. (1977) *Learning to Labour: How Working Class Kids get Working Class Jobs*, Saxon House, Westmead

Woods, P. (1983) *Sociology and the School: An Interactionist Viewpoint*, Routledge & Kegan Paul

Yates, C. and Smith, P.K. (1989) 'Bullying in two English comprehensive schools', in E. Roland and E. Munthe (eds.) *Bullying: An International Perspective*, David Fulton

Young, K. (1990) *Learning through Landscapes: Using School Grounds as an Education Resource*, Learning Through Landscapes Trust, Winchester

Ziegler, S. and Rosenstein-Manner, M. (1991) 'Bullying at school: Toronto in an international context (No. 196R)', *Research Services*, Toronto Board of Education.

Ziegler, S., Charach, A. and Pepler, D.J. (1992) 'Bullying at school' (unpublished manuscript)

Index